Intersectionality, Sexuality and Psychological Therapies

Intersectionality, Sexuality and Psychological Therapies

Working with Lesbian, Gay and Bisexual Diversity

Edited by

Roshan das Nair

Consultant Clinical Psychologist in HIV & Sexual Health,
Department of Clinical Psychology and Neuropsychology,
Nottingham University Hospitals NHS Trust, Nottingham, UK

and

Trent Doctorate in Clinical Psychology,
Institute of Work, Health & Organisations,
University of Nottingham, Nottingham, UK

Catherine Butler

Former Consultant Clinical Psychologist for Infection & Immunology,
Barts and The London NHS Trust, London, UK

and

Senior Lecturer, Department of Psychology,
University of the West of England, Bristol, UK

The British Psychological Society | **BPS BLACKWELL**

This edition first published 2012 by the British Psychological Society and John Wiley & Sons, Ltd.

© 2012 John Wiley & Sons, Ltd

BPS Blackwell is an imprint of Blackwell Publishing, which was acquired by John Wiley & Sons in February 2007. Blackwell's publishing program has been merged with Wiley's global Scientific, Technical, and Medical business to form Wiley-Blackwell.

Registered Office: John Wiley & Sons, Ltd, The Atrium, Southern Gate, Chichester, West Sussex, PO19 8SQ, UK

Editorial Offices: 350 Main Street, Malden, MA 02148-5020, USA
9600 Garsington Road, Oxford, OX4 2DQ, UK
The Atrium, Southern Gate, Chichester, West Sussex, PO19 8SQ, UK

For details of our global editorial offices, for customer services, and for information about how to apply for permission to reuse the copyright material in this book please see our website at www.wiley.com/wiley-blackwell.

The right of Roshan das Nair and Catherine Butler to be identified as the authors of the editorial material in this work has been asserted in accordance with the UK Copyright, Designs and Patents Act 1988.

Library of Congress Cataloging-in-Publication Data
Intersectionality, sexuality, and psychological therapies : working with lesbian, gay, and bisexual diversity / edited by Roshan das Nair and Catherine Butler.
      p. cm.
   Includes index.
   ISBN 978-0-470-97500-8 (cloth) – ISBN 978-0-470-97499-5 (pbk.)
   1. Gays–Mental health.   2. Psychoanalysis and homosexuality.
I. Das Nair, Roshan.   II. Butler, Catherine, 1972–
   RC558.I58 2012
   616.89008664–dc23   2011035238

A catalogue record for this book is available from the British Library.

This book is published in the following electronic formats: ePDFs 9781119967606; Wiley Online Library 9781119967613; ePub 9781119967439; eMobi 9781119967446

Set in 10.5/12.5pt Minion by Aptara Inc., New Delhi, India
Printed in Malaysia by Ho Printing (M) Sdn Bhd

1   2012

To my mother, Janet, who taught me never to be constrained by expected age or gender roles, that love and respect were the most important relationship parameters, and that life was mine to craft and live to the full

—Catherine

To Amma and Dad, for having the courage to let me be me

—Roshan

Contents

Contributors

Catherine Butler

Dr Catherine Butler is currently working in her most challenging role, learning to be a mother, while working part time as a Senior Lecturer in Family Therapy at UWE. Prior to this, she was the Consultant Clinical Psychologist for Infection and Immunology at Barts & The London Hospital Trust. She has worked in HIV and Sexual Health since qualifying and was the research officer on the BPS HIV and Sexual Health Faculty committee. Dr Butler also previously worked as a Clinical Tutor on the Doctorate in Clinical Psychology at the University of East London, as well as in the private and voluntary sector, including as a Couple/Family Therapist at PACE and as a therapist, trainer and Clinical Associate with Pink Therapy. She was previously on the BPS Lesbian and Gay Psychology Section committee and won their Postgraduate Research Prize. She is a member of the Working Party responsible for writing the BPS guidelines on Working Therapeutically with Sexual and Gender Minority Clients. Her previous publications and academic interests include co-editing the book *Sex, Sexuality and Therapeutic Practice*, editing special editions of *The Psychologist, Lesbian and Gay Psychology Review, Clinical Psychology Forum* and numerous book chapters and articles on the topics of minority sexualities, sexual assault, HIV, working with interpreters, and personal/professional integration. She won the London Independent Film Festival 'Best LGBT Film' (2009) for co-producing *Homoworld*, based on her 2004 publication.

Roshan das Nair

Dr Roshan das Nair works as a Consultant Clinical Psychologist in HIV & Sexual Health with the Department of Clinical Psychology and Neuropsychology at the Nottingham University Hospitals NHS Trust, and is a

Research Tutor on the Trent Doctorate in Clinical Psychology programme at the University of Nottingham. He has previously worked in the areas of sex, sexuality, and HIV/AIDS in Zambia and India. Roshan is a board member of the Nottingham Sexual Health Providers' forum. He was the Editor-in-chief of the *Psychology of Sexualities Review* of the British Psychological Society's (BPS) Psychology of Sexualities Section (2007–10). He is also their representative on The International Network on Lesbian, Gay, and Bisexual Concerns and Transgender Issues in Psychology. He has been a member of the Working Party responsible for writing the BPS guidelines on Working Therapeutically with Sexual and Gender Minority Clients. His academic interests include HIV and sexual health in marginalised populations, the interface between ethnicity and sexuality, disability and sexuality, critical theory and cultural studies, and neuropsychological issues related to HIV infection.

Sonja Ellis

Dr Sonja J. Ellis is a Principal Lecturer in Psychology at Sheffield Hallam University where she teaches and researches primarily in the field of gender and sexuality. She has published widely on a range of issues relating to the experiences of lesbians and gay men including homophobia at university, lesbian and gay human rights, and LGB community. Together with Victoria Clarke, Elizabeth Peel, and Damien Riggs she is author of the leading textbook *LGBTQ Psychologies: Themes and Perspectives*.

Sarah Fairbank

Dr Sarah Fairbank is the Clinical Psychologist for the Community Assessment and Treatment Service in Nottingham city, working with people who experience mental health difficulties. She is also a visiting therapist for the Centre for Trauma, Resilience and Growth in Nottingham. She has over ten years experience of working in a variety of mental health settings including adult mental health, learning disabilities, forensic, child and older adults services. She divides her time between clinical, research and teaching commitments on both nursing and clinical psychology programmes. She is the founder and chair of the Sexuality, Relationships and Intimacy Forum for Adult mental health, Nottingham and was the lead trainer for Nottingham on the Department of Health Sexual Abuse training course in 2008.

Her main research interests are sexuality and mental health, service user involvement and the link between trauma and psychosis.

Stuart Gibson

Dr Stuart Gibson is a Chartered Clinical Psychologist who works at a multi-disciplinary mental health service for people living with HIV in south London. For more than 12 years he has practiced clinical psychology, lectured, trained, and conducted research on the psychological aspects of living with HIV in the United Kingdom, Canada and the United States. Stuart also has many years of experience in sexual diversity awareness training in psychology and psychiatry. He is the current Chair of the British Psychological Society's Faculty for HIV & Sexual Health.

Susan Hansen

Dr Susan Hansen is a Senior Lecturer in Psychology at Middlesex University. She has research interests in the application of conversation analysis to sexuality and gender, and to various social problems. She has particular research interests in the negotiation of sexual consent and refusal and in the discrimination and threat to safety gender queer folk may experience in gendered public spaces.

Stephen Higgins

Stephen Higgins is a final year Clinical Psychology trainee at the University of Easy London. His thesis examines the resettlement experiences of Iranian and Iraqi men who have claimed asylum in the UK because of persecution of their sexual identity. Steve has 25 years working in the NHS within mental health and learning disability services.

Adam Jowett

Dr Adam Jowett is a research fellow at the Academic Unit for Elderly Care and Rehabilitation, Bradford Royal Infirmary. His research interests cohere around health, sexuality and social support. His current research uses qualitative methods to investigate longer-term social adaptation after stroke. His PhD thesis examined chronic illness in non-heterosexual contexts and he has also conducted research on Civil Partnership.

Elizabeth Peel

Dr Elizabeth Peel is a Senior Lecturer in Psychology at the School of Life & Health Sciences, Aston University, Birmingham, UK. Her research is located in critical health psychology (particularly chronic illness), sexualities and gender. She is the author, with Victoria Clarke, Sonja Ellis and Damien Riggs, of *Lesbian, Gay, Bisexual, Trans & Queer Psychology: An introduction* (Cambridge University Press, 2010). Her current research centres on dementia care.

Damien W. Riggs

Dr Damien W. Riggs is a lecturer in social work at Flinders University, Australia. His research areas encompass critical race and whiteness studies, gender and sexuality studies, and parenting and family studies. He is the author of *Becoming a Parent: Lesbians, gay men and family* (Post Pressed, 2007), *What About the Children! Masculinities, sexualities and hegemony* (Cambridge Scholars Press, 2010), and (with Victoria Clarke, Sonja Ellis and Elizabeth Peel) *Lesbian, Gay, Bisexual, Trans, and Queer Psychology: An introduction* (Cambridge University Press, 2010). He is also the founding editor of the Australian Psychological Society journal *Gay and Lesbian Issues and Psychology Review*.

Esther D. Rothblum

Prof. Esther Rothblum is Professor of Psychology at San Diego State University. She also serves as Editor of the *Journal of Lesbian Studies*. Her research and writing have focussed on lesbian mental health, and she is former chair of the Committee on Lesbian and Gay Concerns of the American Psychological Association. She received the 1991 Distinguished Scientific Contribution Award from the Society for the Psychological Study of Lesbian and Gay Issues, and also served as President of the division. Prof. Rothblum has edited over 20 books, including *Lesbian Friendships* (New York University Press, 1996), *Preventing Heterosexism and Homophobia* (Sage Publications,

1996), *Lesbians in Academia* (Routledge, 1997), *Boston Marriages: Romantic But Asexual Relationships Among Contemporary Lesbians* (University of Massachusetts Press, 1993) and *Loving Boldly: Issues Facing Lesbians* (Haworth Press, 1989).

Sonya Thomas

Sonya Thomas is a London based freelance writer and equality consultant with over 20 years' experience of equalities work, both in the public and voluntary sectors. She has provided political advice on equalities to local government elected members and political leads and has authored a number of speeches on various aspects of equalities and diversity for Commissioners within the Equality and Human Rights Commission and senior civil servants in the Department of Health. She has an MA in Human Resource Management and post-graduate diplomas in Industrial Relations and Journalism.

Foreword

I feel honoured to be invited by Catherine and Roshan to write the Foreword for this book. Catherine and I have been co-training therapists together for around five years and in recent times have added information on our training programmes on working with clients who have intersecting identities and the impact of various oppressive forces on the individual. We felt it was an absolutely vital component of any training and I feel somewhat ashamed of my lack of knowledge not to have included it in earlier training programmes I have convened. This clearly demonstrates the adage: 'We teach what we know' and as much explains why counselling and therapy programmes in Britain are generally still ridiculously uninformed about the differences experienced by gender and sexual minorities. This is lamentable for two reasons: first, the research which shows poorer mental health in these populations and how Lesbian, Gay, Bisexual and Transgender (LGBT) people are more likely to present for psychological support than heterosexual people, and second, that one in six British therapists have willingly entered into therapy contracts to reduce same-sex attractions, despite there being no evidence based research to show this is possible.

As a therapist who has worked with sexual minorities for 30 years and as the principal author and co-editor of the first British textbook on working with LGB people, it is really gratifying to see the development of a small raft of books in the past year that increasingly reflect the nuances of multiple identities and the complexities of gender and sexual minority identities and their relationships. This book, however, takes things much further in exploring the intersections in various identities (gender, age, race and ethnicity, class, disability, mental and physical health, etc.) and from a largely (though not exclusively) British perspective, which given that many of the issues covered are fairly region-specific, makes the book highly relevant to all therapists working with LGB people here in the UK.

Unlike many books which one can simply dip in and out, this book benefits from reading all the way through since there is much to be learned here; or if I am to own that statement for myself, I personally learned so much. As a white gay man who identifies as disabled and comes from a working class background, living with enduring physical health issues, I have seen my own lived experience recognised and affirmed across many of these pages. I have also learned a lot about the intersecting identities of those clients who have other identities from the research and ideas of the contributors. One example perhaps of an insight for me was thinking that therapists should be transparent about their gender and sexual identity, whereas I now realise this can be both unhelpful (and meaningless) for some therapists coming from Black and Minority Ethnic (BME) communities where they may also face social exclusion from their families and communities if they were to be forced to come out so unselectively.

I think we need to recognise that a one-size-fits-all approach that assumes all LGB people experience the world in the same way is overly simplistic and culturally insensitive. The astute therapist will want to understand the nuances and differences experienced by their clients and how their intersecting identities impact on their sexuality. This book will be a valuable resource into becoming better informed so that the therapist or counsellor is not reliant on having their clients be the sole source of educating them.

Dominic Davies
Director – Pink Therapy
Fellow – British Association of Counselling and Psychotherapy

February 2011

Acknowledgements

If this book is considered a fabric, then many people contributed many threads that we, as editors, have simply woven together. We would like to begin by thanking our clients and friends who shared their stories with us. We thank all our collaborators for willing to contribute to this anthology. We are indebted to Darren Reed from Wiley who was instrumental in getting the project off the ground. We would also like to thank Karen Shield and Tori Halliday at John Wiley & Sons, Ltd for assistance. Dr Tuppy Owens and eirwen yemn edwards from Outsiders, and Dr Andrew Yip from the University of Nottingham have been extremely generous with their time and advice.

Roshan would like to thank Rein Ove Sikveland, the blue-eyed boy from Undheim, for his kindness, encouragement, unfaltering support, and love.

Catherine would like to thank Hazel, Liz and Zoe for distracting Ella so she could work, Ella for her patience, and especially Ray for all his cooking, washing up, childcare and continuous love and 'non-heteronormative' support.

Introduction

Roshan das Nair & Catherine Butler

Lesbian, gay, and bisexual (LGB) literature in health and social sciences is burgeoning. However, much of the early published material focussed on differences between heterosexual and homosexual people, thereby creating a sense of homogeneity of homosexual (and bisexual) lives and experiences. While much of the later work no longer concerns itself with a heterosexual yardstick, and instead explores issues pertinent to LGB lives such as parenting, relationship styles, and so on, much of this work still does not describe the race, ethnicity, social class, or ability of its participants, largely assuming them to be white, middle class and able-bodied (Butler *et al.*, 2010). This book aims to widen the existing psychological and therapeutic literature on LGB issues within a British context. The book unpicks what it means to be LGB by exploring the social-cultural differences within these labels, identities and practices, and how these differences intersect to make being non-heterosexual a unique experience for each person who uses, or chooses not use, these labels or identities.

Intersectionality

Although the concept of intersectionality has been around for many years, and Kimberle Crenshaw is credited with coining the term in 1989, its foray into psychology and therapeutics has been more recent. McCall (2005) hypothesised that this was possibly due to of a lack of guidelines for researchers in psychology to empirically answer complex questions or address multi-faceted issues without fractionating them into their constituent components – holding the complexity is what intersectionality requires. More

Intersectionality, Sexuality and Psychological Therapies: Working with Lesbian, Gay and Bisexual Diversity, First Edition. Edited by Roshan das Nair and Catherine Butler.

recently, however, Cole (2009) has provided us with a framework to help apply intersectionality to psychology. She does this by posing three questions that therapists need to ask when examining any group or social category:

(i)   Who is included within this category?
(ii) What role does inequality play?
(iii) Where are there similarities? (Cole, 2009, p.170).

The first question challenges the perceived homogeneity of a given group on the basis of a single characteristic, and forces us to see the diversity within such a group. The second question introduces power into the equation, and forces us to recognise that the spaces that people exist in and interact with(in) are not level playing fields, but are fluid hierarchies which offer differing levels of 'privilege and power' to some people sometimes. The final question forces us to look for 'commonalities across categories commonly viewed as deeply different' (Cole, 2009, p.171).

Another potential reason for the slow uptake of intersectionality within psychology and therapeutics is perhaps because of the slippery task of attempting to define the concept. As Davis (2008) has suggested, intersectionality has been variously thought of as a theory, a concept or heuristic, or even as a reading strategy. Definitions are also deferred because intersectionality is sometimes simultaneously regarded as 'crossroads', 'axes', or 'dynamic processes' (Davis, 2008). But this lack of a consensus towards a unitary definition of intersectionality does not render it useless to interrogate troublesome questions and social phenomena. In fact, as Davis (2008) paraphrasing Murray Davis asserts, 'successful theories thrive on ambiguity and incompleteness' (p.69).

Phoenix's (2006) definition of intersectionality as a 'catchall phrase that aims to make visible the multiple positioning that constitutes everyday life and the power relations that are central to it' (p.187) is interesting because it highlights at least three key points: (i) making visible multiple identities, (ii) which are relevant in daily life, and (iii) acknowledging that this does not happen in a power-vacuum. Cole (2009) points out that much of intersectionality scholarship has examined the multiple sites of oppression and disenfranchisement of people whose lives fall along the fault-lines of social categories. However, as a theory, intersectionality can also explore issues that pertain to the privileged identities that 'some members of disadvantaged groups . . . (e.g., middle class blacks, white women)' (Cole, 2009. p.171). Therefore, in recognising both disadvantages and advantages of subjectivities, we challenge these frontiers further by examining the possibility for power and agency that these individuals and groups of people experience *because* of their intersectional positions. We feel that this is an avenue that has not received sufficient attention in intersectionality literature, and view it as a way to move out from a position of disadvantage to one of opportunity. This, of course, should have a particular appeal for therapy and therapists.

The importance of intersectionality was highlighted by Kathy Davis (2008) in her paper *Intersectionality as Buzzword*. Although speaking from a Gender Studies perspective, Davis' assertion is applicable to any scholarly pursuit that attempts to understand individual and social phenomena more holistically. She avers, 'any scholar who neglects difference runs the risk of having her work viewed as theoretically misguided, politically irrelevant, or simply fantastical' (p.68). This is a sentiment we share.

The project of intersectionality, however, is one that is forever incomplete, whether in terms of scholarship, activism, and/or service provision. This incompleteness is evident because of the endless possibilities of permutations and combinations of identities and social positions that people inhabit, and because of the amorphous and dynamic nature of these identities and positions. Alice Ludwig (2006) refers to this as the 'Achilles heel of intersectionality' (p.247). Given this assertion, it should therefore come as no surprise that this book is also incomplete. Sites of power differentials can reside within a matrix that covers gender, race, ethnicity, sexuality, dis/ability, nationality, citizenship, creed, class, geographical location, age, landedness, employment, health, caste, and so on. While we have tried to cover some ground in terms of how a constellation of these identities/locations affect individual and group experiences, with sexuality as our primary lens, we recognise that this viewpoint is limited. But limited as it is, it still offers perspectives for therapists (and others) about how various strands of our lives intertwine, like a complex, sometimes jagged, sometimes incomplete, often changing weave; which hitherto have been ignored or silenced.

The impossibility of the intersectional project does not mean that we should abandon the concept of intersectionality or do away with categories that are already in existence, because these very categories that have the power to disenfranchise certain people also have the potential to bring people together to mobilise action. The triumph of intersectionality therefore is its potential to resist the complacency of accepting categories as predetermined, static, and objective truths, and its ability to proactively challenge the composition and limits of these categories. This book demonstrates *intersectionality in action*. From a phenomenological perspective, the voices of the people in this book (authors, clients/patients, therapists, research participants, characters from film, etc.) offer their 'lived experiences' of intersectionality.

The Scope of this Book

We focussed on keeping the book relevant for professionals who offer psychological therapies. We recognise that 'psychological therapies' is a rather broad term, but this reflects the nondenominational flavour of this book, which we believe will appeal to therapists of various persuasions. Each chapter includes a client's story for illustration and ends with guidelines for good practice. We attempted to have all chapters co-authored by at least one therapist, and where this was not possible, there was input from us, as editors who are also practicing NHS therapists. Furthermore, each chapter has reviewed literature that includes both male and female perspectives, to ensure that different genders/sexualities are well represented and tokenism avoided.

This desire to avoid tokenism was one of our reasons for not including Transgender issues in this book, as we felt it was beyond the scope of this book to discuss these issues in any detail. Furthermore, the contributors to this book are specialised in working with issues of sexual orientation and not gender, but we believe that some of the issues discussed here may resonate with some Trans experiences. We also recognise that some of these issues are of direct relevance to Trans people who also identify as LGB. As one of our anonymous reviewers indicated at the outset of this project, it was better to exclude Trans issues rather than 'include Trans experiences into the general body assumptively. A matter for a separate commission perhaps?'. Indeed, we believe these issues, including those related to Intersex, Genderqueer, and other genders and sexualities, need to be dealt with in much greater detail than what can be covered here or in any single book. We are thus aware we sacrificed some important areas for breadth in focus on sexual minorities rather than depth, and recognise that each chapter included here could be extended to a book in itself. However, we hope that the chapters capture the reader's curiosity and act as a springboard for further study if desired. We also believe that the chapters herein do provide sufficient overview to enable therapists to work confidently and competently with non-heterosexual clients presenting with intersecting identity markers and issues.

Given that the anticipated audience for the book is therapists, the chapters focus on *issues* or *problems* that clients may bring to therapy. It could be argued that such a focus results in a 'doom and gloom' perspective on aspects of social difference within LGB lives. The areas of social difference discussed in this book can all be sites of oppression, but we have also suggested ways in which working through these issues of oppression can result in empowerment. Indeed, the vast majority of LGB people are living positive, well-adjusted and happy existences, with no need for therapy to help them work through their daily challenges. Throughout the book, readers are also invited to locate themselves in relation to clients and their issues, and to consider how their own intersectional identities interact with those of their clients in supportive or oppressive ways.

The Structure of the Book

Although we have split the book into chapters for ease of navigation through various topics, the project of intersectionality demands that none of these topics be viewed in isolation. We demonstrate this interconnectedness by cross-referencing topics between chapters. We suggest that readers start from the chapter which is most relevant to their work, or which captures their immediate interest. The highlighted interconnections with other chapters may then lead the reader to further reading, thus expanding their lens and connecting to the complexities that having multiple identities entails.

The book opens with an in-depth exploration of the concept of intersectionality and how it relates to LGB lives; we therefore suggest this might be relevant for all readers. The chapter summarises critiques of essentialist positions on social difference and concepts such as 'cultural competence'. The chapter demonstrates how intersectionality invites incompleteness and ambiguity, for example, one part of a person's identity may involve privilege (e.g., male) whilst another may invite disenfranchisement (e.g., gay). Taken for granted assumptions are thus troubled in the hope that the reader proceeds with an open and questioning mind.

The fractionating of areas of social difference begins with an examination of gender and the various theories which have taken up this challenge, and applying them to LGB individuals, couples and family structures. The assumed hetero-norms of gender are unpicked and alternatives presented. This chapter has a section on Transgender issues, with a focus on Trans people who identify as LGB.

A vacuum in the literature is then addressed with a chapter on issues pertaining to non-heterosexual black and ethnic minority people, who may have good reason not to identify with the labels LGB. This chapter in particular invites the reader into the complexities of intersectionality and non-categorical thinking, presenting thorny issues such as the costs of being visible or invisible within non-heterosexual communities and beyond, as well as the interplay between race, religion and family loyalties. The chapter ends with an invitation to therapists to become an agent for systemic change, exploring the intersections between therapist/activist identities.

The theme of religion is picked up and explored in depth in the next chapter, which critically presents the minimal writing on religion in the lives of non-heterosexuals. The chapter focuses on Islam, Hinduism and Christianity, but the reader is directed to other texts that cover other faiths. This chapter provides insights and guidance to therapists (addressing 'non-believer' therapists in particular) working with clients who are struggling with combining their sexuality and religious beliefs.

Same-sex sexuality (whether linked to an LGB identity or not) is then considered for those seeking asylum, or having obtained refugee status, on the grounds of their sexuality. This chapter describes various contexts that have a fundamental impact on the phases of exile, including the decision to flee and experiences in host countries. These contexts mark the experiences of LGB asylum seekers and refugees as unique compared to those of heterosexuals, and the narrow use of certain diagnostic categories and the application of western models of sexuality are critiqued.

There follows a chapter on social class, a largely neglected topic in LGB and therapy literature, with there being an unspoken assumption of middle-classness. This chapter therefore focuses mainly on the lives of working class non-heterosexuals, pulling together the scant literature and adding insightful and thorough comment. It also troubles the idea of the 'chav' identity, especially in connection with gay spaces, and suggests how this is a vilified, fetishised, and excluded group.

Social class has been strongly linked to health inequalities, and the subsequent chapter on physical health extends these inequalities to consider sexuality. This chapter, while mentioning HIV, makes a point of not having this as its focus as it is already widely considered *the*, and the only, 'gay health issue'. Instead, the chapter discusses influences on poor health, such as smoking, alcohol use and eating disorders, and how these relate to LGB populations. It presents, and critiques, associated theories, such as that of 'internalised homophobia (also referred to in other chapters). It also discusses the prevalence and concerns of chronic health problems and why there are unique issues pertaining to this for LGB people. The chapter ends with considerations for healthcare contexts working with LGB people.

In addition to physical health inequalities, LGB people experience more mental health problems than heterosexuals (King *et al.*, 2008); the next chapter explores the possible reasons for this. The assumed 'healthiness' and well-adjustment of coming out is thrown into question, and issues relating to LGB youth explored. While this chapter covers some common mental health issues, and reasons behind them (such as internalised homonegativity), the bulk of the chapter focuses on how healthcare services perform and what needs to be done to better serve LGB populations with respect, dignity and understanding. The chapter also includes a section on sexual issues for LGB people with severe and enduring mental health problems: an area often neglected as service-users are considered to be asexual (McCann, 2003).

This asexual stereotype is also frequently applied to disability (Morris, 1991) and the chapter on disability challenges this by exploring the lives of disabled LGB people, including issues pertaining to relationships and sex. Prejudice and discrimination in different contexts is described (i.e. the heterosexual mainstream, LGB spaces, and the disability movement) and issues pertaining to growing up with a disability and a developing sexual minority awareness are explored. The chapter ends with sections that specifically focus on learning disabilities and HIV, both areas of potential controversy as some authors argue that these are often missed out from disability texts and campaigns (e.g., Thompson *et al.*, 2001, and Shakespeare *et al.*, 1996, respectively).

The final chapter on social difference focuses on age across the lifespan. The variety of ways of 'doing relationships' is emphasised, with a focus on the importance of friendships and 'families of choice'. Issues relating to bisexuality are explored in detail in this chapter, as is sexuality in later life: both areas often neglected in LGB literature.

Finally, the concluding chapter echoes the point made in this introduction, that LGB lives are not all 'doom and gloom', by celebrating advantages and achievements. This chapter highlights fluidity and complexity, which is the essence of intersectionality, and proposes that acknowledging such fluidity removes the boundaries of self and other. Thus the reader/therapist is once again invited to examine their own position in relation to the issues mentioned in this book.

We recognise that we are limited by our media, in that by writing a book, the captured lived experiences and related reported research become static: frozen in the historic and cultural context in which they are produced. However, this book provides a useful punctuation to pull together existing thinking in this area and introduce therapists to the variety of issues that reflect the heterogeneity of LGB lives. This book perhaps represents a beginning, where several aspects of LGB lives that are brought to therapy are explored through the lens of intersectionality. We therefore invite our readers to join us in expanding the scope of this project by thinking in terms of how sexuality would relate to other issues, such as urban/rural living, non-monogamous relationships, 'kink' or sadomasochistic identities, asexuality, gender variance and the effects of the different permutations and combinations that all these different intersecting identities would have on the individual. In the final analysis, as Crenshaw (1991) suggests, it is only by being aware of identity intersections, that we can acknowledge the differences between us and explore ways in which diversity can be expressed to construct bonding. To this extent, this book is an invitation to celebrate difference in diversity.

References

Butler, C., das Nair, R. & Thomas, S. (2010). The colour of queer. In L. Moon (ed.) *Counselling ideologies: Queer challenges to heteronormativity*. Farnham: Ashgate.

Cole, E. (2009). Intersectionality and research in psychology. *American Psychologist, 64*(3), 170–180.

Crenshaw, K. (1991). Mapping the margins: Intersectionality, identity politics, and violence against women of color. *Stanford Law Review, 43*(6), 1241–1299.

Davis, K. (2008). Intersectionality as buzzword. A sociology of science perspective on what makes a feminist theory successful. *Feminist Theory, 9*(1), 67–85.

King, M., Semlyen, J., Tai, S., Killaspy, H., Osborn, D., Popelyuk, D. & Nazareth, I. (2008). A systematic review of mental disorder, suicide, and deliberate self-harm in lesbian, gay and bisexual people. *BMJ Psychiatry, 8*(70). Retrieved 18 October 2010 from http://www.ncbi.nlm.nih.gov/pmc/articles/PMC2533652/.

Ludwig, A. (2006). Differences between women? Intersecting voices in a female narrative. *European Journal of Women's Studies, 13*(3), 245–258.

McCall, L. (2005). The complexity of intersectionality. *Signs, 30*, 1771–1800.

McCann, E. (2003). Exploring sexual and relationship possibilities for people with psychosis: A review of the literature. *Journal of Psychiatric and Mental Health Nursing, 10*, 640–649.

Morris, J. (1991). *Pride against prejudice*. London: Women's Press.

Phoenix, A. (2006). Editorial: Intersectionality. *European Journal of Women's Studies, 13*(3), 187–192.

Shakespeare, T., Gillespie-Sells, K. & Davies, D. (1996). *The sexual politics or disability: untold desires*. London: Cassell.

Thompson, S.A., Bryon, M. & de Castell, S. (2001). Prospects for identity formation for lesbian, gay, or bisexual persons with developmental disabilities. *International Journal of Disability, Development and Education, 48*(1), 53–65.

1

Intersecting Identities

Damien W. Riggs & Roshan das Nair

The moments when everyday life becomes most vivid or tangible are the moments when most people find themselves living more than one life (Kristin Ross, 1992, p.63).

In June of 2010, renowned theorist Judith Butler was widely reported as having refused the Berlin Pride Civil Courage Prize. Apparently, Butler did so on the grounds that mainstream gay organisations and events continue to fail to adequately address two interrelated issues: (1) the whiteness of their constituency and racism within gay communities, and (2) the complicity of white (primarily middle class) lesbians and gay men with the oppression of non-white and/or non-gender normative people. In so doing, Butler issued a call that has been increasingly made within both academic and activist circles (e.g. Barnard, 2003; Kuntsman & Miyake, 2008; Puar, 2007; Riggs, 2006), namely to recognise how norms function within non-heterosexual[1] communities, and the problematic assumption that there is homogeneity within such communities. Such a call has direct implications for therapists, as elaborated in this chapter (and throughout this book). Specifically, and as the following sections explore in more detail, Butler's call (and those that preceded it) indicates the need for (1) a critical reconsideration of notions of 'cultural competence' when it comes to working with non-heterosexual[2] people, (2) an understanding of the concept of 'intersectionality' (as it

---

[1] The term non-heterosexual is used as an umbrella term, and identity labels such as gay, lesbian, bisexual, etc. are used only when they are quoted as specific descriptors.
[2] Some of the issues related to non-heterosexual people apply to non-gender normative people also.

Intersectionality, Sexuality and Psychological Therapies: Working with Lesbian, Gay and Bisexual Diversity,
First Edition. Edited by Roshan das Nair and Catherine Butler.
© 2012 John Wiley & Sons, Ltd. Published 2012 by John Wiley & Sons, Ltd. and the British Psychological Society.

applies to a broad range of non-heterosexual communities), and (3) an engagement with the work of culturally diverse ethnic minority academics, activists, and others. Having elaborated these points and their implications for therapists, we then turn to examine their application via two case studies that demonstrate the possibility for working intersectionally, and in so doing being mindful of the differential effects of power upon a range of bodies and identities, particularly within the therapeutic context.

Defining Culture

As T.S. Eliot (1958) once said, 'Just as a doctrine only needs to be defined after the appearance of some heresy, so a word does not need to receive this attention until it has come to be misused' (p.13). 'Culture' is one such word that 'needs to be defined' because of the multiplicity of its ab/use. This multiplicity is produced, at least in part, by the abstractness of the word itself. In an attempt to interrogate the concept of culture, Kroeber and Kluckhohn (1952) famously found 164 definitions of the term, and found that these various definitions clustered around several themes. Our conceptualisation of culture in this chapter is related to Fiske's (2002, p.85) definition of culture:

> A culture is a socially transmitted or socially constructed constellation con-
> sisting of such things as practices, competencies, ideas, schemas, symbols,
> values, norms, institutions, goals, constitutive rules, artifacts, and modifica-
> tions of the physical environment.

Fiske's notion of culture is significant because it recognises that culture works at both a conscious and non-conscious level: 'Most of the intangible constituents of culture generally are not accessible to consciousness, reflection, or explicit linguistic expression' (p.81–82).

Therefore, our take on culture includes individual and collective identities carved out from various social markers of culture, which an individual may be able to recognise, acknowledge, affiliate with (and therefore be able to 'articulate'), but may also include those aspects to which he/she feels connected, in a manner which defies reason, and which cannot be communicated through conventional forms of signs and symbols. In our reference to culture, we embrace a wide array of cultural positions and/or identities, which could include race, religion, ability, class, and so forth. Importantly, we are mindful of the immense diversity that exists within cultures, and our intention is to signal that any singular approach to working with any given cultural 'group' will always fail to truly encompass the breadth of experiences that shape what we refer to here as 'culture'. In the following section we take up this point by examining in close detail some of the problematic assumptions that often inform notions of 'cultural competency'.

Cultural Competence

In an insightful article on cultural competency in social work, Pon (2009) argues that cultural competency often functions as a form of 'new racism'[3] (i.e. racism that is more covert and less explicit than more 'traditional' forms of racism, but which is just as damaging). Pon suggests this for a number of reasons. First, he suggests that notions of cultural competency typically treat 'culture' as a neutral or benign concept, rather than one heavily invested with power that operates through the demonisation of certain cultural groups. Second, he suggests that notions of 'culture' within cultural competency typically adopt an essentialist interpretation of culture, where checklists of cultural practices are provided against which it is presumed therapists can assess (and treat) clients from marginalised cultural groups. Third, and compounding the second point, Pon suggests that little attention is given within elaborations of cultural competency to recognising dominant group cultures as also having specific features or practices that require attention. Fourth, Pon suggests that the essentialism that adheres to notions of cultural competency can easily result in the reification of 'cultural conflict' as a 'natural' outcome of 'essential differences' (which again fails to acknowledge the effects of power). Fifth, the reliance upon a 'checklist' type of mentality for cross-cultural practice functions to construct members of marginal cultural groups as 'cultural experts' (which fails to acknowledge differences *within* cultures), thereby homogenising such cultures. In addition to these points we suggest a sixth, namely that cultural competency presumes a sensory-centred understanding of culture, whereby culture is presumed to be easily readable from people's bodies, clothing, language use, or modes of representation. Such notions of cultural competence do not always recognise those who fall in between categories, or those whose lives defy facile categorisations (such as men who have sex with men who do not identify as 'gay', 'bi', or 'heterosexual'). Furthermore, some of these concepts assume stability of categories over time; for instance, notions of 'working class' or 'disability' (or for that matter, 'sexual identity') are not always static concepts. Having listed these concerns raised by Pon, we now explore each briefly with regard to non-heterosexual people, before moving on to explore how the concept of intersectionality may help address these issues.

---

[3] Although Pon specifically addresses 'new racism', the same idea can be transposed to understand 'new classism', 'new disabilism', etc.

Any notion of 'culture' that fails to acknowledge the effects of power will be fundamentally incapable of recognising the impact of homophobia, biphobia, and heteronormativity upon non-heterosexual people. In other words, a view of non-heterosexual cultures as things to be celebrated or affirmed only tells one part of the story; the other part of the story (and often a more important one for many clients accessing psychology and/or counselling services) is recognition of the detrimental impact of social marginalisation and stigma. For example, and as Chapters 7 and 8 of this book suggest, there are considerable negative physical and psychological sequelae of not identifying as heterosexual in a society that privileges this identity category. It must be added here, that such negative sequelae may be equally a problem for non-heterosexuals who do not identify as 'lesbian', 'gay', or 'bi' (LGB) in LGB-dominant spaces, which privilege such identities over other non-heterosexual identities or heterosexual identities. Therefore, what we are identifying here is not only the dominance of the heterosexual identity in clinical and social spaces, but the role that power and context plays in determining what is dominant and preferred in a given setting.

One response to the growing awareness of the effects of social marginalisation has been the development of checklist-type approaches that are aimed at assessing the various challenges that non-heterosexual people face, the support systems they have, and the services that are made available to them. Whilst we acknowledge that such approaches represent an important step forward in the provision of services to these populations, we also share Pon's (2009) concern that such approaches often rely upon an essentialist understanding of non-heterosexual people's cultures. This can have several negative implications. First, there is the potential that any non-heterosexual person who is not easily identifiable as falling into a clear category may be given inadequate service (or even refused service). Second, a checklist approach may bring with it an injunction to rate or rank 'injuries' (to follow Brown, 1994; and Mama, 1995), which can result both in the perpetuation or overemphasis of negative life experiences, and in the screening out of clients who are not assessed as meeting certain 'injury criteria'.

Relatedly, and when it comes to considering the effects of essentialist accounts of culture, Riggs (2007a) has explored how psychological testing typically privileges a very essentialist account of identity, and how psychological tests are primarily normed on white middle class heterosexual samples. The same can be said for checklists, which in most instances are almost certain to take white middle-classness as the norm. Moreover, and as Greene (2007) notes, checklists that *do* attempt to take into account a wider range of identities typically provide highly essentialist accounts of non-white or non-western non-heterosexual communities (such as in the assumption that homophobia is more prevalent in black communities: see Chapter 3).

As we noted above, these points about checklist approaches connect very closely to the failure of some therapists and/or dominant group members to assess their *own* social location. This can mean that professionals (and particularly, though not exclusively, white middle class able-bodied hetero-sexual professionals) fail to acknowledge their classed, raced, (em)bodied and sexed privileges that accord them a significant position of authority and power *in addition to* their privileged position as therapists. A powerful ex-ample of this is provided by Lamble (2008) in her discussion of the murder of gay transman Fred F.C. Martinez. During the trial it was reported that Martinez had been seeing a white gay psychotherapist prior to his murder, and that it was only subsequent to the murder of Martinez that the psy-chotherapist could comprehend the effects of racism *along with homophobia and transphobia* upon Martinez (i.e. the psychotherapist did not recognise the effects of racism arising from Martinez' Navajo identity largely because, as a white man and thus a holder of race privilege, he was not compelled to do so). Thus as Pon (2009) suggests, a checklist-type approach to working cross-culturally maintains a focus on the 'other', and in so doing neglects to encourage an examination of the professional's own identity and social location and its impact upon the therapeutic space.

This brings us to Pon's point about cultural competency's failure to lo-cate individuals in broader (normative) social contexts, and the ways in which this operates to affirm the belief that cultural conflict is inevitable. In the case of non-heterosexual people, this can translate into modes of practice that encourage such groups to solely reconcile themselves to the given social context (i.e. by developing 'safety plans' or developing a 'posi-tive sense of self' through affirmations from peers or professionals), rather than challenging the status quo itself. We of course acknowledge that for some clients simply staying alive and safe may be a necessarily primary focus. However, the concern is that treating conflict as inevitable only serves to legitimate dominant group behaviours that are marginalising (or at the least treats them as a natural, rather than socially determined, 'fact of life').

The last of Pon's (2009) points suggests that dominant understandings of cultural competency typically treat as homogenous any given culture, and in so doing position those seen to be culturally competent members of the given culture as 'experts'. This can be negative in a number of ways in therapeutic settings, primary amongst these being the likelihood that professionals will fail to challenge clients (where appropriate) about stereotypes or norms they may be perpetuating (for example, when gay men perpetuate negative stereotypes about lesbian women or when gay men rely upon norms about gay relationships, such as an assumption of non-monogamy, that may not be appropriate for all men). Whilst there are reasons why non-heterosexual communities may present a relatively unified or internally positive front, in reality such unity is often not the case, with differences amongst members as salient and powerful as those between non-heterosexual communities and other community groups. Treating individuals as 'experts' on their community, whilst important in some instances, in others may fail to make use of the therapeutic space and the knowledge or experience of the practitioner.

Our addition to Pon's (2009) five points is that cultural competency often presumes that bodies and identities are readable markers of culture. The presumption that race, class, gender, ability and so forth are easily readable not only essentialises these categories, but also makes it possible for any failed 'reading' to result in incorrect assumptions or applications of predetermined needs to any given client with little regard to their specific circumstances.

Intersectionality

As is indicated by the problems identified in the previous section regarding cultural competency, much of what is required is for therapists working with non-heterosexual people to *add*, rather than take away, complexity. In other words, reducing the issues faced by non-heterosexual people to simply ones related to gender and/or sexuality (and treating gender and/or sexuality as essential, pre-determined, characteristics) will forever fail to adequately identify all of the issues that clients face. Contrarily, simply adding on more identities (whilst treating them all as separable) will also fail to recognise the complexities of clients' lives. What is called for then, and as has been elaborated by African American feminist scholars such as Kimberle Crenshaw (1991), is an *intersectional* approach to understanding identity/ies. Such an approach suggests that identities should not be seen as problems of addition, but rather as complex sets of interactions that are mutually constituted in a relationship to prevailing social norms. Barnard (2003, p.3) sums this up well in the following example:

> In the United States . . . many contemporary political and theoretical formulations of communitarian subjectivity assume that every identity is merely the accretion of so many other base identities (thus, in popular liberal parlance, a Chicana lesbian is said to be triply oppressed as a woman, a Chicana, and a lesbian), a paradigm that denies the specificity of identity and the inseparability of the supposed constituents of a particular identity (Chicana lesbian might be an identity in itself, rather than a conglomeration of other identities). Consequently, this paradigm normalizes the modes of subjectivity

privileged by material power relations in a particular cultural-historical moment (to compute Chicana lesbian as the sum of Chicana, women, and lesbian, is to establish heterosexual male Chicanoness, white heterosexual femaleness, and white male gayness as the central identities from which the Chicana lesbian draws her constituent parts) and thus erases the experience of those who occupy more than one of the canonized subject positions.

The importance of intersectionality was highlighted by Kathy Davis (2008) in her paper *Intersectionality as Buzzword*, in which she avers, 'any scholar who neglects difference runs the risk of having her work viewed as theoretically misguided, politically irrelevant, or simply fantastical...' (p.68). Although speaking from a gender studies perspective, Davis' assertion is applicable to any scholarly pursuit which attempts to understand social phenomena more holistically.

Other important aspects that intersectionality helps to interrogate are power relations and differentials in interactions. These have not typically been the object of much concern for traditional healthcare practices (van Mens-Verhulst & Radtke, 2006). Even in therapeutic settings, where power dynamics are referred to and attended to, it is easy to sometimes forget this dynamic if we are not used to thinking about it. We are, of course, not advocating for an approach that attempts to claim neutrality in therapeutic encounters (this is not possible), nor are we of the opinion that power differentials are inherently a bad thing. What we are suggesting is that these need to be acknowledged, observed, and used with care. Foucault (1980, p.289) articulates this well:

> The idea that there could exist a state of communication that would allow games of truth to circulate freely, without any constraints or coercive effects, seems utopian to me. This is precisely a failure to see that power relations are not something that is bad in itself, that we have to break free of... The problem [however] in... practices where power – which is not in itself a bad thing – must inevitably come into play is knowing how to avoid... domination effects.

For van Mens-Verhulst and Radtke (2006), one of the most important potential contributions of intersectionality theory is related to power, and the potential it offers therapists to reorient themselves to the client in a way that considers the 'social relational context', and facilitates therapists 'to adopt self-reflexive practices' (p.10). As can be seen in the following quote, they eloquently suggest how applying intersectionality theory to healthcare practice can bring the issue of power to the therapist's attention by posing some basic questions:

> ... 'how are we doing power?', 'who is in a position to exercise power?', 'who is recognized as the expert?', 'who is resisting the regulations and how?', 'whose interests are served by particular regulations and practices within health care institutions?' (van Mens-Verhulst & Radtke, 2006, p.8).

Yet, despite the fact that the concept of intersectionality has been around from the 1970s and its incorporation into healthcare has been seen to be advantageous, its foray into psychology and therapeutics has been more recent. McCall (2005) hypothesised that this was because of a lack of guidelines for psychologists to empirically answer complex questions or address multi-faceted issues without fractionating them into its constituent components – which is what intersectionality requires. More recently, however, Cole (2009) has provided us with a framework to help apply intersectionality to psychology. She does this by posing three questions that psychologists need to ask when examining any group or social category: (1) Who is included within this category? (2) What role does inequality play? (3) Where are there similarities? (Cole, 2009, p.170). The first question challenges the perceived homogeneity of a given group on the basis of a single characteristic, and forces us to see the diversity within such a group. The second question introduces power as a central consideration, and forces us to recognise that the spaces that people exist in and interact with are not level playing fields, but are fluid hierarchies which offer differing levels of 'privilege and power' to some people sometimes. The final question forces us to look for 'commonalities across categories commonly viewed as deeply different' (p.171).

Another potential reason for the slow uptake of intersectionality within psychology and therapeutics is perhaps because of the slippery task of attempting to define the concept. As Davis (2008) has suggested, intersectionality has been variously thoughts of as a theory, a concept or heuristic, or even as a reading strategy. Definitions are also deferred because intersectionality is sometimes simultaneously regarded as 'crossroads', 'axes', or 'dynamic processes' (Davis, 2008). But this lack of a clear consensus towards a unitary definition of intersectionality does not render it useless to interrogate troublesome questions and social phenomena. In fact, as Davis (2008) paraphrasing Murray Davis asserts, 'successful theories thrive on ambiguity and incompleteness' (p.69).

As Cole (2009) points out, much of intersectionality scholarship has examined the multiple sites of oppression and disenfranchisement

experienced by people whose lives fall along the fault lines of social categories. Importantly, however, intersectionality can also explore the ways
in which; 'some members of disadvantaged groups also hold privileged
identities (e.g. middle class blacks, white women)' (p.171). This approach
has recently been developed to also consider how white middle class non-
heterosexual people similarly occupy intersecting identities, albeit ones that
are formed through a relationship both to social privilege (in terms of race
and class) and social disadvantage (in terms of sexuality). Riggs (2010),
extends the intersectional account of identity to encompass a relational account that locates individuals both at the intersections of a range of social
categories, but also in a relationship to other individuals who will likely
occupy different social categories (and specifically focussing on the relationship between the privileged social location of some people and the
disadvantaged social location of others, with the two seen as corollaries)
(see also Erel *et al.*, 2008). Together, intersectionality and relationality provide us with a wealth of responses to the problems raised in the previous
section, as we now elaborate.

In regards to Pon's concern that cultural competency rests upon an apolitical understanding of culture, intersectional approaches are fundamentally
concerned with theorising and investigating how dynamics of power play
out between groups. Crenshaw's (1991) early work in the area examined
how dominant feminist and anti-racist discourses of rape and domestic
violence failed to take account of the experiences of black women. With regards to therapists working with non-heterosexual clients, an intersectional
approach would encourage recognition that issues of power may be com-
pounded for clients who experience multiple marginalisations, and that the
interventions appropriate will be highly contingent upon the effects of this
multiplicity. McDermott's (2006) excellent work on class and race and their
relationship to employment options for lesbian women is a clear example
of this. McDermott suggests that for white middle class lesbians, workplace
discrimination can potentially be addressed by challenging employers, or
if necessary, finding alternate employment. For poorer non-white lesbians,
however, the often tentative nature of paid positions and relative lack of
employment opportunities can result in being forced to stay in a compro-
mised position (such issues are further taken up in Chapter 6). Addressing
the needs of these differing groups of women will require specific strategies from professionals that would not be possible were power not taken
into account.

Utilising both an intersectional and relational approach to understanding identities can afford practitioners the scope to consider not just the
complex intersections of identity categories, but also the broader context in

which those categories circulate and the norms that accompany them. An intersectional approach that takes into account a relational understanding of identity permits the acknowledgment of the position of professionals and/or dominant group/individuals vis-à-vis the client, and challenges the assumption that cultural conflict is 'inevitable'. Therapists who adopt such an approach to cultural competency would ensure that they locate themselves and their practice within a historical and cultural context in which power differentials between groups continue to play out to the benefit of dominant groups (often through the construction of categories of 'good' and 'bad' cultures). Locating oneself in a relationship to clients means acknowledging one's complicity with dominant social hierarchies that one may belong to and the investments that all individuals have in maintaining in-group/out-group practices (and how these are always negotiated in wider social hierarchies and power relations). Patricia Hill Collins (2000), in her discussion of the 'matrix of domination', examines subject locations as crisscrossing 'systems of oppression'. Finding ways out of such matrices of domination, Collins (2000) suggests, requires us to examine how our own 'thoughts and actions uphold someone else's subordination' (p.287). This awareness, she suggests, is necessary to ensure that the oppressed do not become the oppressors, for instance black heterosexual men discriminating against black non-heterosexual men.

As the preceding example suggests, the presumed homogeneity of any social category needs to be interrogated. It is vital that practitioners acknowledge the heterogeneous nature of all cultural groups, and refrain from treating any individual as an expert on their cultural groups. Importantly, this is not the same as refusing to treat an individual as an expert on *their view* of their cultural groups – it will be appropriate in many instances to accept as legitimate a client's view of their cultural memberships. This does not mean, however, that professionals cannot challenge clients' broader assumptions about speaking for all members of their cultural groups. Adopting an intersectional approach can encourage both practitioners and clients to talk up front about their views or standpoints within their cultural groups, and to consider from there what the views of other members who stand in a different relationship to cultural group norms might be. Working with clients to voice their specific standpoints can help to recognise both strengths and limitations, and to build upon these for the client's specific needs.

Indeed, intersectionality, it must be noted, may not only be related to matrices of oppression, but may also afford agency to individuals to negotiate their multiple identities in a manner whereby all these identities do not cause them distress (Fisher, 2003). Whilst for some clients this may mean that certain aspects of their identity are kept separate from other aspects

(Halbertal & Koren, 2006), an intersectional approach is nonetheless vital for understanding how potentially competing identity categories relate to one another and how clients can best negotiate these. This is a point we will come back to later in this chapter.

Not Reinventing the Wheel

Before going on to present our clients' stories, we take up the call made by Butler in the introduction by extending the previous section by outlining some of the academic histories that we believe should inform therapeutic practice, but which often are left unmentioned (see also Butler *et al.*, 2010, for more on this). The key area we mention, and one that has long been elaborated by African-American (e.g. hooks, 1989) and Indigenous Australian (e.g. Moreton-Robinson, 2003) feminists in regards to feminist movements more broadly, refers to what has often been a repeated failure to acknowledge the roots of current rights movements or critical theorising in the works of earlier, most often non-white, theorists and activists. McBride (2005) makes a similar claim in relation to queer theory, which he suggests, along with other 'cutting-edge scholarship', 'could scarcely have been imagined before the advent of African American studies, ethnic studies, gender studies and so forth' (p.8). Acknowledging the academic legacy of the long history of work by African American, Indigenous, and other black feminist scholars means, for therapists, that there is a wealth of critical knowledge about a wide range of areas relevant to professional practices that may not typically appear in academic or specifically mental health outlets, but which nonetheless deserve considerable attention. Resources such as those provided in this book and the references in this chapter represent a considerable opportunity to engage with these knowledges and to use them to examine the assumptions inherent to much of the psychological literature about working cross-culturally (see also Riggs, 2007b).

Importantly, writers such as Roberts (2002) remind us that social reform relating to issues such as racial equality still lags a long way behind laws intended to prevent discrimination. The same can be said about (homo)sexuality: with the majority of the world's nations not permitting or recognising same-sex unions; and even so-called developed nations, such as the UK, keeping the institution of marriage a privilege only for heterosexual couples. Therefore, whilst laws may claim to operate to allow 'justice for all', the ability to enact such 'freedom' is highly contingent upon one's social location, with those located outside the privileged location of able-bodied, healthy, financially stable, white male heterosexual middle-classness often having less than sufficient resources to enable full participation in social life. The fact that many white middle class non-heterosexual people can push for equal rights in the present is thus a legacy not only of the fact that previous rights claims have been made, but that such rights claims continue to be denied to certain marginalised groups (Riggs, 2006).

Adopting an intersectional approach can also further the engagement of therapists with previously subjugated (marginalised) knowledges and voices. As Baldwin (1987, cited in Běrubě, 2001) states so well: 'I think white gay people feel cheated because they were born, in principle, into a society in which they were supposed to be safe. The anomaly of their sexuality puts them in danger, unexpectedly' (p.256). Our point is obviously not that white gay people (for example) do not experience violence or danger. Rather, our point is that intersectional analyses can be used to examine the often unmarked privileges of 'majority minorities' (i.e. members of marginal communities who also occupy a very dominant social location), compared to *metaminorities* (minorities within minority positions).

Thomas (2007), claiming a Pan-Africanist perspective, argues that western binary models of gender fail to appreciate the fact that relationships between people within Africa prior to slavery and colonisation were structured in highly different ways from relationships between people living in colonial nations. As a result, he argues that it is nonsensical (and potentially offensive) to use western gender and sexuality categories to account for the historical (and potentially also contemporary) experiences of African people. Doing so, he claims, can result in the inability to actually see individual differences within African communities on their own terms, as he suggests in the following quote: 'There are never, ever merely girls and boys, men and women, without race and class. Analytically speaking, there are instead a legion of genders and sexualities, so to speak; and they cannot be reduced to the anatomy of any one white racist elite' (p.68). Epple (1998), speaking specifically about gender, suggests that the ways in which western researchers read the identities of First Nation and Indigenous people forces their bodies (and embodiment) into a western framework, where particular markers (such as forms of dress, ways of movement, terms of reference) are taken as symbolising the same things, rather than having potentially different meanings across cultures. This kind of reading can be found in other aspects of identity related to sexuality for instance. Western researches, including queer researchers, (particularly in the past) often misread homosocial activities amongst some South Asian men as homosexual behaviour (e.g. men holding hands or hugging in public).

Finally, therapists would do well to note research on the effects of marginalisation on certain communities. Specifically, research continues to identify the marginalising effects of racism on the part of white LGB people toward black non-heterosexual people (e.g. Kuntsman & Miyake, 2008), negative attitudes amongst LGB people toward bisexual people (e.g. Israel, 2001), anti-Muslim sentiment within gay communities (e.g. Abraham, 2009), and erotic economies within non-heterosexual communities that operate to marginalise non-white people (e.g. Han, 2006; McBride, 2005). Acknowledging the complex issues that arise from contestations over who is allowed to belong within non-heterosexual communities is an important aspect of understanding the social contexts in which these groups live, and the implications of these contexts for therapeutic practice.

With all of the points we have raised thus far in mind, we now present two stories of clients we have worked with, and a discussion of them in order to illustrate some of the complexities we have identified, and the utility of a relational and intersectional approach to addressing them.

Aaron, Mark and John's Stories

Aaron and Mark, a white middle class gay couple in their early 50s, presented for couples counselling in relation to issues over Mark having a relationship with a third person, John, outside of the couple context. Mark reported that from the beginning of their relationship they had negotiated to be able to have casual sex outside of the relationship, but Aaron emphasised that this was supposed to be 'casual', not 'meaningful', and that Mark's relationship with John had crossed over into the latter category. Aaron also expressed concern that Mark was his first partner since coming out when he turned 50, and that he felt Mark (who had come out when he was 20) often took advantage of this by insisting upon making decisions because 'he knew better'. Three weeks after counselling began Mark asked if John could attend a session on his own as he felt he had much to contribute to the work. When John – a young Malaysian man in the country on a working visa – presented for counselling, he went to great lengths to note that he had not intended to enter into a relationship with Mark, but that due to difficulties in maintaining paid employment he had become reliant upon Mark for financial support.

Cases such as this bring with them a number of complex issues that require attention from therapists, namely: the couples' negotiations over sex with other partners and the boundaries of their relationships, Aaron's experience of coming out later in life, Mark's claims to authority within the relationship, and John's position within his relationship to Mark.

Of course none of these issues can be easily read in isolation from any of the other issues or in isolation from the social location of all three individuals. Further, it is important to resist stereotyped or normalising interpretations of the individuals themselves. So whilst on the one hand it is important to recognise the vulnerable positions that both Aaron and John may potentially be in, it is also important to recognise any potential strengths they both have (i.e. the desire and ability to speak of their concerns and to address them).

In regards to the relationship between Aaron and Mark, it would appear important to recognise that whilst both men identify as white and middle class, their experiences are likely to be relatively different due to the time in which they each came out. Research suggests that men who come out later in life experience considerable challenges including (1) having to re-evaluate their life-long views of themselves as well as any potential stigma they have about non-heterosexual identities, (2) having to negotiate a place within non-heterosexual communities that may often be youth-orientated, and (3) having to 'learn the rules' of interacting with other non-heterosexual people in the absence of clear role models (see Meisner & Hynie, 2009). For Aaron, these issues could mean that he is positioned in the relationship as the 'student' who is required to defer to Mark as more knowledgeable or experienced. One implication of this could be that their original negotiation of an open relationship was not necessarily Mark's desire. Of course this should not be presumed by the practitioner, but would need to be carefully explored in order to determine what both Aaron and Mark are looking for in a relationship, and how their individual needs are being met (or not) in the current relationship.

If Mark and Aaron were to both express a desire for an open relationship, then the practitioner would work with them to establish ground rules that are acceptable to both men, and which take into consideration safer sex concerns and provide tools for both men to use to continually reassess the effects of having an open relationship. Importantly, the practitioner may seek to affirm that many gay men do engage in open relationships, and that this is neither inherently pathological nor damaging, but at the same time affirm that the prevalence of open relationships amongst gay men does not necessarily mean that all gay men engage in open relationships (see Clarke *et al.*, 2010, for a summary of non-heterosexual relationship styles). Placing Aaron and Mark's relationship in the context of other non-heterosexual relationships may help both to affirm their experiences as well as open a space for discussions about the degree to which their own desires match up with, or differ from, what a large proportion of other gay men may do in their relationships.

In addition to working with Aaron and Mark, it would also be important to work with them both (and Mark specifically) in his relationship to John. Whilst it would be important not to presume automatically that John is in a vulnerable position as a Malaysian man in relation to Aaron and Mark as white men, it would nonetheless be important to consider how racialised economies of desire operate amongst white men toward men seen as 'Asian', and how this can often function to the detriment of the latter (Han, 2006; and Chapter 3 in this book). For John, his concerns over his economic status must be taken seriously, particularly if he feels unable to make choices about his relationship with Mark because of his precarious position. Working with Mark in this regard could entail encouraging him to consider the privileged position that he holds as a white middle class man and that regardless of his intentions, this privilege comes at the expense of people not located within this category (including people such as John). Of course the point of doing this would not be to pathologise Mark's desire for John, but rather to examine how inter-racialised desire operates and how this places an injunction upon those who occupy dominant social locations to acknowledge the relative power they hold and the potential for this to be misused. For John, the role of the practitioner may be both to listen to his concerns but also to advocate for his needs. This would not be in a paternalistic fashion, but rather so as to acknowledge the position of authority that practitioners hold, and the injunction this produces to use such authority responsibly.

As we have suggested here, the issues that Aaron, Mark, and later John present with are complex, and need to be viewed through an intersectional and relational lens. Importantly, this is not simply the case because of the racialised differences between Mark and John, but also because Mark and Aaron have differing experiences as white middle class gay men that highlight the importance of acknowledging the differences *within*, as well as *across*, identity categories. Of course, in all these interactions, the identities, and especially visible markers of such identities, of the therapist must feature in the equation. Therefore, therapists would do well to recognise their own subjective positions and be mindful of how these might affect the therapeutic process and outcome.

Alia's Story

Alia presented to social services reporting a range of concerns about her current carer. Alia is a young South Asian Muslim lesbian woman who, due to an accident in childhood, is a wheelchair user. Alia has a strong relationship to her family and Muslim communities in the local suburb where she lives, however, they are not supportive of her lesbian identity. She is reliant upon a professional carer who supports her independent living and access to social life. Alia reported that her carer had grown increasingly unwilling to help her access lesbian events, and had twice failed to attend a home visit that had been planned to facilitate Alia's attendance at a lesbian pride weekend. Alia noted that she had made increasing use of social networking sites to meet other women but was frustrated by the difficulty in meeting up with women in real life, both due to limited support from family and her carer, but also due to the hyper-visibility (because of her minority ethnic status) and invisibility (because of her wheelchair) that she experienced at some of the venues she wished to attend, and the attitudes that Alia suspected exists amongst some of the white able-bodied lesbian women she had encountered at these events.

Working with Alia requires attention to a range of competing issues, including: the lack of support from her family in regards to her lesbian identity, but her ongoing strong connection to family and community as a South Asian Muslim woman, her needs as a wheelchair user, her needs as a lesbian, the concerns about her carer's lack of support, the inaccessibility of some LGB venues and the attitudes of people in them.

Working intersectionally with Alia is vital to ensure that her location within a range of identity categories is recognised. As a South Asian Muslim woman with a strong connection to family and extended family, it is vital that the therapist acknowledges the possible Islamaphobia and xenophobia that Alia and her family may have experienced, and which will likely serve as a strong bond between them. Thus in contrast to some literature which emphasises the importance of non-heterosexual people developing supportive family relations *outside* of birth families in order to combat the effects of discrimination *from within* birth families (e.g. Weston, 1991), for non-white cultural groups this may not be a welcomed suggestion. Working with Alia's family may of course be one possibility for understanding and addressing their issues, potentially by encouraging recognition of the diverse narratives about gender and sexuality held across non-white and Muslim communities about non-heterosexuality and non-gender normativity (Beckett, 2010; and Chapter 4 in this book).

In regards to Alia's concerns about her carer, this requires immediate attention. Refusing to support Alia as a lesbian represents a significant instance of homophobia, and one that is clearly preventing Alia from having her social needs met. Research suggests that non-heterosexual people living with disabilities often face the powerful effects of the beliefs of carers who have the capacity to prevent those in their care from accessing services. This can include threatening to 'out' clients or preventing their attendance at relevant events (Bennett & Coyle, 2007; Chapter 9 in this book).

An intersectional approach to working with Alia would involve acknowledging the many spaces in which she may feel she does not belong (i.e. not wholly supported by her family, not easily able to access or feel welcomed in lesbian venues), and identifying ways in which a range of opportunities may exist for having her needs met (i.e. connecting with South Asian and Muslim communities, advocating for better access to and treatment in venues, finding a more suitable carer, working with her family to better understand their beliefs). Working relationally also requires the therapist to examine their own location in regards to histories of prejudice and discrimination and their ongoing effects, and to be responsible for the privileged location(s) that they hold. Such a relational approach would also be important in addressing Alia's concerns about the views of some of the white lesbian women she has encountered, and that rather than pathologising her concerns as 'conspiracy theories', to instead acknowledge the racism that does occur within predominantly white LGB communities, and to talk with Alia about the impact of this upon her as a South Asian Muslim woman.

Conclusion: Moving from Matrices of Oppression to Conditions of Possibility

Throughout this chapter we have elaborated an intersectional and relational approach to therapeutic practice with non-heterosexual and/or non-gender normative people that takes up Butler's challenge to assess how norms function within these communities. In so doing, we have not sought to provide a negative picture of such communities *per se*, but rather to highlight that despite assumptions of homogeneity, there is infinite diversity within such communities, diversity that can at times be a source of strength and growth, but at other times can have a negative impact, particularly for those who experience a 'metaminority' status (see Butler *et al.*, 2010; das Nair, 2006, for more on this).

The two client stories presented illustrate the need for 'adding complexity' to therapeutic practice, rather than seeking simplistic explanations and responses. Non-heterosexual and/or non-gender normative people, like *all* people, inhabit a complex and intersecting range of social locations that exist within a relationship to broader social norms that carry with them the weight of historically and contextually constructed hierarchies. Adding complexity thus requires practitioners to examine the intersections not just of a range of identity locations, but also the intersections of privilege and oppression in the lives of clients (Riggs, 2011). A relational approach is important in this regard, as it can facilitate working with clients to locate them within a range of social contexts, some of which may be productive of privilege, whilst others may be productive of marginalisation. And of course this is just as applicable to practitioners, who must locate themselves in a relationship both to the privileged location they hold as practitioners, but also as members of social categories that will almost certainly differ (at least in some aspects) from those of their clients.

Furthermore, we recognise that much of what has been written here (and elsewhere) about intersectionality refers to how people who find themselves at the fault lines of multiple, sometimes conflicting identities, can be dis-advantaged. While this is no doubt the case for many people, we also feel that there is ample scope for therapists to employ intersectional positions to understand, or even develop, these identities. This of course should not be taken as suggesting that intersectionality can operate as a vehicle for change that is open to everyone at all times. Fisher (2003) describes a location where people who are cognisant of their intersecting identities reside (or 'hybrid identification', to use her terms), which can produce a space that is simultaneously inside and outside of the margins defined by the majority culture(s). Alongside this location, she also describes how such people use 'the liminality of the "closet"' as a strategy and 'a space in which sexuality cannot be easily fixed and identified, as a way to complicate the relationship between centre and periphery' (p.173).

Drawing upon de Certeau's (1984) differentiation between 'strategies' and 'tactics' (where the former relate to institutions and structures of power, and the latter are what individuals use to create spaces for themselves in structures and locations defined by the former), Fisher (2003) examines how non-heterosexual people who also belong to other minority cultures negotiate their daily lives without compromising or forsaking their multi-ple identities, often by pluralising the self. Fisher interrogates hyphenated identities and lives as they are lived in the hyphens. By deploying certain 'tactics', she suggests individuals with metaminority identities/positions can use 'their hyphenated identities to weave together a combination of cultural elements appropriate for the moment, while simultaneously safeguarding their desire to suitably (re)position themselves in the next moment (thereby) move(ing) along a trajectory of locations' (Fisher, 2003, p.174). As such, it must be recognised that such pluralised selves not only posit risks, but also afford opportunities for linkages and leakage between and into different identity groups and practices. In the context of the therapeutic space, it is both the therapist's and client's skill that will enable the latter to identify these potential threats and opportunities, and foster the use of tactics that will ultimately allow the client to live their multiple lives in ways that allow them to acknowledge their varying standpoints and to do so with minimum conflict.

To conclude, whilst current understandings of cultural competency may be limited, as Pon (2009) notes, this does not mean that therapists cannot provide competent and positive services. What is required is an approach to practice that moves beyond the simple application of checklists or essentialist understandings of culture, and toward one where both the complex issues and complex identities that clients present with are recognised and taken into account in the provision of services.

Guidelines for Good Practice

- Therapists should examine their own assumptions about what constitutes 'culture' and assess their own location(s) in regard to social norms.
- Intersections of privilege and disadvantage should be recognised in the therapeutic space and discussed with clients. However, therapists should be mindful of ethical boundaries and potential misinterpretation when considering whether to disclose personal information to clients.
- Both therapists and clients should aim to identify their own standpoints to one another and consider their impact upon other parties.
- Therapists should not assume that a client's cultural values and/or sexual values and identities can be easily read by their appearance or mode of self-representation.
- Therapists should understand the impact of metaminority status(es) and the existence of marginalisation within non-heterosexual and/or non-gender normative communities.

References

Abraham, I. (2009). 'Out to get us': Queer Muslims and the clash of sexual civilisations in Australia. *Contemporary Islam, 3*, 79–97.

Barnard, I. (2003). *Queer race: Cultural interventions in the racial politics of queer theory.* New York, NY: Peter Lang.

Beckett, S. (2010). Azima ila Hayati – an invitation to my life: narrative conversations about sexual identity. In L. Moon (Ed.) *Counselling ideologies: Queer challenges to heteronormativity.* Surrey: Ashgate.

Bennett, C. & Coyle, A. (2007). A minority within a minority: Experiences of gay men with intellectual disabilities. In V. Clarke and E. Peel (Eds.) *Out in psychology: Lesbian, gay, bisexual, trans and queer perspectives.* Chichester: John Wiley & Sons, Ltd.

Běrubě, A. (2001). How gay stays white and what kind of white it stays. In B.B. Rasmussen, E. Klinenberg, I.J. Nexica & M. Wray (Eds.). *The making and unmaking of whiteness.* Durham: Duke University Press.

Brown, W. (1994). *States of injury.* Princeton, NJ: Princeton University Press.

Butler, C., das Nair, R. & Thomas, S. (2010). The colour of queer. In L. Moon (Ed.), *Counselling ideologies: Queer challenges to heteronormativity.* Surrey: Ashgate.

Clarke, V., Ellis, S.J., Peel, E. & Riggs, D.W. (2010). *Lesbian, gay, bisexual, trans and queer psychology: An introduction.* Cambridge: Cambridge University Press.

Cole, E. (2009). Intersectionality and research in psychology. *American Psychologist, 64*(3), 170–180.

Collins, P.H (2000). *Black feminist thought: Knowledge, consciousness, and the politics of empowerment* (2nd edn). New York, NY: Routledge.

Crenshaw, K. (1991). Mapping the margins: Intersectionality, identity politics, and violence against women of color. *Stanford Law Review, 43*, 1241–1299.

das Nair, R. (2006). *Metaminorities and mental health: A model of vulnerability for black and minority ethnic queer folk.* Retrieved 13 October 2010 from http://kc.csip.org.uk/viewdocument.php?action=viewdox&pid=0&doc=3493 0&grp=447.

Davis, K. (2008). Intersectionality as buzzword. A sociology of science perspective on what makes a feminist theory successful. *Feminist Theory, 9*(1), 67–85.

de Certeau, M. (1984). *The practice of everyday life.* (Trans. S. Rendall). Berkeley, CA: University of California Press.

Eliot, T.S. (1958). *Notes towards the definition of culture.* London: Faber and Faber Ltd.

Epple, C. (1998). Coming to terms with Navajo nádleehí: A critique of *berdarche,* 'gay', 'alternate gender', and 'two spirit'. *American Ethnologist, 25*(2), 267–290.

Erel, U., Haritaworn, J., Rodriguez, E.G. & Klesse, C. (2008). On the depoliticisation of intersectionality talk: Conceptualising multiple oppressions in critical sexuality studies. In A. Kuntsman & E. Miyake (Eds.) *Out of place: Interrogating silences in queerness/raciality.* York: Raw Nerve.

Fisher, D. (2003). Immigrant closets: tactical-micro-practices-in-the-hyphen. *Journal of Homosexuality, 45*(2/3/4), 171–192.

Fiske, A.P. (2002). Using individualism and collectivism to compare cultures – A critique of the validity and measurement of the constructs: Comment on Oyserman *et al.* (2002). *Psychological Bulletin, 128,* 78–88.

Foucault, M. (1980). *Power/Knowledge.* New York, NY: Pantheon.

Greene, B. (2007). Delivering ethical psychological services to lesbian, gay, and bisexual clients. In K.J. Bieschke, R. Perez & K.A. DeBord (Eds.), *Handbook of counseling and psychotherapy with lesbian, gay, and bisexual clients,* 2nd Edn. Washington, DC: APA.

Halbertal, T.H. & Koren, I. (2006). Between 'being' and 'doing': Conflict and co-herence in the identity formation of gay and lesbian orthodox Jews. In D.P. McAdams, R. Josselson & A. Lieblich (Eds.), *Identity and story: Creating self in narrative.* Washington, DC: American Psychological Association.

Han, A. (2006). 'I think you're the smartest race I've ever met': Racialised economies of gay desire. *ACRAWSA e-journal, 2*(2). Retrieved 4 June 2010 from www .acrawsa.org.au.

hooks, b. (1989). *Talking back: Thinking feminist, thinking black.* Boston: South End Press.

Israel, T. (2001). Training counselors to work ethically and effectively with bisexual clients. In B.A. Firestein (Ed.), *Becoming visible: Counseling bisexuals across the lifespan.* New York, NY: Columbia University Press.

Kroeber, A.L. & Kluckhohn, C.K. (1952). *Culture: A critical review of concepts and definitions.* Cambridge, MA: Harvard University Press.

Kuntsman, A. & Miyake, E. (Eds.) (2008). *Out of place: Interrogating silences in queerness/raciality.* York: Raw Nerve.

Lamble, S. (2008). Retelling racialised violence, remaking white innocence: The politics of interlocking oppressions in Transgender Day of Remembrance. *Sexuality Research and Social Policy, 5,* 24–42.

Mama, A. (1995). *Beyond the masks: Race, gender and subjectivity.* London: Routledge.

McBride, D.A. (2005). *Why I hate Abercrombie and Fitch: Essays on race and sexuality.* New York, NY: New York University Press.

McCall, L. (2005). The complexity of intersectionality. *Signs, 30,* 1771–1800.

McDermott, E. (2006). Surviving in dangerous places: Lesbian identity performances in the workplace, social class and psychological health. *Feminism & Psychology, 16*(2), 193–211.

Meisner, B. & Hynie, M. (2009). Ageism with heterosexism: Self-perceptions, identity, and psychological health in older gay and lesbian adults. *Gay and Lesbian Issues and Psychology Review, 5,* 51–58.

Moreton-Robinson, A. (2003). I still call Australia home: Indigenous belonging and place in a white postcolonizing society. In S. Ahmed, C. Castañeda, A. Fortier & M. Sheller (Eds.) *Uprootings/Regroundings: Questions of home and migration.* Oxford: Berg.

Pon, G. (2009). Cultural competency as new racism: An ontology of forgetting. *Journal of Progressive Human Services, 20,* 59–71.

Puar, J. (2007). *Terrorist assemblages: Homonationalism in queer times.* Durham: Duke University Press.

Riggs, D.W. (2006). *Priscilla, (white) queen of the desert: Queer rights/race privilege.* New York, NY: Peter Lang.

Riggs, D.W. (2007a). Recognising race in LGBTQ psychology: Privilege, power and complicity. In V. Clarke and E. Peel (Eds.) *Out in psychology: Lesbian, gay, bisexual, trans and queer perspectives.* Chichester: John Wiley & Sons, Ltd.

Riggs, D.W. (2007b). Queer theory and its future in psychology: Exploring issues of race privilege. *Social and Personality Psychology Compass, 1,* 39–52.

Riggs, D.W. (2010). On accountability: Towards a white middle-class queer 'post identity politics identity politics'. *Ethnicities, 10*(3), 344–357.

Riggs, D.W. (2011). Queering evidence-based practice. *Psychology and Sexuality, 2*(1), 87–98.

Roberts, D. (2002). *Shattered bonds: The color of child welfare.* New York, NY: Basic Books.

Ross, K. (1992). Watching the detectives. In F. Barker, P. Hulme & M. Iverson (Eds.), *Postmodernism and the re-reading of modernity.* Manchester: Manchester University Press.

Thomas, G. (2007). *The sexual demon of colonial power: Pan-African embodiment and erotic schemes of empire.* Bloomington, IN: Indiana University Press.

van Mens-Verhulst, J. & Radtke, L.H. (2006). *Intersectionality and health care: Support for the diversity turn in research and practice.* Retrieved 14 January 2011 from http://www.vanmens.info/verhulst/en/wpcontent/Intersectionality%20 and%20Health%20Care-%20january%202006.pdf.

Weston, K. (1991). *Families we choose: Lesbian, gays, kinship.* Columbia, NY: Columbia University Press.

2

Gender

Sonja J. Ellis

Gender refers to the ascribed (attributed) and prescribed (set or agreed) behaviours associated with the categories 'women' and 'men'. In Western societies, certain contrasting but complimentary characteristics are attributed to men and women respectively. For example, men are commonly perceived to be tough, strong and dominant; while women are perceived to be emotionally sensitive, nurturing and passive. Of course not all (if any) men and women fit these archetypal patterns, but these are socially constructed versions of what men and women should be.

In theory, sex and gender are constructed as distinct: sex as the biological differences, and gender as the culturally/socially constructed differences, between men and women. Despite this theoretical distinction, the terms 'sex' and 'gender' are often conflated in practice (Speer, 2005). This is, in part, because the distinction between biological and socially constructed differences is not necessarily as apparent as it may at first seem. More importantly though, gender and sex have historically been constructed as dichotomous and therefore assumed to map neatly onto one another; sex (male/female) thus mapping directly onto gender (masculinity/femininity).

The premise on which the construction of gender is based is that men and women are fundamentally different as a direct function of biological sex. While in contemporary society it is generally accepted that gender boundaries are somewhat blurred, extreme deviation from these norms is often considered sufficient to question one's sex. An example of this is the recent controversy surrounding the (female) South African runner Caster Semenya. Following her victory at the 2009 World Championships, questions were raised about her gender on the grounds that it was not feasible

Intersectionality, Sexuality and Psychological Therapies: Working with Lesbian, Gay and Bisexual Diversity,
First Edition. Edited by Roshan das Nair and Catherine Butler.
© 2012 John Wiley & Sons, Ltd. Published 2012 by John Wiley & Sons, Ltd. and the British Psychological Society.

for a woman to run at such record-breaking speeds. Having ruled out drug use as a possible cause, the International Association of Athletics Federations (IAAF) ordered an investigation into her gender to determine whether she had a rare medical condition giving her an unfair competitive advantage. This is a clear illustration of how gender attributes are presumed to map directly onto biological sex. However, the construction of gender in this way rests heavily on the assumption that sex (and therefore gender) is robust, comprising two (and only two) mutually exclusive categories which are fixed (cannot be changed) and are stable (do not vary across time and context).

The assumption that there are two distinct sex categories is in itself problematic. While (arguably) the vast majority of people have bodies which are 'unequivocally' female or male in their appearance and in their hormonal and chromosomal composition, this is not *universally* the case. A relatively small number of individuals vary in the extent to which they are biologically defined as male or female. For example, some have atypical chromosomal patterns (as in Klinefelter's Syndrome and Turner's syndrome), while others have genitalia which are neither definitively female nor definitively male (i.e. are intersex). However, because of the deeply ingrained belief that people are (and should be) either male or female, the latter are often surgically sex-reassigned in infancy.

Equally problematic is the assumption that gender maps directly onto biological sex. While not the main focus of this chapter, the clearest example of this is individuals who self-define as Trans. For Trans people, gender does *not* map onto biological sex. While these individuals were born in a body which designated them as biologically either male or female, they understand themselves to be a gender other than this. For example, even in childhood, an individual might be born with a body which is clearly male in appearance (and is perhaps consistently male in hormonal and chromosomal composition) yet *feels* that he is actually female and trapped in a male body (see Sanger, 2008 for a full discussion of Trans). However, even in the absence of such clear-cut examples, assuming that there are agreed behaviours that we can attribute distinctly to males and to females belies the considerable similarities between the two. It also does not stack up when we look at the extent of difference within the 'male' and 'female' gender/sex categories.

The focus of this chapter, in the main, is to explore the way in which social constructions of gender impact on the identities and lived experiences of LGB people. With some reference to LGB sexualities, the main psychological and sociological theories/perspectives on gender that are used in various therapies will be outlined, followed by an exploration of the way in which heteronormativity (or heterosexual bias) impacts on LGB people. The latter part of the chapter will look specifically at the relationship between gender and LGB sexualities, followed by a brief overview of how gender impacts on Trans people who identify as LGB.

Gender and (Mainstream) Psychology

Within mainstream psychology 'men' and 'women' have been presumed to be fundamentally different. On this basis gender is constructed as a robust and meaningful category around which to organise comparative research. Consequently, across the wide range of topics it is common to find statistical analyses comparing men and women and attributing the findings to innate and biological 'differences' between them as if those categories were unproblematic. This body of work is known as the study of sex (or gender) differences and its specific aim is to determine what is distinctly different about men and women. However, feminist psychologists (e.g. Fine & Addelston, 1996; Wilkinson, 1997) have frequently argued that far from being neutral and investigative, this work is highly political and (in most cases) designed to reinscribe gender differences that position men as superior to women. This goal is accomplished by using values and attributes traditionally ascribed to men as the baseline against which to compare women. For example, there is a considerable body of early research that explored brain function, hormones and personality to establish that women are inferior to men and to attribute this to biological factors such as menstruation, emotional instability, etc. This work has then historically been used to justify women's exclusion from and/or limited achievement in education and certain occupations (Wilkinson, 1997).

The notion that biology underpins gender differences has also been extended to explain same-sex attraction as a deviation from gendered norms. For example, the scientific studies of Simon LeVay (1991) purported to find distinct differences in the brain structure of gay men compared with their heterosexual counterparts. In particular, a part of the hypothalamus was found to be smaller in gay men than in heterosexual men and of a similar size to that in heterosexual women. This is a good example of how a two-category system of gender gets unproblematically mapped onto a two-category sexuality system (i.e. that gay men are like heterosexual women, and lesbians are like heterosexual men). In addition, it makes the (erroneous) assumption that 'heterosexual men' and 'gay men' (and likewise 'heterosexual women' and 'lesbian women') are distinct and homogenous categories[1]. However, regardless of whether these categories are defined by sexual experience, self-definition, or on any other basis, individuals within those categories are neither the same, nor behave in the same ways, making the categories somewhat arbitrary.

In the absence of adequate tangible evidence for biological explanations, alternative explanations have been developed around the *attribution* of differential characteristics to men versus women. For example, researchers (Stern & Karraker, 1989) presented neutrally clothed infants to adults and although there was some variation in responses to the infants, more often than not the adults engaged in stereotypically gendered play with the child based on the sex they believed the child to be. Thus, there is some evidence to suggest that gender differences are a function of social processes rather than real (and discernable) differences.

Social Learning Theory

In the 1960s the innateness of gender began to be questioned. Social Learning Theory (Bandura & Walters, 1963) suggested that gender was primarily the product of socialisation rather than biology: that is, that gender is *learned*. This theory was based on the observation of children in societies where gender roles were highly demarcated. In such societies girls tended to stay with their mothers, and boys with their fathers, watching the behaviour of their same-sex parent and imitating it. He argued that these behaviours then became internalised so that boys and girls came to identify with the parent of the same sex. Gender differences therefore came to be understood as the result of the acquisition of gender roles. Despite the plausibility of this theory, it only partially explained gender socialisation. In societies which are less gender segregated, most young children, both boys and girls, spend a disproportionate amount of time in the presence of *female* role models (e.g. mothers, nannies, childminders, teachers, etc.). So, for Social Learning Theory to make sense, boys must at some stage shift their identification to male role models. Although there are potentially lots of explanations for this, it has been argued that children basically learn to associate certain kinds of behaviour with one or other gender (Bandura, 1986). Identification with the behaviour associated with one's own sex is then rewarded and thus reinforced.

---

[1]   This kind of research is further complicated by the fact that identifiers such as 'gay' are culturally subscribed and do not necessarily generalise across all cultures and historical times (see Chapter 3 on Race and Ethnicity for more discussions on the construction of LGB identities).

Since gendered socialisation is based heavily on a heterosexual model of relating, it can be problematic when used to understand same-sex relationships. For example, it has been argued that because men are typically socialised to be competitive, sexually active and aggressive there is perhaps more potential for conflict, sexual difficulties and anger/violence in same-sex relationships between men (Hawkins, 1992). This is, however, a rather simplistic application of gender norms which assumes that gendered characteristics manifest themselves identically in same-sex relationships to how they are assumed to operate in heterosexual ones.

Classical Psychoanalysis

Congruent with Social Learning Theory, same-sex attraction has been explained in terms of a failure in the early socialisation of LGB persons. For example, in psychoanalytic work (e.g. Goldsmith, 2001) the development of a gay (male) identity has been attributed to the failure of the individual to successfully identify with male role models (usually fathers) and come to see women as an object of their affection. Similarly, the development of a lesbian identity has been attributed to having been raised by an overly-dominant mother and a passive or emotionally absent father (e.g. Wolff, 1971). In this respect, sexuality is therefore seen as closely tied to gender socialisation, with LGB sexualities arising from some problem or dysfunction in the socialisation process.

Gender Schema Theory

Employing the model of schematic processing, the cognitive phenomenon enabling individuals to impose structure and meaning onto stimuli, Sandra Bem (1981) developed Gender Schema Theory. This theory proposed that sex typing is derived from gender-based cognitive processing, or the processing of information on the basis of sex-linked associations. That is, because we expect men and women to behave in ways consistent with their sex-typed gender we evaluate their behaviour in relation to those gender norms. This frequently results in the same behaviour being evaluated differently when exhibited by a man than a woman. For example, a man who is sexually promiscuous is viewed as a 'stud' whereas a woman who is sexually promiscuous is viewed as a 'slag'.

The use of gender schemata directly informs gender stereotyping: a 'set of beliefs about the psychological traits and characteristics and the behaviours expected of (and seen as appropriate for) men and women' (Stainton-Rogers & Stainton-Rogers, 2001, p.50). Stereotyping is generally seen as a bad thing because it socially constrains or restricts the ability of individuals to deviate from so-called gender norms. The solution suggested by Bem (1981) was for society to be aschematic in its orientation to gender. A further observation was the way in which our schematic processing of gender is underpinned by heterosexuality (Ingraham, 2006). By heightening the differences between men and women through the dichotomous construction of gender, we facilitate the generalisation that men and women are (and should be) different from one another. The very foundation of heterosexuality is, in part, that 'opposites attract' or that the alleged differences in characteristics of men and women mean that they complement each other physically and emotionally.

Based on this premise, same-sex relationships are problematised on the grounds that gender similarity inevitably results in problems relating within the couple dyad. For example, it is commonly assumed that because women are regarded as emotional, sensitive and nurturing, lesbian couple relationships are characterised by high levels of closeness, intimacy, and emotional intensity. Rather than being viewed as a relational strength, this is generally constructed as a bad thing because of the risk of fusion/merger (the blurring of boundaries between individuals). However, this construct has been heavily critiqued on the grounds that it applies a heterosexual model of gender resulting in the pathologisation of lesbian relationships (e.g. Hill, 1999).

The Impact of Critical Social Psychology

While mainstream psychology continued to study sex differences and socialisation, the emergence in the mid 1980s of a critical social psychology enabled gender to be theorised and researched in other ways. This approach to the study of gender was primarily advanced by the work of feminist social psychologists, including Bem's later work. The main argument brought to the fore was that hidden assumptions embedded in social institutions and cultural discourses perpetuate male power and disadvantage women and sexual minorities. Bem (1993) argued that there were fundamentally three cultural assumptions (or lenses) which underpin the institutionalisation of gender differences. The first lens, androcentrism (male-centredness), functions to define males and male experience as the norm from which women deviate. As a result, women's values, achievements and qualities are undervalued while men's are promoted. The second lens, gender polarisation, works to impose gender differences on every aspect of human experience so that our focus on difference is heightened, making small differences appear much larger than they actually are. The key assumption is that the most salient feature about gender is across-group (i.e. males vs. females) rather than within-group (Ingraham, 2006) or the potential similarities between men and women. Biological essentialism (the third lens) works to reinforce the other two lenses by treating gender differences as the inevitable consequence of innate biological differences between men and women. According to Bem, these assumptions not only shape our perceptions of social reality, but are instrumental in shaping gender differences in our material worlds from unequal pay right through to sexual conduct. LGB persons are again compared to these heterosexually prescribed norms and found lacking.

Gender and Sociology

In contrast with (mainstream) psychology, sociology has been concerned with gender as socially defined and separate from the individual. Consequently, rather than being the product of biology and socialisation, gender was primarily viewed as 'scripts' that people learn and follow; referred to as *gender roles*. Gender roles are the social and behavioural norms considered to be appropriate for individuals of a specific sex in the context of the culture in which they live. For example, in western culture in the 1950s-60s the gender role of women was to be a good homemaker, wife and mother, while the role of a man was to earn a living to support his family and to contribute to public/social life outside of the home. While gender role norms have shifted somewhat over the ensuing decades, these scripts still tend to underpin social understandings of gender and gender difference.

Gender Role Theory

Gender Role Theory (formerly known as *Sex Role Theory*) was developed by Talcott Parsons (Parsons & Bales, 1953) to explain how men and women come to acquire these roles and how society benefits. According to Parsons, boys and girls learn gender appropriate behaviours and attitudes from their families and the overall culture in which they grow up; so non-physical differences were viewed as the product of early socialisation. Moreover, sex-differentiated behaviour was viewed as underpinning the division of labour within society and therefore essential for helping society 'work' effectively. Labour was thus divided along gender lines based on the characteristics attributed to men and women, resulting in a role segregation in which men were encouraged (and expected) to seek career advancement, assume responsibility for decision-making, and provide for their families; while women were encouraged (and expected) to take responsibility for house-keeping and childcare. Based on the archetypal heterosexual relationship, men and women were seen as working in a partnership in which their complimentary but different roles brought mutual benefit.

One of the ways in which gender roles manifest themselves is in the value afforded work done by men in comparison to women. While traditionally women's labour (usually in the home) was unpaid, today it is underpaid in relation to men's labour. The *gender pay gap* between men's and women's earnings also operates differentially (and unequally) on LGB people. While it is difficult to access accurate statistics disaggregated on grounds of both gender and sexuality, studies (e.g. Schmitt, 2008) seem to indicate an 'earnings penalty' for gay/bisexual men in comparison with their heterosexual counterparts. The reasons for this could be many and varied, but it is certainly a disincentive for men to be 'out' as gay/bi. Similarly, some women may find it difficult to come out as lesbian/bi, particularly if they are financially dependent on a male partner with whom they are raising children. So, while the wealth of the so-called 'pink pound' is associated with LGB people, it applies mainly to (a subgroup of) gay men (see Chapter 6 for how this relates to different social classes).

Gendered subjectivity

For both women and men, subjectivities (people's opinions/beliefs/judgements about and the way they experience themselves and others) are constructed within a framework of gender difference. Therefore, gender becomes the reference point for measuring how we fit, or how we deviate from, gender norms, and the basis on which our gender conformity/difference is policed. Arguably, it is easier for girls/women to move between gender-differentiated positions than it is for men. For example, women who dress/behave in ways that deviate from standard feminine norms are (in most cases) far less stigmatised than men who dress/behave in ways that deviate from accepted norms of masculinity. This explains why effeminate gay/bisexual men experience greater levels of stigmatisation and are more often the victims of hate-motivated violence than lesbian/bisexual women. More often than not it is gender transgression rather than sexuality *per se* which is the focus of prejudice against LGB people.

Gendered subjectivity is heavily underpinned by discourses of heterosexuality, one of the most common discourses being that of the *male sex drive*

(Hollway, 1984). Based in a biological determinist framework, this discourse constructs men's sexuality as directly produced by a biological drive (aimed primarily at reproduction). Men are thus constructed as being innately predisposed to want sex and that this desire is relatively uncontrollable. Based on this premise, it is presumed that gay/bi men *as men* will be subject to this same biological drive and thus same-sex relationships between men will be dominated by sex. While research evidence seems to suggest that gay men *do* have more sex than other groups, this is largely the bi-product of the way in which men generally are constructed as sexually promiscuous.

The other common discourse of sexuality is the *have/hold discourse* (Hollway, 1984). This discourse encompasses ideals about monogamy, partnership and family life and positions women as asexual: deriving sexual pleasure from fulfilling a man's desire and the prospect of bearing children (thus fulfilling her maternal instinct). This heavily biologically-based heterosexual norm assumes that women are not themselves sexually motivated. This discourse constructs men as protectors of women and 'good' women as maternal rather than sexual. By extension, women in same-sex relationships are consequently constructed as fundamentally asexual or at best having a low sex drive and not motivated by the prospect of motherhood (something not substantiated by the growing number of lesbian mothers). This demonstrates the application of heterosexual norms to same-sex relationships between women in a way that denies women a sense of sexual agency and marginalises the sexuality of lesbian women both as women and as lesbians. Furthermore, the notion of monogamy as a feminine ideal results in the positioning of lesbian women as more likely to commit to long-term relationships than to more casual sexual encounters.

The traditional western construction of sexuality in a dualistic scheme (underpinned by the gender dichotomy) is also complicit in shaping the subjectivities of bisexual men and women. Within this dualistic scheme, heterosexuality and homosexuality are perceived as the only 'real' and valid forms of sexual orientation which, by default, positions bisexuality as a 'mixed' form of sexuality (Klesse, 2005). From this standpoint, a person can only be considered bisexual if he/she maintains relationships with persons of the same and other genders at the same time. This reinforces stereotypical notions (and forms) of bisexuality as necessarily non-monogamous. Those who identify as bisexual but do not practice non-monogamy are therefore frequently positioned as 'in denial' (i.e. really lesbian/gay) or 'just experimenting' (i.e. really heterosexual) discourses which marginalise and make invisible bisexuality as a legitimate sexual identity. However, bisexual women who do practice non-monogamy are equally problematised on the grounds that non-monogamy is (erroneously) equated with promiscuity: a quality stereotypically viewed as undesirable in women.

Hegemonic masculinity

Hegemonic masculinity refers to the culturally dominant (and idealised) form of masculinity that men are strongly encouraged to embody. As well as the propensity to dominate other males and to subordinate females, this particular form of masculinity is characterised by aggressiveness, strength, drive, ambition and self-reliance; characteristics which are encouraged (and rewarded) in men, but discouraged in women. Rather than being a description of a 'real man', a personality type or character, hegemonic masculinity is an aspirational goal articulated through a set of prescriptive social norms (Connell, 1987). These norms are reinforced through popular media representation through the depiction of the white, heterosexual, successful masculinity of *the hero* (Speer, 2005). However, framing masculinity as a singular (and monolithic) construct masks the role of social context in shaping individual subjectivities and fails to recognise that not all individuals have equal access to such a narrow idea of masculinity. Furthermore, it positions itself in direct opposition to a singular notion of femininity thus reinforcing a dichotomous notion of gender.

One of the products of the sociology of gender was the development of gender theory beyond simply the study of hegemonic masculinity. Instead of talking in the singular, writers started to talk about there being multiple forms of masculinity and femininity: hence the shift in language to talking about masculini*ties* and feminini*ties*. However, work on gender has suggested that some forms of masculinity and femininity are more socially valued than others (Wetherell & Edley, 1999). For example, while new masculinities have emerged such as the 'Sensitive New Age Guy' or 'SNAG' (a man who is timid, sensitive and listens to his partner) and the 'Metrosexual' (a heterosexual man who pays attention to his appearance and is aesthetically groomed and fashioned), the archetypal form of masculinity (the man who is strong, dependable and stoic) is still the most highly valued within western society.

Although there is considerable diversity in the way gay/bisexual men (and indeed men generally) *do* masculinity, gay men in particular are commonly perceived to be effeminate and therefore the direct opposite to dominant representations of masculinity. This can be particularly problematic for certain groups of gay men (e.g. gay men who are also fathers) and especially for bisexual men. As well as defying traditional masculine ideals by being romantically/sexually attracted to other men, gay/bi men are affected by masculine ideals that restrict the expression of emotion and affection between men (Sánchez *et al.*, 2009).

Because in western society masculinity is heavily policed, it can be important for gay/bi men to be socially accepted and affirmed as men. While there is a risk that they may be victimised by heterosexual men for their non-conformity to the 'masculine ideal', gay men are frequently idealised by heterosexual women precisely because they do not typify hegemonic masculinity (i.e. they are 'safe' social companions who will not approach them sexually), while lesbian women may perceive them to be allies in a heteronormative world. For bisexual men the picture is more complex. Given that bisexual identity is itself marginalised (and largely invisible) within the dichotomous structures of gender and sexuality, bisexual men may feel a greater imperative to be socially validated in terms of their masculinity. A study of bisexual men by Stokes and colleagues (2002) found that masculine ideology was played out in their sexual encounters to avoid their manhood being questioned. Masculinity was therefore manifested through emphasising physical pleasure rather than emotional intimacy, being the 'insertive' partner in sexual contact, and treating relationships as 'just sex'.

Dominic's Story

Dominic is a single man in his mid-thirties. Although he is attracted to and has had sexual relationships with both men and women, he feels more strongly drawn to men and has recently started to think of himself as gay rather than bisexual. In sexual relationships he has a preference for being the passive/submissive sexual partner. In his relationships with women he has explored ways of being that are not heteronormative, but the relationships have not lasted because he has not lived up to masculine expectations demanded of him by his heterosexual female partners. This, together with his preference for being submissive in gay male sex, has caused considerable distress for Dominic as it made him question his maleness. Consequently, he has sought alternative ways of asserting his masculinity through heavy drinking and acts of aggression.

One therapeutic approach in this case would be to unpack the meaning of masculinity that Dominic holds. Exploring meanings associated with such constructs exposes notions of hegemonic masculinity. Framing masculinity in the plural often provides clients with alternative ways of being a man, all 'real'. Such explorations may also highlight the inherent belief systems that Dominic has and how these link to the expectations of his social networks.

Performativity

Possibly the most significant contribution to the sociology of gender is the poststructuralist work of Judith Butler. Butler (1990) proposed the radical view that there is no real distinction between sex and gender and therefore the so-called naturalness of the male-female dualism that under-pins gender difference is questionable. Instead, Butler theorised gender in terms of *performativity*. She characterised gender as the effect of repeated acting that produces the effect of a static gender, while obscuring contradic-tions and instability of the gender acts at an individual level. Butler argued that the natural-seeming coherence of categories of sex and gender (and sex-uality), were therefore culturally constructed through consistently stylised bodily acts (i.e. performances). So, rather than being the function of actual differences, their repetition makes them *appear* as essential. Furthermore, her work challenged biological accounts of dichotomous sex categories by conceiving the sexed body as itself constructed within 'regulative discourses', which in turn shape the construction of gender and sexuality.

While much of the theory outlined this far has troubled the concept of gender (and, by implication, sexuality), some have argued that it does not go far enough. Arising from sociology, *Queer Theory* (De Laurentis, 1991) aims to 'denaturalise' sex, gender and sexuality (and the supposed relationship between them) and to abandon these categories altogether as a means of resistance (Clarke & Peel, 2007). Instead of being defined by sex/gender/sexuality categories, Queer Theory is defined by an opposition to heteronormativity. Without reference to labels, it therefore encompasses sex, gender and sexuality in whatever forms and fluidity it takes so long as it does not conform to heteronormative ways of being. Queer approaches to gender (and sexuality) therefore recognise the fluidity of lives, identities and practices and affirm the individual choices that people make (Butler & Byrne, 2008; Clarke & Peel, 2007).

Sexism, Heterosexism and Heteronormativity

Sex discrimination (or sexism) refers to 'the unequal and harmful treatment of people because of their sex' (Benokraitis, 1997, p.7). Blatant sexism (e.g. sexual harassment, sexist language/jokes, etc.) is the most obvious form of sexism, but it also includes more subtle forms of sexism. One of the most prevalent forms of subtle sexism is sexual objectification[2]. This form of sexism commonly treats women as possessions or sex objects; often through images of women as asexual body parts, or by treating women's bodies as trophies (Benokraitis, 1997). Women are therefore seen as visual stimulation for heterosexual/bisexual men and judged in ways that fulfil heterosexual/bisexual men's sexual objectives or fantasies:

> Women become objects as men become objectifiers. As the culture has granted men the right and privilege of looking at women, women have been expected to accept the role of stimulators of men's visual interest, with their bodies becoming objects that can be lined up, compared and rated (Brooks, 1995, p.3).

While this applies to women generally, it is frequently extended to include lesbians as sexual objects for the gratification of men. For example, many heterosexual men find the idea of lesbian sex a 'turn-on' and contend that what lesbians need is a 'man to finish off the job'. Constructing lesbian/bisexual women in this way relies heavily on gendered notions of women being sexual objects for men's pleasure and having no sexuality of their own.

Subtle sexism also occurs when cultural assumptions about the dichotomous and normative conceptions of 'essential manly and womanly natures' (West & Zimmerman, 1987) are challenged. As childcare is culturally defined as 'women's work' and therefore culturally devalued, men who work in childcare are seen as transgressing a sacrosanct gender boundary and therefore treated with suspicion. Such action may call into question a man's competence as a teacher/caregiver as well as his manhood and sexuality. As 'gay' is constructed as a sexualised identity, 'when a man admits to being, is discovered to be, or is suspected of being gay his gay identity may define everything else.' (Murray, 1997, p.149-150). He is often then seen as someone guided by (and preoccupied with) sexual thoughts and feelings and consequently as a 'risk' to vulnerable children. This is despite overwhelming evidence that the majority of paedophilic acts are perpetrated by heterosexual men.

Heterosexism (Herek, 1990) is a very particular kind of sexism, which relates to the wider social structures (institutions, customs and history), as well as individual attitudes and behaviour, that constitute prejudice on the grounds of sexuality, itself a function of gender prejudice. While

---

[2]   It should be pointed out that sexual objectification also occurs based on other demographics, such as race (see Chapter 3) or class (see Chapter 6).

heterosexism can be perpetrated at an individual level (usually referred to as *homophobia*), it is more often a socio-cultural artefact of the way in which society is structured around gender norms which are underpinned by heterosexuality. Discursive studies (e.g. Gough, 2002; Speer & Potter, 2000) have shown that incidences of heterosexism are commonly delivered in the course of everyday interaction, a phenomenon referred to as *mundane heterosexism* (Peel, 2001). These are instances of prejudice which are subtle to the point of being unnoticed or unnoticeable because they are socially normative: a phenomenon referred to as *heteronormativity* (Warner, 1991). Heteronormativity refers both to the perceived reinforcement of certain beliefs about sexuality within social institutions and policies, and to the practices and institutions that legitimise and privilege heterosexuality and heterosexual relationships (Cohen, 2005). Beliefs might include, for example, the idea that sex equals penis-in-vagina intercourse, or that 'family' constitutes a man-woman couple and their children. The practices or institutions that stem from this then might be the criminalisation (or pathologisation) of forms of sexual behaviour that are not about penis-in-vagina intercourse (e.g. oral or anal sex), the availability of the institution of marriage only to heterosexual couples, and the pathologisation of asexuality.

Heterosexuality is not inherently heteronormative in that some forms of sex and relationships between men and women challenge taken-for-granted heteronormative assumptions, for example, 'queer heterosexuals' (Thomas, 2000). Conversely, some forms of non-heterosexual sex and relationships may conform to heteronormative assumptions, for example, 'straight-acting queers' (LGB people who do not exhibit stereotypical LGB appearances or practices). However, heteronormativity is not simply about sexual practices, but rather the 'ways in which heterosexual privilege is woven into the fabric of social life, pervasively and insidiously ordering everyday existence' (Jackson, 2006, p.108). Therefore, LGB people are more readily included in society when their lifestyles mirror that of normalised heterosexuality (e.g. their appearance is gender conventional and their relationships are romantic, monogamous, committed). So, rather than simply focussing on heterosexist practices, the ways in which heterosexuality functions to reinforce gendered norms and constrain behaviour becomes the keystone for understanding how LGB sexualities are marginalised (and controlled) through heteronormativity.

In 1980, Adrienne Rich wrote a classic article *Compulsory Heterosexuality and Lesbian Existence* in which she highlighted how heterosexuality is institutionalised as both normative and natural. She claimed that rather than being natural, (most) women become heterosexual through the promotion of romance, the eroticisation of the male body, rape and the censoring of lesbian pleasure. This is not a conscious process, however, but the by-product of a society in which gender difference is eroticised and rewarded to the point that heterosexuality *appears* to be natural and normal. Heterosexuality is therefore promoted and rewarded in ways that ensure that other forms of sexuality (and gender representation) are at best marginalised if not erased altogether. This is played out in everyday social interaction where regardless of what a person's gender or sexuality might be, they are routinely read as being male or female (based on their physical appearance) and assumed to be heterosexual.

The existence of heteronormativity means that there is no social imperative to identify oneself as heterosexual in conversations. When strangers speak together they formulate their talk in ways which automatically assume that the recipient(s) of that talk is(are) heterosexual. However, for anyone who lives as a non-heterosexual, every conversation is likely to disrupt this norm, as any discussion about partners, marriage, or everyday lives invariably invokes the assumption that one's partner is of a different sex. While heterosexuals continually and routinely present themselves and others as heterosexual within ordinary conversations, which are not ostensibly about sexuality or relationships (Kitzinger, 2005), heteronormativity presents non-heterosexuals with an interactional 'problem' that necessitates them either (inadvertently or deliberately) coming out or passing up the opportunity to come out. While for some individuals this is relatively unproblematic, for others it can foreground fears of ostracism, homophobic abuse, or the risk of being exposed (or 'outed'). Therefore, those who do not wish to be out need to deploy careful use of personal pronouns (e.g. he, she) when referring to their partner(s). While they may simply collude in the assumption made by the person they are speaking with, or use phraseology that avoids the use of personal pronouns, this requires active close monitoring of sentence construction and syntax, which can be quite challenging.

Another way in which heteronormativity is embedded in society is the way in which language is used to police sexual (and gender) identities so as to normalise heterosexuality. Terms such as 'poof', 'dyke' and 'gay' are used as put-downs when a person is seen not to conform to gender norms, rather than being about sexual identities *per se* (Sharpe, 2002). In this respect, homophobic behaviour is about policing gender boundaries to ensure that compulsory heterosexuality is maintained. This is also evident in studies of colloquial terms used to describe lesbians and gay men (e.g. Peel, 2005). Colloquial terms for lesbians (e.g. 'lettuce licker', 'rug muncher') and gay men (e.g. 'turd burglar', 'shit stabber') are predominantly sexualised and negatively framed, while there is an absence of such terms to describe heterosexual ('straight'[3]) persons. Heteronormativity is, therefore, promoted and reinforced by constructing non-heterosexual identities as both 'other' and as undesirable.

Gender and Minority Sexuality

Theory, research and practice are underpinned by taken-for-granted norms about gender that relate primarily to a heterosexual context. However, it is not just heterosexuals who are subject to gender norms and expectations, but gender is frequently overlooked in relation to LGB people, identities and practices. Sexuality is assumed to be the salient factor around which LGB people's lives are organised and therefore LGB people are treated as a homogenous group with little/no reference to gender differences. However, gender is equally important in understanding the lived experiences of LGB people. For example, when general trends are viewed, lesbian/bisexual women are markedly different from gay/bisexual men in aspects of their mental and physical health (e.g. see Chapters 7 and 8) as well as in their social and emotional needs. Furthermore, society reads bisexual men and women differently, mapping their sexuality onto the gendered sexual behaviour of men and women respectively (e.g. bisexual men as 'adventurous' and bisexual women as 'licentious'), which in turn impacts differently on their experiences.

Relationships

Because same-sex relationships comprise two persons of the same sex, these relationships are presumed to operate around gender similarity which, by and large, appears to be the case. For example, research on purchasing decisions (e.g. Wilkes & Laverie, 2007), division of domestic labour (e.g. Dunne, 2000) and interests (e.g. Kurdek, 1995) consistently suggests that same-sex couples are more egalitarian in the way they organise their lives. This pattern of relationship functioning may be attributed to the fact that people of the same sex are likely to have been similarly socialised in terms of gender (e.g. Metz *et al.*, 1994). It could therefore be expected that they would be similar in their values, beliefs and behaviours than that of two people of different sexes. However, this simply reinforces the way in which gender is prioritised over other issues in assessing relationships. Furthermore, it does not shed any light on the way in which shifting between heterosexual

---

[3]   'Straight' as opposed to the homosexual person being 'bent'.

and lesbian/gay relationships may shape or alter the way in which bisexual people's relationships might be organised, nor does it allow for differences within same sex couples.

The alleged sameness between same-sex couples can be an issue in the functioning of relationships. For example, Blumstein and Schwartz (1983) suggest that while heterosexual couples often face problems arising from their differences, same-sex couples' issues often arise from the 'sameness of gender'. For heterosexual couples there is a heteronormative 'script' to fall back on, or at least to organise ones lives in relation to (even resistance to traditional gender norms). However, for same-sex couples there are no established scripts and consequently LGB people often rely on heterosexual scripts (e.g. marriage) or variations of them (e.g. civil partnerships) to or-ganise and conduct their relationships. While the lack of non-heterosexual scripts may be one reason for using or adapting heterosexual scripts, it is often the case that LGB people feel (or are told) that only if they adopt those scripts can they be accepted. While (perhaps because of this) the relation-ships that most LGB people form conform to these norms, some LGB people are happy with relationship configurations that can be non-monogamous, polyamorous, or 'open' coupled relationships. However, rather than being seen as alternative ways of *doing* relationships, these are seen as deviant, resulting in the marginalisation of LGB people, particularly subgroups of bisexual men and women, who do not organise their relationships around a mutually exclusive coupled structure.

Although gendered norms and assumptions impact in many ways on the lives of all LGB people, one of the situations where they really come to the fore is domestic violence in same-sex relationships. Theories of aggression and dependency are heavily gendered and infused with the assumption that men are invariably the perpetrators of violence while women are its victims. Therefore, it is widely assumed that domestic violence could not occur (or is not as serious) between two women; and that where it does occur in same-sex couples, they are equally culpable because they are 'matched' on their aggressiveness because of their shared gender (Simpson & Helfrich, 2007). For lesbian women in particular, it has been very difficult to talk about domestic violence. This is because the myth that women are naturally less aggressive than men has been perpetuated by feminists in their quest to argue that violence against women is a by-product of male dominance (Ristock, 2003). Exposing women-on-women violence would therefore run the risk of derailing the feminist project of promoting lesbian relationships as havens of harmony and egalitarianism. Conversely, gendered norms and perceptions operate against gay men who find themselves in a situation of domestic abuse. Because the norms of gendered masculinity position men as strong and as protectors, gay male victims of domestic violence may feel that they can/should not disclose this information because it calls into question their masculinity (Letellier, 1994).

Parenthood and family

While in contemporary western society families come in a range of forms, it is still the nuclear family headed by a heterosexual couple that is considered the archetypal family. For same-sex parents (and their children) to be accepted as a family they must work around the dominant cultural understanding of the family and negotiate the social (and often legal) obstacles to being recognised as a family. Socially accepted notions of 'family' and 'parenthood' are heavily underpinned by heterosexual gender norms. For this reason, raising a family as a same-sex couple presents a number of challenges in terms of gender norms and expectations. 'Lesbian mothers' and 'gay fathers' are often subject to the contestation that it is essential for every child to be raised by *both* a mother and a father on grounds that it is 'unhealthy' and potentially detrimental to a child's wellbeing to not have direct access to both a male and a female role model (Clarke, 2006). For lesbian/bisexual women raising children in a same-sex relationship, the role of mother is more readily accepted (although certainly not immune to scrutiny and prejudice) on the grounds that women are naturally nurturing. Conversely gay/bisexual men raising children in a same-sex relationship often have more difficulty being accepted as credible parents. Since hegemonic forms of masculinity construct men as emotionally detached and not particularly nurturing, gay men are often deemed inadequate role models for children (Clarke, 2006), despite the fact that they are also considered 'feminine' by large sections of society. This creates a double bind for such men.

The other factor that impacts on LGB people raising children is the notion that biological heritage is paramount in defining family. For this reason, same-sex couples face the challenge of their respective contribution as parents being socially (and legally) recognised and valued. Routinely it is the biological mother/father within the same-sex relationship who is recognised as the parent, while the absent donor/surrogate parent is often afforded a greater parental status than the 'social mother/father' (i.e. the same-sex partner of the biological parent). Here, gender plays out in the reinforcement of gender roles as stemming from biological bases. This is also reflected in law in that the same-sex partner is not legally recognised as having parental rights over those of the sperm donor unless the couple are civilly partnered (thus reflecting a heterosexual relationship norm) (Human Fertilisation and Embryology Act, HMSO, 1990).

Gendered embodiment and the resistance of gender norms

Gender is also directly relevant to LGB people at an individual level. This is manifested in the stereotyping of lesbian women as 'butch' (e.g. short hair, masculine dress and aggressive) and gay men as 'camp' (ostentatious, exaggerated, affected, theatrical and effeminate). Furthermore, lesbian and gay couples have also been commonly stereotyped according to a heteronormative pattern of appearance and behaviour, for instance, that one is 'the dominant one' and the other the 'submissive one' (both socially and sexually). Portrayals of gender are not arbitrary, but rather structure (lesbian/bisexual) women's and (gay/bisexual) men's expectations within and for relationships (Moore, 2006). LGB people not only operate within a gender-centred heteronormative society, but organise their lives in ways which respond to this as acts of conformity and/or resistance.

Within LGB communities there are some subgroups in which gender is portrayed (or played out) in ways that resist and/or reclaim elements of gendered embodiment. For example, 'Bears' (large mature gay men with hairy bodies and facial hair) and 'bear culture' is tied to the workings of hegemonic masculinity. Essentially it is a rejection of mainstream gay culture that privileges slim/athletic, youthful, hairless men, while redefining masculinity in a way that is more closely allied to (but distinct from) a more traditional form of masculinity (Hennen, 2005; Gough & Flanders, 2009). Likewise, more recent iterations of feminine forms of lesbianism such as 'femme' (e.g. wears dresses/skirts or form-fitting jeans, low cut tops, make-up and jewellery), or 'lipstick lesbian' (e.g. a lesbian/bisexual woman who exhibits 'feminine' attributes such as wearing make-up, dresses and high heeled shoes), are an attempt to define as both lesbian and feminine. This is a direct response to the stereotype of a lesbian as masculine (or 'butch'), having short-hair and wearing clothes that are not form-fitting. While in the 1950s, when same-sex relationships were heavily stigmatised, pairing as 'butch' and 'femme' was a common way of 'passing' as a male-female couple and helped to define roles (and expectations) within the relationships. In particular, it helped to structure romantic interpersonal interactions in the community in a similar way to that which biological sex does for heterosexuality (Levitt & Hiestand, 2005). Today, they are seen both as a response to the more androgynous (or gender-blending) embodiment of lesbian feminists (Moore, 2006), as well as a play on cultural representations of gender as a form of conformity and/or resistance to gendered womanhood.

While these manifestations play with gender, they are not a form of role play as such. In a postmodern society these are about blurring the boundaries of gender, and to some extent *queering* gender and therefore do not necessarily translate into matched gendered practice. The purpose is to get outside the gendered structure altogether, a phenomenon which is captured very well by Robin Maltz (1999) in her description of 'Daddy', a *stonebutch*[4] woman. In this instance the female body itself is queered through the practices of 'packing' (the wearing of a harness and soft prosthetic penis and scrotum) and 'binding' (the bandaging of the breasts to make them flattish) to represent 'heightened masculinity foregrounded on a subverted female body' (p.84). Since a stonebutch-femme pairing replicates the binary structure of heterosexual orientation, sexual practice and lifestyle; it is often read through the gendered lens as being a re-enactment of heterosexuality in which the femme partner is viewed as 'really heterosexual' (desires a man) and the stonebutch partner as 'really Trans' (believes herself to be male in a female body and desiring women *as a man*). However, what they are actually doing is queering what is seen as normal or natural that 'brings into relief the utterly constructed status of the so-called heterosexual original' (Butler, 1990, p.31).

Some of these forms of gendered embodiment are quite subversive; they form a wide repertoire of non-normative ways of being LGB. However, it is important to remember that these culturally mediated representations are not equally accessible (or even desirable) to individuals across cultural contexts. While some of these displays of gender (and sexuality) are prevalent in non-western contexts (e.g. 'butch' in East Asia; 'lady-boys' in Thailand), there is often a risk that these are read and understood according to western norms and codes of conduct and therefore misread. This can be particularly frustrating for men and women who have to constantly reassert their gender and sexuality (see Chapter 3 on Race and Ethnicity for a further discussion of these issues).

Gender and LGB Trans People

Trans persons are diverse in their sexual identity/orientation (e.g. Nuttbrock *et al.*, 2009). However, they are often (erroneously) assumed to be attracted to people of the same sex and therefore are assumed to claim they are another sex and/or seek gender reassignment because they cannot accept their homosexuality. As well as being untrue this is disrespectful to the ways in which Trans people experience their own subjectivity and how they

---

[4]   A 'stonebutch' is a woman who is strongly masculine in character and dress, who tops her partner sexually (sometimes emotionally) and who does not wish to be touched genitally.

choose to conduct their lives (Denny & Green, 1996). While some Trans people identify as heterosexual, others do not. For example, a recent study of Trans men (female-to-male Trans people) (Bockting *et al.*, 2009) found that participants had a strong cross-gender identity and also a strong attraction to men. For some this made them question their gender identity and their desire for sex reassignment. What this demonstrates is the hegemonic way in which heterosexual norms shape the way in which people think about their own (and others' gender).

While LGB Trans people often associate with wider LGB communities, they experience their gender quite differently from those within LGB communities who are not Trans (Bockting *et al.*, 2009). One of the key contributing factors here is that in being Trans their experience of gender socialisation is quite different to that of LGB people who unequivocally identify as male or female. For most Trans people, the gendered norms they were exposed to growing up will have been based on their natal sex and therefore at odds with their proclaimed gender resulting in an atypical experience of gender socialisation. This also means that when as adults they are able to live as their proclaimed (rather than natal) sex/gender (with or without anatomical surgery) their sense of themselves is founded on an atypical, rather than normative, experience of that gender. So, for example, a Trans man will have been raised and socialised as a girl and therefore will not have experienced socialisation as a boy in the way that male-born males will have been. While in itself this is not a problem, it is made problematic because of the way in which gender is constructed as congruent with biological sex. Because gender socialisation and proclaimed gender do not map onto one another for LGB Trans people, this can make it socially difficult for the Trans person to affirm their gender identity and sexuality (Nuttbrock *et al.*, 2009) in the way that non-Trans LGB people might more easily be able to.

For most LGB Trans people, their sexual identity is consistent with their proclaimed gender but this is not universally the case. For example, in a recent study (Schleifer, 2006) 'Tony' and 'Phil' (female-to-male transsexuals) report having been attracted to women prior to transitioning. However, after transitioning they found themselves attracted to men. This would seem to indicate that for LGB Trans people gender and sexuality are somewhat more fluid than is suggested by binary models (Schleifer, 2006). Despite this, conventional labels of sexuality are often applied to Trans people as if they were unproblematic.

As a function of gender variation, LGB Trans people may also experience their sexuality in ways that are distinct from that of their non-Trans counterparts. In one study (Bockting *et al.*, 2009), despite identifying as lesbian/bisexual, male-to-female Trans persons described experiences that went beyond conventional notions of lesbianism and bisexuality. For example, while experiencing themselves socially and sexually as male, some incorporated their female genitalia (vulva and vagina) into their sexual activities. This led them to question the binary construction of gender and to describe their identities in ways that were distinctly Trans rather than organised around conventionally sexed bodies.

Taken-for-granted understandings of gender are also challenged through the way in which Trans people (and their partners) conduct their relationships. Few Trans people are attracted solely to other Trans people, and commonly form relationships *in spite of* being Trans rather than *because* they are Trans (Denny & Green, 1996). In some cases Trans people have entered a relationship with someone of another sex and have subsequently transitioned (sometimes without undergoing sex-change surgery) and have continued to remain in that relationship post-transition. While this appears to illustrate not only a change in gender, but also a shift in the nature of the relationship (i.e. from heterosexual to lesbian/gay), this interpretation only makes sense within a western dichotomous construction of sex/gender and sexuality. The imposition of such labels may make no sense to either the Trans person or their partner. Therefore, the problem with conventional understandings of gender, and the way in which sexuality is presumed to map neatly onto this, is that they act as a straitjacket that impedes our understanding of our (and others') gender in ways that are both diverse and fluid.

Summary

This chapter has focussed on the ways in which the social construction of gender as a binary impacts on the identities and lived experiences of LGB people. One of the key issues that has been highlighted is the way in which categories of sex, gender and sexuality are inextricably linked and assumed to map neatly and unproblematically onto each other. While it has frequently been assumed that sexuality is *the* most salient and defining feature of LGB sexualities, it is evident that our social understanding of sexuality is heavily underpinned by taken-for-granted norms around gender. Consequently, gender is as, if not more, salient in understanding LGB identities and experiences as sexuality is, not least because categories of 'lesbian', 'gay' and 'bisexual' make no sense without a binary gender system. Essentially, human beings are attracted to human beings and without constructs of gender and sexuality there are only bodies and the joining and friction between them (Denny & Green, 1996).

Guidelines for Good Practice

- Try to disaggregate sex, gender, and sexuality in order to better understand how these apply in the particular context of the client. Do not assume a simple mapping of these constructs onto one another.
- Do not assume that LGB people are fundamentally one group with very similar experiences. Consider instead the way in which hegemonic forms of masculinity might impact on gay and bisexual men *as men*; and conversely, how dominant discourses of femininity might impact on lesbian and bisexual women *as women*.
- Avoid making assumptions that gender norms operate the same way in same-sex relationships as they (predominantly) do for heterosexual couples.
- Appearances are deceiving! Be aware that the appearance of an LGB person does not necessarily imply anything about their gendered subjectivity in social contexts or emotionally and sexually in relationships.
- Remember that there are multiple ways of performing gender and conducting relationships. Clarify the sexual and relational choices that each member makes and validate and support those decisions on the clients,' own terms.

References

Bandura, A. (1986). *Social foundations of thought and action.* Englewood Cliffs, NJ: Prentice Hall.

Bandura, A. & Walters, R.H. (1963). *Social learning and personality development.* New York, NY: Holt, Rinehart and Winston.

Bem, S.L. (1981). Gender schema theory: A cognitive account of sex typing. *Psychological Review, 88*(4), 354–364.

Bem, S.L. (1993). *The lenses of gender: Transforming the debate on sexual inequality.* New Haven: Yale University Press.

Benokraitis, N.V. (1997). Sex discrimination in the 21st century. In N.V. Benokraitis (Ed.), *Subtle sexism: Current practice and prospects for change.* Thousand Oak, CA: Sage.

Blumstein, P. & Schwartz, P. (1983). *American couples.* New York, NY: William Morrow.

Bockting, W., Benner, A. & Coleman, E. (2009). Gay and bisexual identity development among female-to-male transsexuals in North America: Emergence of a transgender sexuality. *Archives of Sexual Behavior, 38*(5), 688–701.

Brooks, G.R. (1995). The centrefold syndrome: Mixed prospects. *Population Bulletin, 45,* 3–41.

Butler, C. & Byrne, A. (2008). Queer in practice: Therapy and queer theory. In L. Moon (Ed.), *Feeling queer or queer feelings? Radical approaches to counselling sex, sexualities and genders.* London: Routledge.

Butler, J. (1990). *Gender trouble: Feminism and the subversion of identity.* New York, NY: Routledge.

Clarke, V. (2006). 'Gay men, gay men and more gay men': Traditional, liberal and critical perspectives on male role models in lesbian families. *Lesbian and Gay Psychology Review, 7*(1), 19–35.

Clarke, V. & Peel, E. (2007). From lesbian and gay psychology to PGBTQ psychologies: A journey into the unknown (or unknowable)? In V. Clarke & E. Peel (Eds.), *Out in psychology: LGBTQ perspectives.* Chichester: John Wiley & Sons, Ltd.

Cohen, C.J. (2005). Punks, bulldaggers, and welfare queens: The potential of queer politics? In E.P. Johnson and M.G. Henderson (Eds), *Black queer studies.* Durham, NC: Duke University Press.

Connell, R.W. (1987). *Gender and power.* Cambridge: Polity.

De Laurentis, T. (1991). Queer theory: Lesbian and gay sexualities. *Differences: A Journal of Feminist Cultural Studies, 3*(2), iii–xviii.

Denny, D. & Green, J. (1996). Gender identity and bisexuality. In B.A. Firestein (Ed.), *Bisexuality: The psychology and politics of an invisible minority.* Thousand Oaks, CA: Sage.

Dunne, G.A. (2000). Opting into motherhood: Lesbians blurring the boundaries and transforming the meaning of parenthood and kinship. *Gender & Society, 14*(1), 11–35.

Fine, M. & Addelston, J. (1996). Containing questions of gender and power: The discursive limits of 'sameness' and 'difference'. In S. Wilkinson (Ed.), *Feminist social psychologies: International perspectives.* Buckingham: Open University Press.

Goldsmith, S.J. (2001). Oedipus or Orestes? Homosexual men, their mothers, and other women revisited. *Journal of the American Psychoanalytic Association, 49*(4), 1269–1287.

Gough, B. (2002). 'I've always tolerated it but. . .': heterosexual masculinity and the discursive reproduction of homophobia. In A. Coyle & C. Kitzinger (Eds.), *Lesbian and gay psychology: New perspectives.* Oxford: BPS Books/Blackwell Publishing Ltd.

Gough, B. & Flanders, G. (2009). Celebrating "obese" bodies: Gay "bears" talk about weight, body image and health. *International Journal of Men's Health, 8*(3), 235–253.

Hawkins, R.L. (1992). Therapy with the male couple. In S.H. Dworkin & F.J. Gutierrez (Eds), *Counseling gay men and lesbians: Journey to the end of the rainbow*. Alexandria, VA: American Counseling Association.

Hennen, P. (2005). Bear bodies, bear masculinity: Recuperation, resistance, or retreat? *Gender & Society, 19*(1), 25–43.

Her Majesty's Stationery Office (1990). *Human Fertilisation and Embryology Act*. London: HMSO.

Herek, G.M. (1990). The context of anti-gay violence: Notes on cultural and psychological heterosexism. *Journal of Interpersonal Violence, 5*(3), 316–333.

Hill, C.A. (1999). Fusion and conflict in lesbian relationships? *Feminism & Psychology, 9*(2), 179–185.

Hollway, W. (1984). Gender difference and the production of subjectivity. In J. Henriques (Ed.), *Changing the subject: Psychology, social regulation and subjectivity*. London: Routledge.

Ingraham, C. (2006). Thinking straight, acting bent: Heteronormativity and homosexuality. In K. Davis, M. Evans & J. Lorber (Eds.), *Handbook of gender and women's studies*. London: Sage.

Jackson, S. (2006). Gender, sexuality and heterosexuality: The complexity (and limits) of heteronormativity. *Feminist Theory, 7*(1), 105–21.

Kitzinger, C. (2005). Heteronormativity in action: Reproducing the heterosexual nuclear family in after hours medical calls. *Social Problems, 52*(4), 477–98.

Klesse, C. (2005). Bisexual women, non-monogamy and differentialist anti-promiscuity discourses. *Sexualities, 8*(4), 445–464.

Kurdek, L.A. (1995). Predicting change in marital satisfaction from husbands' and wives' conflict resolution styles. *Journal of Marriage and the Family, 57*, 153–164.

Letellier, P. (1994). Gay and bisexual male domestic violence victimization: Challenges to feminist theory and responses to violence. *Violence and Victims, 9*, 95–106.

LeVay, S. (1991). A difference in hypothalamic structure between heterosexual and homosexual men. *Science, 253*, 1034–1037.

Levitt, H.M. & Hiestand, K.R. (2005). Gender within lesbian sexuality: Butch and femme perspectives. *Journal of Constructivist Psychology, 18*(1), 39–51.

Maltz, R. (1999). Toward a dyke discourse: The essentially constructed stonebutch identity. *Journal of Lesbian Studies, 3*(3), 83–92.

Metz, M.E., Rosser, B.R.S. & Stapko, N. (1994). Differences in conflict-resolution styles among heterosexual, gay and lesbian couples. *The Journal of Sex Research, 31*(4), 293–308.

Moore, M.R. (2006). Lipstick or timberlands? Meanings of gender presentation in black lesbian communities. *Signs, 32*(1), 113–139.

Murray, S.B. (1997). It's safer this way: The subtle and not-so-subtle exclusion of men in childcare. In N.V. Benokraitis (Ed.), *Subtle sexism: Current practice and prospects for change*. Thousand Oak, CA: Sage.

Nuttbrock, L.A., Bockting, W.O., Hwang, S., Rosenblum, A., Mason, M., Macri, M. & Becker, J. (2009). Gender identity affirmation among male-to-female transgender persons: A life-course analysis across types of relationships and cultural lifestyle factors. *Sexual and Relationship Therapy*, *24*(2), 108–125.

Parsons, T. & Bales, R.F. (1953). *Family socialization and interaction process.* London: Routledge & Kegan Paul.

Peel, E. (2001). Mundane heterosexism: Understanding incidents of the everyday. *Women's Studies International Forum*, *24*(5), 541–54.

Peel, E. (2005). Effeminate 'fudge nudgers' and tomboyish 'lettuce lickers': Language and the construction of sexualities in diversity training. *Psychology of Women Section Review*, *7*(2), 25–36.

Rich, A. (1980). Compulsory heterosexuality and lesbian existence. *Signs: Journal of Women in Culture and Society*, *5*, 631–660.

Ristock, J.L. (2003). Exploring dynamics of abusive lesbian relationships: Preliminary analysis of a multisite, qualitative study. *American Journal of Community Psychology*, *31*(3-4), 329–341.

Sánchez, F.J., Greenberg, S.T., Liu, W.M. & Vilain, E. (2009). Reported effects of masculine ideals on gay men. *Psychology of Men and Masculinity*, *10*(1), 73–87.

Sanger, T. (2008). Queer(y)ing gender and sexuality: Transpeople's lived experiences and intimate partnerships. In L. Moon (Ed.), *Feeling queer or queer feelings? Radical approaches to counselling sex, sexualities and genders.* Hove: Routledge.

Schleifer, D. (2006). Make me feel mighty real: Gay female-to-male transgenderists negotiating sex, gender, and sexuality. *Sexualities*, *9*(1), 57–75.

Schmitt, E.D. (2008). Discrimination versus specialisation: A survey of economic studies on sexual orientation, gender and earnings in the United States. *Journal of Lesbian Studies*, *12*(1), 17–30.

Sharpe, S. (2002) 'It's just really hard to come to terms with': Young people's views on homosexuality. *Sex Education*, *2*(3), 263–277.

Simpson, E.K. & Helfrich, C.A. (2007). Lesbian survivors of intimate partner violence: Provider perspectives on barriers to accessing services. *Journal of Gay and Lesbian Social Services: Issues in Practice, Policy and Research*, *18*(2), 39–59.

Speer, S.A. (2005). *Gender Talk: Feminism, discourse and conversation analysis.* London: Routledge.

Speer, S.A. & Potter, J. (2000). The management of heterosexist talk: Conversational resources and prejudiced claims. *Discourse & Society*, *11*(4), 543–572.

Stainton-Rogers, W. & Stainton-Rogers, R. (2001). *The psychology of gender and sexuality.* Maidenhead: Open University Press.

Stern, M. & Karraker, K.H. (1989). Sex stereotyping of infants: A review of gender labelling studies. *Sex Roles*, *20*, 501–22.

Stokes, J.P., Miller, R.L. & Mundhenk, R. (2002). Toward an understanding of behaviourally bisexual men: The influence of context and culture. In A.E. Hunter & C. Forden (Eds.), *Readings in the psychology of gender: Exploring our differences and commonalities.* Needham Heights, MA: Allyn & Bacon.

Thomas, C. (Ed) (2000). *Straight with a twist: Queer theory and the subject of heterosexuality*. Champaign, IL: University of Illinois Press.

Warner, M. (1991). Introduction: Fear of a queer planet. *Social Text, 9*(4), 3–17.

West, C. & Zimmerman, D.H. (1987). Doing gender. *Gender & Society, 1*, 125–151.

Wetherell, M. & Edley, N. (1999). Negotiating hegemonic masculinity: Imaginary positions and psycho-discursive practices. *Feminism & Psychology, 9*, 335–356.

Wilkes, R.E. & Laverie, D.A. (2007). Purchasing decisions in non-traditional households: The case of lesbian couples. *Journal of Consumer Behaviour, 6*(1), 60–73.

Wilkinson, S. (1997). Feminist psychology. In D. Fox & I. Prilleltensky (Eds.), *Critical psychology: An introduction*. London: Sage.

Wolff, C. (1971). *Love between women*. London: Duckworth.

3

Race and Ethnicity

Roshan das Nair & Sonya Thomas

I remember how being young and black and gay and lonely felt. A lot of it was fine, feeling I had the truth and the light and the key, but a lot of it was purely hell. There were no mothers, no sisters, no heroes. We had to do it alone (Audre Lorde, 1982, p.176).

Much of lesbian, gay and bisexual (LGB) literature has been written in a race and ethnicity-vacuum (Butler *et al.*, 2010). Issues of developing an LGB identity and living LGB lives have been mostly documented from white perspectives, without taking into account how these sexual identities interact with racial, ethnic and cultural identities, and the privileges and problems such intersecting identities pose. Black and Minority Ethnic (BME) groups form over 14% of the population of the UK (Office for National Statistics [ONS], 2001) and therefore form a large minority in terms of absolute numbers. Just as there have been studies which have indicated poor physical and mental health of LGB people (see Chapters 7 and 8; albeit, the research being largely based on non-BME samples), BME groups in Britain are also known to have higher rates of mental health problems compared to their white counterparts (Bhui *et al.*, 2003). The reasons for the high incidence of physical and mental health problems in specific minority groups has been related to the relative social exclusion, disadvantage and prejudice they face. Despite the high rates of these problems reported in both LGB and BME groups separately, research that looks at membership to both these groups *in combination* is still nascent. Published research has mainly focussed on challenges such groups face, but many BME LGB/non-heterosexual individuals have been able to negotiate their sexuality and ethnicity in creative

Intersectionality, Sexuality and Psychological Therapies: Working with Lesbian, Gay and Bisexual Diversity,
First Edition. Edited by Roshan das Nair and Catherine Butler.

ways, thereby minimising the negative effects of their multiple minority statuses and capitalising on the various options that belonging to multiple and diverse groups offer (see Fisher, 2003).

This chapter will first attempt to unpack the construct of ethnicity and challenge some of the preconceived notions of needing sexual identity labels (especially LGB labels) within BME populations, and by extension a 'homonormative' pressure to 'come out' to lead a 'healthy, actualised existence', and explore some alternative ways of being that are as authentic and legitimate as any other dominant (predominantly white middle class) options for non-heterosexual people. This chapter will also interrogate the coming out process and what understanding it can bring to therapists working with BME clients who identify as LGB. To this extent, we also refer the reader to Chapters 4 and 5 of this book, which deal with Religion and Refugees and Asylum seekers respectively. While we do not deny BME people use and benefit using LGB labels, we will also explore the particular challenges BME individuals face in their own ethnic groups and in dominant/majority LGB communities and how therapists can help them negotiate their multiple, sometimes conflicting identities to foster a healthy, fulfilling life.

Throughout this chapter we utilise examples that we have come across, not only from scholarly texts, but also from media reports, films, web forums, client reports, stories from friends and from our own experiences. There are two reasons for using such a myriad palate. First, as we have suggested, there has not been much psychological research that taps into sexuality issues of BME groups and therefore we felt that dipping into other 'texts' (or textual data) would be useful to add to this limited knowledge-base. Second, we do not feel that the production of 'scholarly knowledge' is free from power and prejudice, which in itself has the potential *to cause* a paucity of such research being conducted and published. The following quote exemplifies the point we are making:

> I once had a manuscript returned to me unreviewed by a top journal . . . because the editor informed me that his readers were not interested in research on black lesbians. He implied my sample must be biased, because it was difficult to imagine that my research team could find 600 black lesbians to fill out questionnaires in the first place (Solarz, 1999, p.143).

Therefore, BME LGB people not only have to defend their position and existence, but also have to deal with ignorance and prejudice from the gatekeepers of certain forms of knowledge transfer. Such practices of disbelief continue to make invisible research that arguably would have contributed to reversing the trend of invisibility. Therefore, we do not believe that only certain knowledges and certain vehicles of communicating these knowledges (such as peer-reviewed journals), are the sole sources of credible and/or useful information.

Finally, in this chapter we use the term 'LGB' only when referring specifically to lesbian, gay, and/or bisexual identities, and use the term 'non-heterosexual' to refer to other sexual identities and/or practices that are not labelled as LGB. We feel this distinction is important because not all BME non-heterosexuals identify as LGB and some actively distance themselves from such identity labels, preferring other terms, or at times preferring not to label their sexual identity at all. It must be remembered that different societies and communities have different ways of understanding sexual identities, orientations and practices. For instance, *dogana*, which refers to 'doubling' or 'two-ness', is both a verb referring to female-female sexual activity 'as well as women given to such activity' (Vanita & Kidwai, 2000, p.220). Also, in some instances, certain cultures do not make the same categorical distinction between gender and sexuality akin to the Western notions of these terms. The Thai *phet* categories are a good example of this, where gender and sexuality are closely intertwined (Jackson, 2000).

Unpacking Ethnicity

The concept of ethnicity is troublesome, not least because it is variously defined, understood, assessed and (ab)used. An early definition of ethnic group by Schermerhorn (1978, p.12) suggested that it was a:

> collective within a larger society having real or putative common ancestry, memories of a shared historical past and a cultural focus on one or more symbolic elements defined as the epitome of their peoplehood. Examples of such symbolic elements are: kinship patterns, physical contiguity (as in localism or sectionalism), religious affiliation, language or dialect forms, tribal affiliation, nationality, phenotypical features, or any combination of these. A necessary accompaniment is some consciousness of kind among members of the group.

Given the broad scope of such a definition, it should come as no surprise that different individuals selectively use and report only certain aspects of this construct. Phinney (1990) suggested that there were at least five components of this construct that can be delineated:

   (i)   *ethnicity* (a person's heritage, parents' ethnicity),
  (ii)   *ethnic self-identification* (which may be different from their ethnicity),
 (iii)   *ethnic belonging* (a sense of belonging to the self-identified ethnic group/s),
  (iv)   *ethnic involvement* (participation and cultural practices, language spoken, etc.), and
   (v)   *ethnic attitude* (positive or negative feelings towards the self-identified ethnic group).

   For BME non-heterosexuals, each of these aspects is a potential site of consternation and strife. Therefore, therapists should be mindful of the complexities of defining ethnicity itself and the client's multiple connections and disconnections from each of these aspects before mapping these onto the fabric of his/her sexuality. This is an invitation to complexity which cannot be overlooked. In fact, the unpacking of such constructs, although problematic, can be 'of great importance if it is used to produce multi-dimensional instead of categorical representations of culture and ethnicity' (McKenzie, 1998, p.278).

Multiple Sites of Oppression

When considering race and ethnicity, we need to be clear that this forms only one thread in a complex weave of what constitutes personhood within the fabric of larger society. For instance, the role of race and religion with reference to many BME non-heterosexuals is intertwined in many ways. One way is related to their own negotiating of these multiple identities and how the idea of 'culture' and 'heritage' for some BME people are in-separable from their religion. Another way is how such BME people are read by others (especially non-BME people) and how in their (mis)reading there is a conflation of race and religion. One of our clients reported that she got called a 'fucking Mozzie [Muslim] Paki [Pakistani]' when she was exiting a gay nightclub by a group of white and black men, also coming out of the same venue. For this client, her Sri Lankan national identity and her Catholic religious identity were obfuscated by the mere colour of her skin. Such instances reflect the multiple sites of oppres-sion that BME non-heterosexuals experience being members of multiple minority groups.

The Multiple Oppression website[1] states:

> People of color, women, and individuals with disabilities are some of the groups that often experience dual or multiple oppression. Members of these groups who also identify as LGB often feel torn when they try to determine which community is truly their home. Women may find themselves sorting out relationships among how they are treated as women, as people of color, and as lesbians. Often it can be difficult to find a support system that will value all aspects of an individual's experience.

There is a tendency for those who are victims of oppression to compare their experience of oppression with those of other groups. The intention is often to derive some form of ranking: a kind of who is the greater oppressed. This discussion, spurious in truth, lends itself to feeding the notion of one oppression being greater than the other and this easily leads to a discussion about what is and is not acceptable. Is homophobia, for example, more acceptable than racism? For someone who is both non-heterosexual and BME such a question is of little value, serving no real purpose in attending to their overall experience of oppression.

We exist on multiple levels and such multiple identities allow for us to have multiple sites of oppression. However, oppression itself serves a purpose in terms of power. Even outside the aggressive acts that both individuals and states perpetrate, there are the small everyday actions that multiply to form a layer of weight upon the lives of those caught in the margins, whose lives and identities exist outside of the mode of white heternomativity. This is where the idea of intersectionality is useful.

BME Folk and LGB Identity

> The categories gay and lesbian are not universal at all and can only be universalized by the epistemic, ethical, and political violence unleashed on the rest of the world by the very international human rights advocates whose aim is to defend the very people their intervention is creating (Massad, 2007, p.41).

Western ideas about LGB identities do not necessarily apply to all non-heterosexual BME people. Words used to describe sexual identities may be absent and can be different for different cultural groups. Yet, some

[1] https://www.msu.edu/~eavesoli/mult_opp.html offers some good references to LGB intersectionality issues.

published academic and popular media reports attempt to simplify BME non-heterosexual sexual identity labels and experiences by assuming that everyone is LGB, or worse, *forcing* everyone into the 'LGB' category. While this may be appropriate for BME people who self-identify as LGB, not recognising other non-heterosexual sexual identities in BME groups can alienate and further make invisible those already living 'liminal' lives. This, it can be argued, is one form of cultural and 'identity violence'.

Joseph Massad's (2007) *Desiring Arabs* demonstrates how even the binary oppositions of sexual identity (as homosexual/heterosexual, let alone LGB identities) is in fact a historical fabrication of colonialism that has in contemporary times been both exported to non-heterosexual individuals and groups in the Global South and BME groups/diaspora in the West. In an unadapted and culturally insensitive manner, this would ultimately do more harm than good. We believe there is some truth in Massad's argument. However, where this analysis falls short is perhaps related to Masad's reluctance to engage with the issue of globalisation, which has meant that some non-heterosexual BME people in the West and those in the Global South, have already adopted and will continue to adopt LGB-identified labels to describe their desires and themselves. There is no need for 'the Gay International'[2] to coerce same-sex desiring individuals to claim LGB identities, because Western cultural practices and ideologies have several routes by which they can be transmitted, with or without coercion, for example, via the internet, film, literature, and so on. In the final analysis, the backlash and homophobia that individuals face, whether they identify as 'LGB' or 'homosexual', cannot be ignored and the crimes committed against them because of their sexuality, cannot be viewed as anything but crimes. A case in point is the hanging of two youths in Iran (Iran Focus, 2005), allegedly for their same-sex sexual actions. The Western media covering this story referred to the youths as 'gay' and 'homosexual': identity markers which were attributed to them without evidence to suggest that these were the terms they would have used to self-refer. However, irrespective of what they called themselves or how they identified sexually (if they did in the first place), the outcome was death.

The problem of framing ethnic minority sexual desires in LGB terms can be explored further through a critical reading of a film like *Fire* (Director, Deepa Mehta, 1996). *Fire*, written and directed by an Indian-born Canadian film maker, was received with a mixture of kudos (from Indian dailies such as *The Hindu* calling it 'pathbreaking' and *The Times of India* referring to it as 'gutsy') and derision and horror. A crude synopsis first: the film tells the

---

[2]   Massad's term for International LGB organisations.

story of two sisters-in-law (Radha and Sita), who find themselves in loveless, 'arranged', heterosexual marriages to brothers, Ashok and Jatin. Ashok, on advice from his spiritual guru, has not had sex with 'his' Radha for 13 years; and Jatin is in love with his girlfriend who he continues to have an affair with even after his marriage to Sita. Radha and Sita embark on a romantic and sexual relationship. On Ashok finding out about this liaison, they argue, Radha's sari accidently catches fire and Ashok steps away watching her burn. Radha manages to put the fire out and leaves Ashok and their home. In the final scene, Sita and Radha unite.

Nowhere in the film is there mention of the words 'lesbian' or 'bisexual', yet the film was branded a 'lesbian' film by commentators in India and the West (the BBC Online ran with the headline: 'South Asia Lesbian film sets India on Fire'; Lak, 1998). Mehta herself said that she didn't know why *Fire* had come to be labelled a 'lesbian film' and asserted that '*Fire* is not a film about lesbians' (Verma, 1997). The negative reactions that the film elicited from the Hindu Right (from both men and women) and Left-leaning Indian feminists make for interesting analysis. The Right was scandalised by the 'immoral and pornographic' nature of the film and that it was 'against Indian tradition and culture', with some leading Right-wing activists suggesting the same-sex desire depicted was 'a sort of a social AIDS' (Bearak, 1998). Conversely, some feminists and lesbians came out in support of the film and to claim an Indian lesbian existence. However, some other Left-leaning feminists also argued that by framing the characters as 'lesbian' or 'bisexual', what the film did was to deny the existence of indigenous sexualities and risked the obliteration of homosocial spaces and interactions (that allow for some slippage between homosocial and homoerotic experiences) which are found in many South Asian communities. They also objected to the notion that lesbian identity was a *result* of a failed heterosexual identity. In fact, Kishwar (1998) suggests that '[b]y crudely pushing the Radha-Sita relationship into the lesbian mould, Ms Mehta has done a big disservice to the cause of women' (p.11), and goes on to say:

> I suspect that the net result of this political tract of a film, determined to create programmed individuals, will be to make many women in India far more selfconscious than earlier in their relationships with other women. There is a danger that many of those exposed to this controversy will learn to view all such signs of affection through the prism of homosexuality.

The issue of *naming* sexual identity is in itself interesting. In the film *Fire*, Sita articulates this to Radha as: 'There is no word in our language to describe what we are to each other'. Some South Asian lesbians (mainly in the

US) have adopted the word 'anamika' (Sanskrit for 'nameless' or 'without name') to name this relationship in an affirmative way (Shah, 1993).

The reactions to this film demonstrate how complex the idea of an identity label is, and how if deployed and imposed on cultures which do not subscribe to these sexual identity labels or even on the basis of sexual preference/practices, can potentially alienate those most vulnerable, and in some cases is simply inept. Gopinath (1998), for instance, refers to the 'resistance' to label some women's homoerotic relationships as homosexual or lesbian, not because it is 'a failure to articulate queerness', but rather as an 'acknowledgement of the inadequacy of such articulation in expressing the range and complexity of nonheteronormative sexual practices and allegiances as they emerge within sites of extreme heteronormativity' (p.634). Thus, cultural sensitivities around the notions of relationship patterns, sex and sexuality are crucial and need to be considered, particularly when dealing with BME non-heterosexuals who may have recently migrated to the West.

Coming Out and BME People

Coming out is complex, tough, emotional experience that can have lasting consequences in terms of long-term emotional health. Friends are lost, discovered or rediscovered; relationships with family are strengthened or temporarily weakened (if not permanently broken). It is, however, widely acknowledged that coming out can be positive and healthy (e.g. Rosario *et al.*, 2001). A great deal of writing exists, both creative and non-fiction, to help deepen the knowledge of and understanding of the coming out experience, but psychological literature about LGB identity, identity formation and the processes and transition to 'coming out' is often silent on the issue of LGB/non-heterosexual BME folk. Their invisibility from the content and bodies of work that exist to aid understanding and meaning to therapists working with clients means that their experience is overlooked, disregarded and misunderstood. However, these issues have been captured in film, literature, and the stories of our friends and clients[3].

The process of BME LGB identity development and transition to disclosure is affected by heterosexism and the pervasive culturalism and racism that are inherent in society. The extent to which both understanding and support is available to those who identify as LGB or non-heterosexual can

---

[3]   We direct the interested reader to Moore (2009), *Does your mama know: An anthology of black lesbian coming out stories.*

in part depend on the attitudes of immediate family and friends as well as the cultural groups to which they may belong.

Coming out, staying in, and stepping in and out of the closet

It is largely conceptualised that, much like the process of bereavement, the coming out process happens in stages. Some psychologists believe and have argued that the development of an LGB identity changes in accordance to and across ethnic, cultural and racial lines (e.g. Chan, 1989; Chung & Katayama, 1998). In fact, coming out Beckett (2010) attests, is a 'game of truth' (cf. Foucault, 1988) that the majority LGB communities play. Although originally a 'Western' concept, it has found a place in the Global South also, predominantly amongst those who have the (financial, and perhaps the language) resources to engage in some of the performances related to coming out, such as self-identifying as LGB, or attending Pride marches. However, as a game of truth, it is intrinsically linked to power, which perhaps explains why it is not a game that everyone has equal access to.

Ravichandran (2010) eloquently summarises the sometimes perilous road of coming out for BME LGB people. He exposes some of the specific dilemmas that BME LGB people need to consider and negotiate when thinking about coming out. Added to these pressures, such folk also have to contend with being accused of not being 'true to oneself' or 'authentic' for *not* coming out. Because coming out is sometimes marketed as a valorised position that is to be attained by all self-respecting non-heterosexuals, this can lead to considerable stress for some who may feel torn between an urge to 'be like other gays' or to 'be like other Indians' (for instance). This dichotomous thinking is fostered by both majority LGB communities and heterosexual BME communities, as demonstrated by their common discourse of: 'Are there gay Caribbeans?' or, 'Are there gay Muslims?' (for instance).

We are family

I'd rather be black than gay because when you're black you don't have to tell your mother (Charles Pierce, American actor, 1980).

das Nair (2006) poses three questions in relation to BME coming out:

(i)   Is coming out necessary in the first place?
(ii) If yes, who does the BME individual come out to, and
(iii) Where does he/she come out (in)to?

These questions are pertinent especially when BME people consider coming out to family because family relationships, filial responsibility and ethnic kinships play a major role in BME life, particularly for youngsters. A recent British study by Maynard and Harding (2010) found that BME groups were more likely to visit friends and relatives and go other places as a family compared to white groups. Family activities were, however, important independent correlates of psychological well-being for all groups in this sample. While for some, the family may be a safe harbour from a whirlwind of emotion that can accompany some coming out experiences, for others, it might be the very eye of the storm. Another British study by McKeown *et al.* (2010) found different challenges that disclosure posed to different BME groups. South Asian gay men for instance expressed considerable regret in not being able to fulfil family expectations regarding marriage and having children. Black gay men, however, McKeown *et al.* (2010) discovered, believed that 'same-sex behaviour subverted cultural notions related to how masculinity is configured' (p.843). This further illustrates our point about the complexities and multi-factorial nature of categories such as 'gay' or even 'BME', which can easily be forgotten under the guise of inclusiveness.

While much of the literature focuses on gay men, there are narrative accounts of similar difficulties that bisexual women and lesbians also face. One such account (Goldberg, 2010) was provided by a British-Arab woman in her twenties who tried to come out to her parents:

> I tried to introduce it [her sexuality] to them, because I knew it was a thing you don't talk about. It's forbidden. But once you mention 'homosexual' the discussion is over. You can't go into detail about it.

This disclosure led to this person being subjected to physical abuse from her family, forced (heterosexual) marriage and encouragement to kill herself because she had brought disrepute to the family. What is interesting is that the damage to the family honour was not perceived to be directly related to the woman's *sexual desire*, but because she 'was making the family look like a *modernised, westernised*, filthy family' (our emphasis, no page number). This further relates to the point we were making about the impact sexual identity labels have in different cultural contexts.

Expulsion from the family and ostracisation from the ethnic community are commonly reported in clinics and amongst friends we know, when people come out. Negative family reactions can take on various forms, from denial and repression of the LGB person's disclosure and/or behaviour, to praying for change (of sexual orientation), to bribing, to emotional blackmail, to severing of ties, to punishment, and to coercion and forced marriage.

The Forced Marriage Unit (FMU), a joint UK Home Office/Foreign Office body, reported that the number of calls they received from men had increased by 65%, from 134 in 2008 to 220 in 2009 (Hill & McVeigh, 2010). Most of these men were of South Asian origin (mainly from Pakistan), while others were from the Middle East, Africa and Eastern Europe. Their families attempted to get them married not only because they came out, but also because their families *suspected* they were gay or bisexual. There have also been reports of non-heterosexual BME women in the UK being forced into heterosexual marriages to protect the 'honour' of the family (Goldberg, 2010). Therefore, the family may not be a safe space for some BME people to come out to.

We must also remember that for LGB BME people the disclosure environment (or the 'framing environment') in which coming out takes place is often heterosexual and also predominantly white; one in which culturalism and racism takes place. This has consequences over and beyond the homophobia which is rooted in their BME experience within a predominantly heterosexual environment. This further complicates the coming out process, because the family and ethnic community are seen as shields from such racism.

The 'othering' stories that reflect some BME non-heterosexual experiences indicate the existence of in-groups and out-groups within mainstream LGB communities. This relates to das Nair's (2006) third question: Where does the BME LGB person come out (in)to? When considering how the boundaries of such sexual in-groups and out-groups are charted, we may find a corollary in the multilevel process theory of racial boundaries (Wimmer, 2008, p.970). This theory assumes that:

> ... boundaries are the outcome of the classificatory struggles and negotiations between actors situated in a social field. Three characteristics of a field – the institutional order, distribution of power, and political networks – determine which actors will adopt which strategy of ethnic boundary making.

Wimmer's theory offers a dynamic model of understanding actors, actions and boundaries, which can fluctuate over time. This fluidity is appealing because it represents the malleability of individual and group identity and also suggests some form of agency on the part of the actors. However, this agency it could be argued, is mediated by the distribution of power that is inherent to groups. Because groups not only define themselves in terms of what is common between members of the group, but also in terms of how they differ from other groups, it is in the interest of some groups to keep their membership exclusive. Keeping people out is a shared group activity that strengthens in-group bonds. If race is considered a grouping category, then maintenance of racism can also work along these lines. Therefore, for some BME non-heterosexuals, coming out into dominant LGB groups could be tinged with trouble, if they then experience racism and exclusion from a group that they thought they belonged in.

This said, we do not doubt the importance of coming out and the positive effects it has had (and continues to have) for many people, including BME folk. We are only suggesting that we need to be careful not to indiscriminately *prescribe* it as a rite of passage for all non-heterosexuals. This is a view that Beckett (2010) also endorses. She takes the idea of coming out further, and proposes a 'coming-in' option for BME non-heterosexual people. By coming-in, she refers to 'the conscious and selective invitation of people into one's "club of life"' (Beckett, 2010, p.204). One of Beckett's clients explains this well:

> Even if I don't tell certain members of my extended family about my sexuality, I don't view myself as in the closet, in a dark place that I must escape from. Far from it, this 'closet' is full of precious things, like things you could never afford to buy! It's my treasure chest. The way I see it, rather than me needing to move out of the closet, to make my sexuality public to everyone, including my grandparents, instead I get to choose who to open the door to, and who to invite to 'come in' to my life (Beckett, 2010, p.210).

This, we find, is an exceptionally powerful idea to work with clients who may feel compelled to come out simply because they are made to believe that it is the only way to lead a fulfilled non-heterosexual life authentically. Therefore, coming out, staying in, and stepping in and out of the closet, should all be seen as valid options for non-heterosexuals.

Linking Race and Homophobia

Homophobia exists in all communities regardless of how they are racially or ethnically defined. However, BME groups often stand accused of possessing a form of homophobia that can be distinguished from the wider homophobia of other majority groups, by its virulence and aggressiveness. Even highly regarded human rights activists, who hold positions of significant reputational capital, have fallen victim to the lazy thinking that attributes different worth to certain displays of homophobia. This means the yardstick used to gauge homophobia is changeable and becomes dependent on the cultural and ethnic status of the persons accused of it. This inevitably leads to cultural stereotyping and the stigmatisation of certain BME groups, where they are labelled as being more homophobic than the white, majority groups. The de facto position appears to be that the homophobia of non-BME communities is rendered innocuous when held up against the caustic, savage words and deeds of the minority cultural group. In essence, a different standard of judgement is brought into force.

Good examples of this can be seen in recent newspaper articles. For instance, in reading Alex Petridis' article (Petridis, 2004), which covers his travels to the Caribbean where, the by-line tells us, he 'discovers a culture that can't see a problem, let alone a solution' to the contentious issue of dancehall music and lyrics that incite hatred and murder of gay men. The reference to the term 'culture' here serves as a significant broad-brush, used to envelope the Afro-Caribbean community as a whole rather than to understand elements within it. Decca Aitkenhead's article (Aitkenhead, 2005), however, offers a more nuanced understanding of homophobia as it exists within the black community and seeks to debate the issue without being blinkered about the historical factors that are invariably at play. She looks behind the macho posturing of some BME males, to understand the forms that homophobia takes within black communities and why. She puts forward the view that 'slavery laid the foundations for homophobia' and that 'the sodomy of male slaves by their owners as a means of humiliation' is part of the history of Jamaica. She goes on to state that its legacy can be seen in the 'overexaggerated masculinity of many men in Jamaica'.

These reports add to the growing and well-established perception of the Caribbean, and therefore Caribbeans, as being home to a virulent form of homophobia not found anywhere else. The symbolism and allusion is that African-Caribbeans embody something darker, and all the more menacing in their homophobia, warranting harsher commentary and woeful denunciation within the press and beyond. It must be noted that similar claims of vituperative forms of homophobia have also been levelled against people from Asian and the Arab world (see Massad, 2007).

Such thinking can lead to more pronounced invisibility of BME LGB/non-heterosexuals as they are not seen as being distinct from homophobic BME people. Therefore, they are often seen to be the aggressors, the targets of condemnation rather than the genuine beneficiaries of support that is generally offered to those who are considered to be affected by homophobia. This said, there is evidence that suggests that even people who regard themselves as 'gay' *and* 'Black Caribbean' regard their ethnic group as being relatively more homophobic than their white counterparts. For instance, in the McKeown *et al.* (2010) study, black participants themselves reflected on their own ethnic group's homoprejudice. Therefore, while homophobia is present in many BME communities, we need to be mindful of the effects of being continuously fed with the idea that homophobia mainly exists, or only exists in, BME communities. Such thinking is dangerous because it has the potential to abbreviate a complex phenomenon into a simplistic equation of:

$$Black + Heterosexual = Homophobia.$$

Linking Sexuality and Racism

Whiteness is a 'powerful place that makes invisible, or re-appropriates things, people and places it does not want to see or hear, and then through misnaming, renaming or not naming at all, invents the truth – what we are told is "normal", neutral, universal, simply becomes the way it is' (Mirza, 1997, p.3).

The range of literature on LGB experiences offers the notion of commonality, of a normative, collective experience, which is largely left unproblematised. Where there is mention of BME it is often only to eulogise the image of the black male, sexualising and contorting the image to one of objectification rather than looking beyond the physical to the individual (Butler *et al.*, 2010). The gap, with nothing to fill in, leaves open the assumption that the default position is white with all the privileges that 'whiteness' brings. This default position then becomes the 'central organising category' around issues discussed, the profiles within the LGB community and specifically by therapists working professionally with LGB clients. White then becomes the gold standard by which 'gayness' is assessed.

There is often a perception that race and racism itself is absent from within LGB communities, which some presume explains its absence from LGB literature. This position sits on a frail notion that had once been the backbone of a movement of Pride within the LGB communities: that of not passing on the oppression. It was a laudable moral concept that sought to ensure that as a group with far too much experience of the pain and hurt of oppression, it could not justify in any way being party to the oppression of others. This position is at odds with the experience of many BME LGB people (e.g. Buttoo, 2010; McKeown *et al.*, 2010).

An ongoing survey being conducted on a British website (www.ukblack out.com), which is a 'virtual community and editorial website for gay and lesbian people of African and African-Caribbean descent in the UK and beyond', found that over 46% of their sample of 650 respondents reported that they had 'experienced racism on the gay scene' and almost 20% had experienced this more than once. Much of the research literature related to BME non-heterosexuals refers specifically to Black African and Caribbean men. There is scant available literature on South Asian and East Asian non-heterosexual experiences (McKeown *et al.*, 2010) or of the experiences of Asian women, despite both these ethnic groups forming a large proportion of the British population. It must be pointed out that it is not only African and African-Caribbean men who report racism on the gay scene in Britain but also women and other BME groups. A recent article in the BBC Online, for instance, covered the problems faced by South Asian gay men when accessing the gay scene in the North of Britain (Buttoo, 2010). Gay South Asian men reported: 'We get looked at in a funny way. We don't get served in bars unless we protest and we get called Paki or have to deal with comments like "here come the suicide bombers"', and '[b]efore we can go into a club bouncers ask us to kiss other men to prove we are really gay. White men are not asked to do this so I just don't bother going out anymore, it's not worth it'.

A qualitative study by McKeown *et al.*, (2010)[4] makes advances in this respect by examining the experiences of 'Black and South Asian gay men in Britain'. This is an important study in many respects; not only because it begins to unpick some of the issues faced by non-heterosexual men identifying as 'gay' and 'black' or 'Asian', but also because this study uses an interesting data collection method, viz. the use of email exchanges between the interviewer and the interviewee which forms the corpus of the data to be analysed. This approach is particularly valuable when researching groups that have been typically considered 'hard to reach'. However, this approach is at once an asset and a limitation of this study, which because of the methodology employed, would necessarily exclude certain voices and these voices are perhaps the less heard voices amongst a group whose voice is seldom heard. While the authors recognise the limitations of using such online methods to recruit and collect data, we feel this issue needs to be further highlighted: online communities and samples come from a relative position of privilege.

In many studies of this type, there is the temptation to show similarities and differences between (white and non-white) groups, but most studies do not pay sufficient detail to exploring intra-group variations. This is problematic on at least two counts:

(i) although perhaps not intentional, there is the lure of grouping people based solely on one parameter (e.g. race), thereby essentialising the

---

[4]   We only introduce this study here, but discuss its findings later.

experience of people who fall into that group, and (ii) perhaps as a result of this, those who are most likely to be marginalised and disadvantaged are not given due recognition. Therefore, there is the risk that such people are doubly disadvantaged by both the systems that do not recognise their experiences and needs, and by ventures that purport to understand and appreciate these. Thus, a caveat and reminder: such research should emphasise 'the importance of theorising social location when examining the intersection of ethnicity and sexuality' (McKeown *et al.*, 2010, p.12).

An overriding assumption that therapist should avoid is one that invokes the so called 'LGB community':the notion of assumed similarities and experiences, which is acultural, ahistorical and apolitical. It is easily understood that a group that is generally marginalised by the dominance of heterosexuality can, in deriving support and emotional enrichment, come together under a single banner: that of non-heterosexuality. But the banner heading assumes one common shared experience that allows the inter- and intra-grouping within that banner to become less visible. Invariably, this process of 'making absent' contributes to the general failure to recognise the contribution that LGB/non-heterosexual BME people have made to LGB issues. This has contributed to the lack of understanding of the needs and concerns of non-heterosexual BME people.

The Costs of Visibility and Invisibility

> It is a matter of making conflicts more visible, of making them more essential than mere clashes of interest or mere institutional blockages. From these conflicts and clashes a new relation of forces must emerge whose temporary profile will be a reform (Foucault, 1994, p.456–457).

A double-bind operates for those who identify as BME and LGB. The hyper-visibility afforded by their skin colour makes them target of 'interventions' (read 'racial profiling') by the state (black people and Asians, under Section 60 of the Criminal Justice and Public Order Act 1994, are 26.6 and 6.3 times respectively, more likely than white people to be stopped and searched by police in England and Wales; Townsend, 2010). However, sometimes, it is their very skin colour that makes them invisible as sexual (minority) subjects. This double-bind is further extended because in order to claim their sexual subjecthood, they need to subscribe to a pre-scripted Western sexuality label (such as LGB), which some of them may not be comfortable with (see Chapter 5 on Refugees and Asylum Seekers). This is not merely a question of wanting to have one's cake and eat it too, but expecting a right to be accepted on one's own terms.

Interestingly, just as there has been an increase of BME people being stopped and searched by the police over the last few years, over the past 20 years several studies have reported that a disproportionate number of BME people are compulsorily detained under the Mental Health Act, 1983; and are more likely to be treated with psychotropic medication (Bhui *et al.*, 2003; Churchill *et al.*, 1999; Morgan *et al.*, 2004). Certainly, racism and the context within which racism is discussed and understood, has changed since some of the initial research in this area was carried out. This change has partly been brought about by improved legislation (e.g. the Race Relations (Amendment) Act, 2000) that deals with discrimination at various levels, including institutional racism.

When referring to invisibility, we need to remember that certain ethnicities can also be made invisible in the larger BME discourse. The Irish in the UK are one such group that is sometimes not considered as an ethnic minority, perhaps because of their skin colour. And yet, 11.8% of ethnic Irish men (compared to the national average of 9.9% of adult males) report having a limiting long-term illness; and also have greater than national average rates of unemployment (ONS, 2001). Keogh *et al.* (2004) record the importance that family and religion play for such groups and how these factors mediate sexual expression. These authors found that, like some of the other ethnic minorities mentioned in previous sections, Irish men were also concerned about shame and dishonour their coming out would bring to their families.

Racial stereotypes also have the potential to make invisible certain sexual identities and preferences. For instance, East Asian gay and bisexual men are consistently thought of as effeminate and therefore 'bottoms' ('passive'/receptive partners in anal intercourse) (e.g. Han, 2006; 2010). Therefore, even with the visibility that an identity label like 'gay' or 'bisexual' affords, there is a predetermined judgement made on what that identity entails for the person. This links to the performance of sexuality and how the racialised body is read in terms of sexual identity and desire (discussed later). Again, like the negative stereotypes other ethnic minorities were faced with, Irish men had to contend with the general public perception that they had 'little control over their alcohol consumption, to be stupid or poorly educated' (Keogh *et al.*, 2004, p.35). Such racial stereotypes about South Asian lesbian and bisexual women have also been reported. Kawale (2003), for instance, found that BME lesbian and bisexual women thought it was important to make themselves visible in largely white LGB spaces, because this was essential to create and enforce their visibility. But they also spoke of the discomfort they experienced in such venues, which made them consider organising their own spaces. Spaces such as Kiss (www.planetkiss.org.uk) and Club Kali (www.clubkali.com) provide this safe heaven where BME non-heterosexuals can 'exert control over seeing and being seen' (Kawale, 2003, p.191). Another interesting finding from Kawale's study is how South Asian lesbian/bisexual women enjoyed being in the presence of gay/bisexual Asian males, while her white respondents preferred to be in women-only spaces. The bond that the Asian women felt with the men present at these venues was a proxy-kinship bond, which (re)created images of family and community. One respondent referred to it as a 'homey feeling' (p.191).

Consider the following quote from an Asian lesbian:

> If you're really, really, really, really, really stupid, and think the whole world is completely heterosexual, and that every single woman with long hair, no matter how she acts, is heterosexual, then you could probably assume that I'm heterosexual . . . And I think it has a lot to do with, not only because I have long hair, but because I'm an Asian woman, and the stereotype of an Asian woman with long hair. In their eyes, I cannot be anything but a heterosexual woman. Which is fucked up, you know, because I can be many things, and I am (quoted in Lee, 1996, p.121).

What this quote and other literature in this section suggests, is that invisibility can be in the form of both sexuality and ethnicity for some people, based on cultural and ethnic grouping, and other ways in which the BME body is read in public and private spaces.

The Body in the Sexuality/Ethnicity Nexus

The sexuality/ethnicity nexus is problematic for some BME non-heterosexuals, who are sometimes challenged to demonstrate the *authenticity* of their racial/ethnic background because they are not heterosexual. In some instances, heterosexual BME people feel that the LGB BME person is 'selling out' to what is sometimes referred to as a 'white preoccupation' or worse still, being infected by a 'white disease'. Some BME South Asians are accused of being 'coconuts' ('brown on the outside, but white inside') and East Asians are similarly called 'bananas' (das Nair, 2006). McKeown *et al.* (2010, p.5) record one of their BME participants having said:

> [I] [h]ave a black female friend who . . . complained that I was focusing too much on being gay and not enough on being black. It is assumed by her that

the black identity is superior and not complementary, and the implication in her voice and manner suggested that I was 'letting the side down'. She and other associates seem to struggle with the idea that you can be both simultaneously'.

We have previously described the relation between the body and the erotic purchase power that such a body has, particularly in gay and bisexual male spaces (Butler *et al.*, 2010). In this work, we have also discussed the reduction of the back male body and the individual to the 'big black dick' (to use the words of one of McKeown *et al.*'s participants). McKeown *et al.* (2010) similarly describe the eroticisation of the black (African and Caribbean) body by white men, which some black men found discriminatory, because while they were looked at as potential sex interests, they were not considered as potential romantic partners.

McKeown *et al.*'s (2010) study peripherally explores the racial and sexual relations and performances that black men encounter when they are sexually involved with a non-black man. Their data suggests a replaying of racial power-play in sexual encounters, where the black man is treated in a subservient manner, almost recreating a colonial master-slave interaction and invoking this discourse. As one participant recalled, 'He [white sexual partner] would say things like "fuck me nigger" or "suck my dick nigger", "love my white dick nigger", "love ur master"'. However, the inverse of such racial/sexual power-play has also been narrated to us by some of our friends and clients. One white client reported how he enjoyed playing the 'sub' (submissive male) when he had sex with black men (but not with white men), because he wanted to be the 'slave'. This client further reported how his black sexual partners also enjoyed being the 'master' in such encounters. Such master-slave dialectics and inverse re-enactments and role-plays are interesting because they deploy a subject-object relationship or encounter in sex play. The master's subjectship takes control over the object (slave). The materiality of object positions creates a space for the objectification (and fetishisation) of some racialised bodies; and by virtue of the fetishisation, some bodies become trophies, while others are viewed as ordinary or less than ordinary.

The exclusion of Asian male bodies from popular consumption (either sexually in real life or in the media) has been documented before (e.g. Chuang, 1999; McKeown *et al.*, 2010). This exclusion occurs in both physical and online spaces (such as LGB social networking sites). One Indian participant in the McKeown *et al.* (2010) study reported: 'I am . . . attracted to English (Caucasian) men and often find it frustrating when I read things like "no brown men please" on their Gaydar profiles' (p.9). At a basic level, this quote illustrates the frustration experienced by many Asian LGB men who feel undesired because of their ethnicity. However, at another level, this quote is interesting because it demonstrates another type of 'othering' that is at play. This participant says that he is 'attracted to English men', which the authors clarify mean 'Caucasian'. One wonders whether then this person is also saying 'no brown men please' to other Asian men who may wish to enter into a relationship with him. Consider another response by another Indian man:

> I only like white guys. I personally find that brown guys are a bit too easy too [sic] score. But moreover, my primary sexual attraction is to white guys. I've been trying to change this, after feedback from some friends, but find it similar to not wanting to be gay in general (McKeown *et al.*, 2010, p.9).

What this discourse does is to equate desire for a specific gender (male) to desire for a specific race/ethnicity (white) as stemming from the same (presumably inherent) basis (or origins), thereby distancing the person from having a 'choice'. The rhetoric employed here is reminiscent of a gay man trying to become straight, because it is not what he or society wants and not succeeding. In a similar vein, here this person claims that he has tried 'to change this, after feedback from some friends', but finds that like his sexual orientation, he cannot change the preference of the *type* of man he desires. This discourse is replicated in a response from another British Asian participant, who clearly suggests a biological predisposition for his predilection, by saying, 'I don't think it's a "preference"; it's just the way I'm wired' (McKeown *et al.*, 2010, p.10). For this participant, the roles of colonialism, socialisation, politics and the media are discounted for a more essentialist origin of his desire: one of wiring, one of biology. Would this preference for one racial type and the active distancing of other (and their own) racial types be considered racism? Or is this perhaps an indication of 'internalised racism'? These are questions that require further interrogation.

We have anecdotal evidence to suggest that some Asian men prefer white men and disprefer other Asian men and regard the white body (person) as the most sought after prize. Parallel evidence also comes from a study by Chuang (1999) who examined this phenomenon with East Asian non-heterosexual men in Australia. Perhaps then it is not surprising when McKeown *et al.* (2010) suggest that '[w]hatever the reasons given, no participant in the study said that they saw themselves having a man of the same ethnicity as themselves as a long-term partner' (p.10).

Compared to the literature available on BME non-heterosexual men and their bodies and desired bodies, there is much less written about non-heterosexual women in this area, and even less written about BME non-heterosexual women (Cohen & Tannenbaum, 2001).

However, there are some parallels with BME gay men's experiences that have been observed. For instance, South Asian women are more likely to be read as 'bisexual' or 'heterosexual', rather than as 'lesbian' (Kawale, 2003, p.186). Similarly, the exoticisation of the BME female body by other lesbian or bisexual women has been reported (e.g. Walker, 1993). Beverley Greene (1996), a pre-eminent scholar on BME LGB issues, refers to 'lesbians of color' in terms of 'triple jeopardy' for being black, woman, and lesbian. Furthermore, even the *type* of lesbian identity that some BME women subscribe to can be denied to them because of what their ethnic bodies look like to other (white) people, including white lesbians. This is clearly the case when Bannerji (1993, p.60–61) states:

> As a lesbian of Indian origin . . . My breasts, hips, and long hair were not seen by everyone as symbols integral to my identity as an Indian woman; they were reinterpreted by white lesbians as manifestations of my being a 'femme'.

The BME body, therefore, becomes the site of conflict to assert and claim a non-heterosexual (e.g. LGB) identity, but at the same time becomes the site where LGB identities are enforced. This goes beyond the hetero/homosexual binary and includes the way in which ethnic minority LGB bodies are mis/read in terms of their specific LGB identities and practices, for example, butch/femme.

Sadanand's Story

Sadanand is an Indian student in his late twenties who moved to the UK to complete his PhD. He currently identifies as gay. Although he has had sexual encounters with men in the past, he had never felt romantically attached to men and did not consider himself gay. While he was in India, he had had a few girlfriends. He felt that he was, truly in love, with his last girlfriend in India, and considered getting married and having a family with her. The couple did not want to engage in sex before marriage. The relationship, however, came to an end because she did not want to have a long-distance relationship with him, and also because her parents were eager for her to get married soon.

Here in the UK, Sadanand has been meeting men online, and having sex with them. So far he has only been able to meet 'old, white men' (who he is not attracted to) for sex. He feels that younger men (both Asian and white) don't want to have sex with him, and his sexual offers and advances have been rebuked on numerous occasions online. Some of these rebukes have been associated with racial slurs. He feels that he is not attractive.

He still does not see himself being romantically involved with men and wants to get married to a woman when he returns to India. He feels he doesn't 'fit in' with the other gay people he has met (including other Indian gay men he has met here). He has not discussed his sexual encounters with his friends. Some of his 'sex-mates' have been asking him to come out. He feels pressured to come out, but doesn't want to. He has been told that he is 'living a lie' and is 'living a double life' if he doesn't come out. This has made him question his identity, and has caused him significant distress. He says he was happier in India, where he was with his girlfriend, had 'masti' (fun) with some men from time to time and had a dream (of heterosexual marriage) that he and his parents were going to make into a reality. He acknowledged that there were obviously a lot of issues that need unpicking. However, the most pressing issue for Sadanand at this point was the issue of coming out and his sexual identity.

Using a social constructivist perspective, the imperative to come out and affirm one stable sexual identity that is both ahistorical and acultural is problematised and other ways of *being* are explored in therapy. By referring to other ways of being, this is not to suggest that Sadanand should identify as 'bisexual' or even 'non-heterosexual', because these would be other categories that would be imposed on him. Instead, therapy can set him on a journey of exploration that would help him seek answers to questions such as: How did this pressure to come out come about? How is he different from those who are forcing him to come out? How are his circumstances and situations in life different from those who are urging him to come out? Why does he feel compelled to come out now? The therapy room becomes the site for a form of psychoeducation, which seeks to broaden the view of the problem and apply a critical lens to it. The therapist may help him explore these difficulties through their dialogue, but also through homework assignments which could include providing him with carefully selected reading material on the subject (bibliotherapy). The exploration would not just be from an individual perspective, but from sociological, historical, political, (post)colonial discourses that situate him in a complex web of interactions.

The Therapist as an Agent of Change

The therapist has a key role in fostering change within their clients, themselves, the organisations they work in and the systems they are in contact with. This is another interesting intersection: therapist meeting activist[5]. Jones (2010) explores the role conflict she faced, when exploring the grieving process that families went through when a family member was on death row, as a therapist, activist and researcher/academic. She also describes the challenges, obstacles and the triumph of working in such an intersection. Jones concludes her article with a plea:

> Activist academics, as well as those who possess clinical skills, must continue the discussion of various ways to address the conflicts that arise among their roles in order to maximize the potential advantages that they each bring as we strive to create progressive social change (p.57).

We believe this includes dealing with homophobia and racism in therapy and outside of it. While it is not always possible to keep all these roles at the fore of one's consciousness, there are times when they can be seen as coexisting. Take for instance, talking about sexual prejudice using a social constructivist or certain narrative approaches to therapy. Here, the therapist works with the client to understand how systems of power play a role in framing categories of being (e.g. homosexual/heterosexual), how hierarchies of dominance and subservience are created and maintained, how a sickness role is applied, how the power seeps into the therapy room (between therapist/client), the functions that these processes serve, and for whom. We believe this is an avatar of activism which is just as legitimate and important as taking placards and slogans to the streets, signing petitions, speaking out against injustice.

Laszloffy and Hardy (2000) make suggestions for how white *and* BME therapists can guard against racism in therapy and how they can sensitively

---

[5] We direct readers interested in therapy and activism related to LGB issues to Glassgold & Drescher (2007) *Activism in LGBT Psychotherapy Practice*; Silverstein (2007) *Wearing Two Hats: The Psychologist as Activist and Therapist* and Singh & Burnes (2011) *Feminist Therapy and Street-Level Activism: Revisiting Our Roots and "Acting Up" in the Next Decade.*

challenge clients who make racist comments in therapy. While this process has been written from a therapist-client perspective, it also translates to supervisor-supervisee relationships and interactions. They advocate a three-step process of:

(i)   *validation* (therapists 'find some aspect of their clients' disclosures that warrants affirmation'),

(ii) *challenging* (therapists begin to ask questions or make statements that 'encourage clients to examine critically the connections between their verbal disclosures, their racial ideology, and if possible, the presenting problem'), and

(iii) *request* (therapists 'pull issues and themes together and make a request that translates this information into a concrete direction for where to proceed next')(p.45–46).

We end this chapter with Judith Glassgold's words of wisdom:

> In order to incorporate liberation psychology into our own work, we need to start with self-analysis. Without applying critical consciousness to our profession, our organisations, and our own lives, any attempt to transform others will fail (2007, p.53).

Glassgold (2007) challenges us to reclaim the original meaning of the word 'deviance', meaning 'off the road', and suggests that we need to be 'path breakers' and to 'expand meanings, not to limit them', if we are to be therapists who can 'embrace the diverse possibilities for human identity, creativity, energy, and love' (p.54). This is no easy challenge, but one that should remain with us both inside and outside the therapy room.

Summary

As Sadanand's story demonstrates, for BME people who may be non-heterosexual, or may not identify in those terms, but have same-sex desires, there are various issues that may bring them to seek help from therapists. Some of these issues, which are covered in this chapter, such as racism, homophobia, sanism, and so on, create the potential for multiple sites of oppression. While these issues are addressed on individual terms, their combined effects are rarely acknowledged in public discourse and in psychological literature. This creates an illusion of 'sameness', a level playing field of desires and experiences that can be applied to all LGB people or all black people, without problematising these categories, thus rendering aspects of people's identities invisible. This is sometimes evident in the discourse that surrounds coming out, where coming out is exalted to a position which epitomises progress, liberation and truth, which all LGB people should aspire to. While invisibility can be deployed as a strategy for some BME non-heterosexuals to negotiate their multiple identities in hostile surroundings, it can also pose a threat to individuality and sexual subjectship. Therefore, when a client comes to therapy with one or many of these issues, the therapist should be mindful of the fact that they not only have the possibility to support an individual but are well placed to influence and challenge systems that create the problems for their clients.

Guidelines for Good Practice

- Therapists should be careful not to assume the meaning or definition of a client's ethnicity or sexuality, or how these interact. Curiosity and respectful questioning will allow an idiosyncratic understanding to emerge. Let the client tell you which identity has the foreground or background in different situations.
- The therapist should be curious about diversity of experience and opinion within communities as well as between then. Systemic questions such as: 'Who else would agree, and who would disagree, with such a position?' are helpful in drawing out such difference.
- A therapist should consider the unique space that therapy provides for ideas, behaviours and identities to be discussed, which may not be possible outside of the therapy room. Given this, ending sessions with clients should be carefully considered in terms of where these conversations can continue in a way that is safe and nurturing for the client.
- White models of psychological health must not be applied to all BME LGB/non-heterosexual clients. For example, if a client describes living two very separate lives (one with their family of origin and one with their friends, the latter being where they are open about their sexuality) a therapist must not assume that it is 'healthy' to combine the two and come out to their family. This may not be safe and may divorce the client from support against racism, and other forms of prejudice they face as a BME person. The concept of 'coming in' is helpful here.
- Listen careful for the issues the client wants to discuss in therapy. They may not explicitly talk about how their sexuality and race interact but it may become part of your formulation. Be transparent about this with the client and decide together on its relevance.

- Reflect on your own attitudes towards various racial and ethnic groups and observe how they influence your therapy. Also remember the power you wield to create change for the better from both individual and systemic perspectives.

References

Aitkenhead, D. (2005, 5 January). Their homophobia is our fault. *The Guardian online*. Retrieved 18 August 2010 from http://www.guardian.co.uk/world/2005/jan/05/gayrights.comment.

Bannerji, K. (1993). No apologies. In R. Ratti (Ed.) *A Lotus of another color: An unfolding of the South Asian gay and lesbian experience*. Boston: Alyson.

Bearak, B. (1998, 24 December). A lesbian idyll, and the movie theaters surrender. *New York Times*, (1998-12-24). Retrieved 05 May 2011from http://query.nytimes.com/gst/fullpage.html?res=9B0DE5DB113CF937A15751C1A96E958260.

Beckett, S. (2010). Azima ila Hayati – an invitation in to my life: Narrative conversations about sexual identity. In L. Moon (Ed.) *Counselling ideologies: Queer challenges to heteronormativity*. Surrey: Ashgate.

Bhui, K., Stansfeld, S., Hull, S., Priebe, S., Mole, F. & Feder, G. (2003). Ethnic variations in pathways to and use of specialist mental health services in the UK: Systematic review. *British Journal of Psychiatry, 182*, 105–116.

Butler, C., das Nair, R. & Thomas, S. (2010). The colour of queer. In L. Moon (Ed.) *Counselling ideologies: Queer challenges to heteronormativity*. Surrey: Ashgate.

Buttoo, S. (2010, 8 March). Gay Asians reveal racism problems. *BBC Online*, Retrieved 28 May 2011 from http://news.bbc.co.uk/1/hi/uk/8555503.stm.

Chan, C.S. (1989). Issues of identity development among Asian-American lesbians and gay men. *Journal of Counseling & Development, 68*(1), 16–20.

Chuang, K. (1999). Using chopsticks to eat steak. *Journal of Homosexuality, 36*(3/4), 29–41.

Chung, Y.B. & Katayama, M. (1998). Ethnic and sexual identity development of Asian-American lesbian and gay adolescents. *Professional School Counseling, 1*(3), 21–25.

Churchill, R., Wall, S., Hotopf, M., Buchanan, A. & Wessely, S. (1999). *A systematic review of research relating to the Mental Health Act (1983)*. Retrieved 26 May 2011from http://www.health.wa.gov.au/mhareview/resources/documents/Systematic_Review_of_MH_Legislation.pdf.

Cohen, A. & Tennenbaum, I. (2001). Lesbian and bisexual women's judgments of the attractiveness of different body types. *Journal of Sex Research, 38*(3), 226–232.

das Nair, R. (2006). Metaminorities and mental health: Pathways of vulnerability for Black and Minority Ethnic queer folk. *Inter-Disciplinary Net*. Retrieved 29 May 2011 from http://www.inter-disciplinary.net/ci/sexuality/s2/nair%20paper.pdf.

Fisher, D. (2003). Immigration closets: Tactical-micro-practices-in-the-hyphen. *Journal of Homosexuality*, 45(2/3/4), 171–192.

Foucault, M. (1988). The ethic of care for the self as a practice of freedom: an interview with Michel Foucault. (J.D. Gauthier, Trans.) In J. Bernauer & D. Rasmussen (Eds.). The final foucault. Cambridge: MIT Press, pp. 1–20.

Foucault, M. (1994) *Power. The essential works vol. 3*. In J. Faubion (ed.), P. Rabinow (series ed.). London: Penguin Books. p.456–457.

Glassgold, J. (2007). "In dreams begin responsibilities" Psychology, agency, and activism. *Journal of Gay & Lesbian Psychotherapy*, 11(3/4), 37–57.

Glassgold, J. & Drescher, J. (Eds.) (2007). *Activism in LGBT psychotherapy practice*. New York, NY: Haworth Medical Press.

Goldberg, A. (2010, 24 October). Tale of gay woman forced to marry to protect 'honour'. *BBC News Online*. Retrieved 5 May 2011 from http://www.bbc.co.uk/news/uk-11613992.

Gopinath, G. (1998). On Fire. *GLQ: A Journal of Lesbian and Gay Studies*, 4(4), 631–636.

Greene, B. (1996). Lesbian women of color: Triple jeopardy. *Journal of Lesbian Studies*, 1(1), 109–147.

Han, C. (2006). Geisha of a different kind: Gay Asian men and the gendering of sexual identity. *Sexuality & Culture*, 10(3), 3–28.

Han, C. (2010). One gay Asian body: A personal narrative for examining human behavior in the social environment. *Journal of Human Behavior in the Social Environment*, 20(1), 74–87.

Hill, A. & McVeigh, K. (2010, 1 July). Gay men become victims of forced marriages. *The Guardian Online*. Retrieved 13 October 2010 from http://www.guardian.co.uk/world/2010/jul/01/gay-men-forced-marriage.

Iran Focus (2005). *Iran Majlis deputies endorse execution of minor*. Retrieved 5 May 2011 from http://www.iranfocus.com/en/?option=com_content&task=view&id=2917.

Jackson, P.A. (2000). An explosion of Thai identities: global queering and reimagining queer theory. *Culture, Health & Sexuality*, 2(4), 405–424.

Jones, S. (2010). When the roles of clinician, activist, and academic collide: Bearing witness within the death chamber. *Journal of Applied Social Science*, 4(2), 43–57.

Kawale, R. (2003). A kiss is just a kiss . . . or is it? South Asian lesbian and bisexual women and the construction of space. In N. Purwar & P. Raghuram (Eds.), *South Asian women in the diaspora*. King's Lynn: Berg, pp. 181–200.

Keogh, P., Henderson, L. & Dodds, C. (2004). *Ethnic minority gay men: Redefining community, restoring identity*. Sigma Research. Retrieved 5 May 2011 from http://www.sigmaresearch.org.uk/files/report2004c.pdf.

Kishwar, M. (1998, 1 January). Naive outpourings of a self-hating Indian: Deepa Mehta's Fire, *Manushi*.. Retrieved 1 September 2011 from http://www.manushi.in/docs/392.%20Naive%20Outpourings%20of%20a%20Self-Hating%20Indian.pdf.

Lak, D. (1998, 13 November). South Asia lesbian film sets India on Fire. *BBC Online.* Retrieved 5 May 2011 from http://news.bbc.co.uk/1/hi/world/south_asia/213417.stm.

Laszloffy, T.A. & Hardy, K.V. (2000). Uncommon strategies for a common problem: Addressing racism in family therapy. *Family Process, 39,* 35–50.

Lee, J.Y. (1996). Why Suzie Wong is not a lesbian: Asian and Asian American lesbian and bisexual women and femme/butch/gender identities. In B. Beemyn & M. Eliason (Eds), *Queer studies: A lesbian, gay, bisexual, and transgender anthology.* New York, NY: New York University Press.

Lorde, A. (1982). *Zami, A new spelling of my name.* Trumansburg, NY: Crossing Press.

Massad, J.A. (2007). *Desiring Arabs.* Chicago, IL: University of Chicago Press.

Maynard, M. & Harding, S. (2010) Psychological well-being in adolescence in the context of time spent in family activities. *Social Psychiatry and Psychiatric Epidemiology, 45,* 115–123.

McKenzie, K. (1998). Ethnicity in psychiatric epidemiology. *British Journal of Psychiatry, 172*(3), 278.

McKeown, E., Nelson, S., Anderson, J., Low, N. & Elford, J. (2010). Disclosure, discrimination and desire: experiences of Black and South Asian gay men in Britain. *Culture, Health & Sexuality: An International Journal for Research, Intervention and Care, 12*(7), 843–856.

Mirza, H.S. (1997). Mapping a genealogy of black british feminism. In H.S. Mirza (Ed.) *Black British feminism: A reader.* London: Routledge.

Moore, L. (2009) (Ed). *Does your mama know: An anthology of black lesbian coming out stories,* 2nd Edition, revised. Washington, D.C: RedBone Press.

Morgan, C., Mallett, R., Hutchinson, G. & Leff, J. (2004). Negative pathways to psychiatric care and ethnicity: The bridge between social science and psychiatry. *Social Science and Medicine, 58,* 739–752.

Office for National Statistics (2001). *Census 2001.* Retrieved 5 May 2011 from http://www.statistics.gov.uk/census2001/census2001.asp.

Petridis, A. (2004, 10 December). Pride and prejudice. *The Guardian Online.* Retrieved 18 August 2010 from http://www.guardian.co.uk/music/2004/dec/10/gayrights.popandrock.

Phinney, J.S. (1990). Ethnic identity in adolescents and adults: Review of research. *Psychological Bulletin, 108*(3), 499–514.

Pierce, C. (1980). Retrieved 1 September 2011 from http://www.allgreatquotes.com/gay_homosexual_quotes.shtml.

Ravichandran, B. (2010, 5 July). Gay community should help South Asians. *The Guardian Online.* Retrieved 5 May 2011 from http://www.guardian.co.uk/commentisfree/2010/jul/05/gay-south-asians%20%20on%2013.10.10.

Rosario, M., Hunter, J., Maguen, S., Gwadz, M. & Smith, R. (2001). The coming-out process and its adaptational and health-related associations among gay, lesbian, and bisexual youths: Stipulation and exploration of a model. *American Journal of Community Psychology, 29*(1), 133–160.

Schermerhorn, R.A. (1978). *Comparative ethnic relations: A framework for theory and research.* Chicago, IL: University of Chicago Press.

Shah, N. (1993). Sexuality, identity, and the uses of history. In R. Ratti (Ed.), *A lotus of another color.* Boston: Alyson, pp-113–132.

Silverstein, C. (2007). Wearing two hats: The psychologist as activist and therapist. *Journal of Gay & Lesbian Psychotherapy, 11*(3), 9–35.

Singh, A.A. & Burnes, T.R. (2011). Feminist therapy and street-level activism: Revisiting our roots and "acting up" in the next decade. *Women & Therapy, 34* (1/2), 129–142.

Solarz, A. (Ed.) (1999). *Lesbian health: Current assessment and directions for the future. Institute of Medicine.* Washington, DC: National Academy Press.

Townsend, M. (2010, 17 October). Black people are 26 times more likely than whites to face stop and search. *The Observer.* Retrieved 2 April 2011 from http://www.guardian.co.uk/uk/2010/oct/17/stop-and-search-race-figures.

Vanita, R. & Kidwai, S. (2000). *Same-sex love in India: Readings from literature and history.* Delhi, India: Mamillan India Ltd.

Verma, S. (1997). *An interview with Deepa Mehta.* Retrieved 10 March 2008 from www.rediff.com.

Walker, L.M. (1993). How to recognize a lesbian: The cultural politics of looking like what you are. *Signs, 18*(4), 866–890.

Wimmer, A. (2008). The making and unmaking of ethnic boundaries. A multi-level process theory. *American Journal of Sociology, 113*(4), 970–1022.

4

Religion

Roshan das Nair & Sonya Thomas

I bought abandon dear
And sold all piety for pleasure.
My own free spirit I have followed,
And never will I give up lust.
(Abū-Nuwās, c.756-786CE; in Kennedy, 1997, p.221).

Religion[1] has for some cultural groups and communities acted as the repository of their faith and hope. It is the balm to their wounds, the emollient to the discrimination and oppression that over the years has skewered their lives. This is no less true for people who are lesbian, gay, or bisexual (LGB). However, when this very sanctuary is turned against LGB people, or they feel estranged from their religion, many experience a sense of loss, angst, anguish, or emotional turmoil. Therefore, religions, faith and spiritualities can also have negative consequences for LGBs, given that at the heart of some of the more dominant and pervasive religions is an unyielding opposition to same-sex desires and/or practices and to those who engage in them. For those religions, the 'sin' of openly entering into a same-sex 'act', is that which demands castigation and denunciation. The rhetoric of 'love the sinner, hate the sin' resonates with such a sentiment.

---

[1]   In this chapter, we mainly refer to religion and not spirituality. There is a separate literature on sexuality and spirituality and we direct the interested reader to texts such as Sweasey (1997) *From queer to eternity: Spirituality in the lives of lesbian, gay, and bisexual people*; Timmerman (1993) *Sexuality and Spiritual Growth*; and Helminiak (2006) *Sex and the sacred: Gay identity and spiritual growth*. We note, however, that there are parallels which can be drawn between religion and spirituality for some of the issues discussed here under religion.

Intersectionality, Sexuality and Psychological Therapies: Working with Lesbian, Gay and Bisexual Diversity, First Edition. Edited by Roshan das Nair and Catherine Butler.

Like any act of denunciation, this exists on a spectrum, with violence at one end and at the other, a mild form of chastisement: one that seeks to understand while withholding approval. But essentially at its heart lies opposition. It could seem entirely incongruous therefore to be both LGB and to hold and have a faith that on the one hand comforts and protects, while on the other, judges and condemns. It would seem to some that the two states cannot coexist and that the dominant religions are so forcefully anti-LGB that staying within them is tantamount to 'sleeping with the enemy' (Yip, 2010, p.42). There is often a great deal of criticism levelled against LGB people of faith for choosing to remain within institutions that actively and systematically seek to exclude them (Yip, 2010). The irony is that the language and actions deployed with such criticism can be equal to and as unrelenting as the very intolerance it rails against.

For some, the idea of religion, faith and spirituality practised and linked to the lives of LGB people is a source of discomfort; a logic that has become tense and fragmented. The LGB faithful, religious and the spiritualised encounter disbelief from those who struggle to, or do not understand how, or why, LGB people would cling to any belief system that so clearly condemns their emotional and sexual lives. The literature of religion and scripture, for example texts in both the Bible and the Qur'an, often act as the authoritative base of much of the invective and bilious prejudice that exists around LGB lives.

In his chapter, *Coming home from the wilderness*, Andrew Yip (2010) provides a comprehensive overview of 'scholarly research' on LGB religiosity and spirituality in the 'West'. By his own admission, much of the literature reviewed is from a gay standpoint, and to a lesser extent, a lesbian one, and it mostly covers experiences from Christian and Muslim (and to a lesser extent, Jewish) perspectives. Our own review of literature finds similar trends in published scholarship in this area. We, however, take a broader view of what 'texts' and 'scholarly' are. For Yip (2010) '[t]ext is neutral, but reading of it is not' (p.41). We are, however, of the opinion that there can be no 'text' without a reader. A text is only a text when it is read or decoded in some fashion and as Iser (1974) suggested, the text only takes on life if it is realised; ergo, no text can be neutral. Similarly, what is a 'scholarly' text for us is not formulated on the basis of where/how the text is produced or who the producer is, but on how it is put to work, used, or deployed. With this formulation, we explore how non-heterosexual people negotiate their religious/spiritual identities.

This chapter focuses on the extent to which religion and religious faith reaches into the lives of non-heterosexual people, how sexuality and religion collide in the lives of those who have same-sex desires and/or identify as LGB. We will seek to explore the lived experiences of religious non-heterosexuals, and the challenges and opportunities that belonging to religious communities bring. This chapter will unpick the contemporary issues surrounding sexuality and religion in non-heterosexual people and will challenge some of the ideological notions of religious and secular LGB identity politics, particularly from Hindu, Muslim, and Christian perspectives. We also touch upon the issues of non-religious (LGB) therapists working with these issues in therapy.

Reading Religious Texts

Yip (2010) skilfully synthesises the literature on sexuality and religion and collapses them into three categories: 'defensive apologetics', '"cruising" texts', and 'turning theology upside down'. Such literature offers the potential for the development of theological capital, which can aid in the formation of a unified sexual/religious identity for religious/spiritual individuals.

The first category of 'defensive apologetics' attempts to 're-contextualise textual passages/verses which have been conventionally deployed as an indisputable basis for the moral exclusivity and authenticity of heterosexuality, and the unacceptability of homosexuality' (p.37). The 'recontextualisation' is achieved by attending to the original (often ancient) languages the texts are written in, and attempting to read them in light of the socio-historical context in which such texts were written and intended for use. To us, this appears to be a highly cognitive exercise. This is perhaps both its appeal and its problem. In therapeutic practice, we often find that most people are able to make the cognitive connections and have a conceptual grasp of their, and others', reading of religious texts. The challenge for most of these people, however, is to incorporate the affective components related to their cognitive integration of their seemingly incongruent sexual and religious identities. Furthermore, reason and logic are not often the language that people with homonegative attitudes understand, nor are they the weapons that can be used against ignorance and hatred from others who do not understand or do not *wish* to understand non-heterosexuality.

Yip's second category of '"cruising" texts' attempts to move beyond apologetics to actively *read* sexuality (and non-heterosexuality) within religious texts and figures. This offers a more affirmative engagement with texts than the previous category, and is often more provocative, but is perhaps only in its infancy with many significant texts yet to be 'cruised'. Again, the charm of this approach to reading and re-reading texts is both its strength and weakness: the agency required of such reading. Furthermore, there is still the cognitive imperative in such an enterprise, but there is nothing to suggest that this cannot be extended to cover other aspects of connecting the text and meaning making to one's lived experience.

Such an approach is perhaps akin to Yip's third category, of 'turning theology upside down', which he sees as a 'bottom-up' approach (p.40), whereby sexuality and 'spirituality' (it is interesting to note that he does not use the word 'religiosity' here) are seen as inseparable, and sexuality is conceptualised as 'not only genital acts' (p.40). There is a nod towards spiritual practices such as tantra, zen, and so on, here. There is an instant appeal to the wholesomeness of such an inherent connection. There is, however, a worry about such a reading also, which prejudices carnal desire (the so called 'genital acts') devoid of an intimate commitment or connection to a place lower in the hierarchy, which may serve to propagate certain heteronormative ideas and practices. Therefore, desires and practices which offend heteronormative sensibilities, such as non-monogamous sexualities, bisexuality, and so on, may be further denounced, thereby creating dissociations between 'good sex' and 'bad sex' (cf. Rubin, 1984). Yip (2010) also acknowledges this when he claims that bisexuality is 'even more subversive of heteronormativity compared to transgenderism and homosexuality' (p.38). The 'bisexual problem' in same-sex religious/spiritual deconstructive efforts/projects causes most discomfort for heteronormativity when it does not conform to dyadic or monogamous relationship patterns. We believe this is related to the inherent problem of religious/spiritual texts being read as asexual texts or as texts which proscribe certain sexual practices, whereby the sex becomes 'incidental' to the main aim of being in a loving, committed, monogamous relationship, even for non-heterosexuals. Therefore, we feel that there needs to be a more transgressive step in the queering of religious texts, moving from just 'cruising' texts to 'sexing' them.

Moving from this framework of reading and re-reading scripture and other religious texts in general, we now turn towards the specifics of sexuality and how it relates to Islam, Christianity and Hinduism, the three largest religious groups in the UK (Office for National Statistics, 2005). We only offer a snapshot of contemporary issues that concern non-heterosexuals belonging to these religious groups, while also providing some background to how non-heteronormative sexualities are perceived. We direct those interested in a more in-depth analysis of some of these issues to Browne *et al.* (2010), who expertly cover various aspects of sexuality in Christianity, the

Quaker movement[2], Islam, Buddhism and other spiritualities. For studies of sexuality and the Jewish faith we direct readers to the works of Balka and Rose (1989) and Beck (1989): the stories in these sources also account for the lived intersections between sexuality, religiosity and ethnicity, as well as disability and working class issues.

Islam

Sexuality and its place in Islam has been the subject of significant interrogation over the centuries, but such scholarship has been diverted by contemporary politics and agenda set by certain men in power, to stifle critical readings of religious texts. In fact, Scott Siraj al-Haqq Kugle (2003) goes so far as to say that '(s)cholars in the contemporary period have not lived up to the standards and frankness of pre-modern Islamic scholars, and much work has yet to be done on the question of sexuality in Islamic scripture, law, and society' (p.191).

As Shannahan (2010) suggests, the narratives of many LGB people suggest 'coming out' as a turning point in their lives, a present break that defines what is (left) in the past and what is yet to come. In such a linear discourse, the seemingly 'traditional' and 'ethnic' aspects of the self are left behind. Religion is also one aspect of life that is positioned as a 'repressive force' (p.674) and thus relegated to the past to create new subjectivities. There is a notion that Islam and homosexuality make for uncomfortable bedfellows, or as Shamira Meghani (2010) deftly stated, there is a 'predominantly assumed opposition between sexual desire and expression, and religious sensibility, that in recent years seems to have reached fever pitch in the representation of Islam and Muslims as necessarily homophobic and misogynistic' (p.713). For people belonging to certain faiths (such as Christianity), the fractioning of the past and the present/future is mitigated by joining a church or community which is LGB affirmative. However, there are no such established LGB affirmative religious spaces for Muslims in the UK. This refocuses the above-mentioned notion to: *certain* religions and homosexuality are incompatible.

Shannahan (2010) appears to suggest that homosexuality, in the public consciousness, is positioned as secular by default. We suggest that this can be taken further in contemporary Britain to suggest: if not secular, then Christian. This exposes the lack of imagination and the deeply ingrained idea about who a Muslim is to the non-Muslim. In fact, 'the Muslim-West

[2] Also see *Towards a Quaker view of sex: An essay by a group of Friends,* Society of Friends (1964).

gap rests on differences in attitudes toward sexual liberalization and gender issues rather than democracy and governance' (Inglehart & Pippa, 2003, cited in Gallup, 2009). In such statements, there is an assumption that there is great homogeneity in both the Muslim and the 'general public' views on such matters. Some of the findings from the Gallup Interfaith Relations study (Gallup, 2009), which surveyed over 1000 people belonging to the 'general public' (non-Muslim) and over 500 Muslims in the UK, is interesting here in disrupting this notion. The study found that while the Muslims surveyed tended to have more 'conservative' views on moral issues, the general public was 'far from monolithic' in their views (p.31). One significant 'moral' issue investigated was the 'acceptability of homosexuality'. None of the Muslims surveyed in Britain thought that homosexuality was morally acceptable, compared to 42 per cent of the British 'general public' who believed that it was *not* acceptable. While these may not be particularly surprising statistics, it is a reminder that a large minority (of the general public) still consider same-sex activities and relations as a moral problem. Interestingly, 35 per cent of Muslims in France thought homosexuality was acceptable. This further exposes the fallacy of there being a monolithic Muslim identity or value system, even within Europe. Therefore, the idea that Islam and non-heterosexuality are antithetical is erroneous. In fact, some of the participants in Yip and Khaled's (2010) study, reported that the very status of being a metaminority (a 'minority within a minority') was a motivating force that led them to a spiritual quest and path which they would not have followed had they not experienced marginalisation.

In the UK, there has been a growing trend amongst some Muslim clerics to forge a better understanding of how homosexuality and Islam can both play a significant role in an individual's life (e.g. Jillani, 2010). While we report this as a trend, it is by no means the experience of the majority of non-heterosexual Muslims, who in our experience, are sometimes unwilling, and some cases unable, to rely on their religious leaders for support. In such times, they look to alternative networks and groups to find emotional support that they can rely on. Groups such as *Imaan* (www.imaan.org.uk) offer support to Muslim LGBT people and their families and friends to help them address issues related to their sexuality and their religion. Other groups such as the *Safra Project* (www.safraproject.org), primarily an online resource, deal specifically with issues related to Muslim lesbian, bisexual women, and transgendered people, with the aims of empowering them to raise issues related to their needs and appropriate service provision, and to irradiate prejudice and discrimination while promoting diversity[3].

---

[3]   Information taken from their websites. Both Imaan and Safra Project have a good list of references on Islam and sexualities on their websites.

Non-heterosexual Muslim women

The Safra Project report (Jivraj *et al.*, 2003) that emerged following consultation with various UK organisations and a two-day conference attended by over 30 women, is illuminating in terms of highlighting the concerns of Muslim non-heterosexual women (particularly lesbian and bisexual women) and their specific needs. Many Muslim lesbian and bisexual women, it was reported, did not know exactly what the Qur'an said about their sexuality, and most found it difficult to access information about this. Available material often focussed only on male homosexuality (Jivraj *et al.*, 2003). Perhaps as a result of this, many women felt that they needed to choose between their religion and their sexuality, and did not see them as being compatible. The report (p.9) quoted one woman as saying:

> When I realised that I was in love with a woman, I thought I would have to go to the other extreme of leaving Islam and leaving my family. But now my faith is stronger, I am still myself and I have more confidence with my children, whereas before I believed I was not good enough to be their mother.

The issues related to family of origin and the women's own children was also explored, with many fearing being forced into marriage with a man if they were single; and/or domestic violence, if their sexuality were disclosed. They feared violence from their families of origin and their husbands and in-laws (see Chapter 3 on Race and Ethnicity). Some non-heterosexual Muslim women resisted the pressures of getting married while others opted to get married, if not for anything but to escape from the pressures of being an unmarried woman in a Muslim household. For those who were married and had children, many feared that their children would be taken away from them, either legally through the courts, or by family members abducting them. Being heterosexually married and having children within these unions (especially at a young age) also poses a particular problem for those non-heterosexual Muslim women seeking asylum in the UK, because asylum decision-makers may take this as a marker of their 'genuine' heterosexuality, without recognising that many of these women would not have had a say in the matter of marriage or pregnancy (Jivraj *et al.*, 2003; see Chapter 5 on Asylum seekers and Refugees).

The women were at times emotionally blackmailed by their families into not disclosing their sexuality, by reminding them of the consequences this would have on the rest of the family: the family's name or honour (*izzat*) would be ruined and this would also potentially jeopardise future marital alliances for the younger siblings (especially female siblings) of the person coming out. This can result in the non-heterosexual woman experiencing significant levels of guilt and shame, which can have deleterious effects on her mental and physical health.

Coming out, therefore, for these women is a treacherous enterprise. Alongside the above mentioned issues, is the possible loss of support from the family in terms of finance, housing, education, protection against racism and Islamophobia, and so on. Given these factors, the decision to come out to the family of origin also appeared to be mediated through social class, with families from middle class backgrounds being seen to be more liberal towards personal freedoms than those from working class backgrounds (also see Chapter 6 on Class). Coming out to their own children was also perceived to be difficult, as one woman in the Jivraj *et al.* study (2003) said:

> My children equate homosexuality with promiscuity because of the way they are being taught and because of the homophobia in their schools. This makes it so hard for me to come out to them (p.13).

The report warned, 'explicitly coming out to family and friends is not, at all times or in all situations, viable or safe' for lesbian and bisexual Muslim women, and that '[t]he gains of coming out . . . do not always outweigh the losses or (physical) risks' (p.13). However, the unavailable opportunities to freely acknowledge one's own sexual identity can cause an extreme sense of isolation for some women. Non-heterosexual Muslim women can sometimes feel that they are the only ones 'afflicted' with such a problem (of same-sex sexual desire). This is one of the reasons why having local non-heterosexual Muslim women's groups is useful. There is tremendous power in the bonding and sharing that people experience in such groups. However, these groups should not be seen as a panacea, addressing all the needs of these women and the communities they live in, but could serve as an adjunct to mainstream and regular public services.

Despite the various issues that non-heterosexual Muslim women experience, their uptake of public services, whether it is offered by the police (e.g. in the case of domestic violence), social services (e.g. in terms of child custody issues), or psychological services, is poor. The reasons for this appear to be three-fold:

(i)   there is generally a low sense of awareness of what services are available, which is probably a result of a paucity of information about these services;

(ii) non-heterosexual Muslim women's negative expectations of these services, which they perceive as being either Islamaphobic/racist and/or homophobic, and therefore, they do not trust these services; and

(iii)   nonexistent or ill-equipped services that do not meet the needs of these women, with some services not being culturally sensitive.

The women's voices in the Safra project suggested that some therapists had a poor understanding of Islam and/or a poor understanding of the women's cultural contexts which led some of them to 'fail to differentiate between patriarchal forces within Muslim communities and cultural and religious values' (p.9). Related to the issue of culturally sensitive services, some Muslim women reported that they would not seek psychological support from LGBT-identified centres, because of the fear associated with being seen going to such spaces, which are visibly marked. Most women reported feeling more comfortable seeking such services from within a gender and/or race-specific centre. Therefore, the low uptake of services is perhaps not because non-heterosexual Muslim women feel that psychological therapies or support groups are unimportant, but because of the threats or perceived threats of accessing such services.

The foregoing discussion is not to suggest that non-heterosexual Muslim women do not access services at all, or are unappreciative of the services that exist to support them. As one of the women in the Safra project said:

> When I came into the refuge, the first thing I noticed was a poster on the wall for the gay and lesbian helpline and I thought: here I can finally be myself and be accepted. It really meant a lot to me and I will never forget that moment of relief (p.21).

For this woman, a poster was all it took to relieve her of her fears and apprehensions of being acknowledged, accepted and welcomed to this service. Posters, we feel, do not need to specifically use sexual identity labels, such as LGB, because these labels themselves may create distance. Instead, the use of sensitive and culturally appropriate visuals can make a great impact, for example, the relationship portrayed in a visual of two women holding hands can be read in multiple ways, as lesbians, lovers, sisters, friends, and so on.

Rereading, reinterpretation, or 'undressing' Islamic texts

One aspect that plays a key role in the reconciliation of religion and homosexuality is that of rereading, reinterpretation, or 'undressing' (cf. Shannahan, 2010) of religious historiography and texts, particularly those parts of the texts which have been used over the years to condemn and vilify non-heterosexual activity, and by extension, non-heterosexual identities.

As Kugle (2003) says: '(w)e must be instantly suspicious of statements like "Islam says..." or "The Shari'ah says..." as if these abstractions actually speak. Things do not speak. Only people speak' (p.194).

His work is particularly noteworthy in that it 'queers[4]' (and offers a method of queering[5]) the Qur'an and *hadith*[6] in a nuanced and scholarly fashion. He attempts to show how patriarchal and heterosexist reading of the Qur'an has come to be perceived as orthodox, which try to limit ambiguities in religious texts and teachings[7]. This then promotes a kind of a 'scriptural determinism' which tries to alienate anyone or any group who are seen to violate the prescribed codes which define the norm. It is interesting to note here that (according to Kugle, 2003) the contemporary idea that homosexuality is incompatible with Islam stems from the European Christian dichotomy of 'natural' and 'unnatural' which has been borrowed by Muslims today, a dichotomy which is not indigenous to the Qur'an.

There is an interesting polemic when considering 'progress', 'modernity', 'sexual liberation' and Islam, with the West currently viewing the Islamic nations (and Islam) as needing to be brought to the 21st Century with regard to ideologies related to gender and sexuality. For us in the West, it is worth remembering though that at another time (medieval and early modern), it was the European Christians who accused the Muslims of being 'sodomitical' and permissive (Kugle, 2003), and thereby being 'backward'.

Christianity and Judaism has since moved on, 'progressively' some might suggest, in varying degrees towards, if not affording complete acceptance of homosexuality, at least by conferring a more liberal understanding of it. This in itself poses, what Brian Whitaker (writing about gay and lesbian life in the Middle East) describes as an intriguing question: Why, given the significance that each religion has to the other, have these changes occurred in Christianity and Judaism but not in Islam? He suggests that it is the historical difference between Muslim and Christian countries in the spread of secularism that provides, in part, an answer. In addition, he believes that changes in Christian attitudes towards homosexuality was partly affected by the 'historical progression, stimulated by a concern for social justice and respect for all human beings' with no equivalent 'progressive Islamic trend' (Whitaker, 2006, p.180). Whitaker goes on to highlight its significance for

---

[4]   Queer used in this context refers to the verb 'to queer', meaning to question, deconstruct, and re-read texts from a non-heterosexist perspective.
[5]   Kugle offers an illustrative case of the story of Lut, and painstakingly shows how meaning-making is dependent on how the text is read.
[6]   Narrations concerning the words and deeds of the Prophet Muhammad.
[7]   Also see Yip (2005).

Muslims 'whose sexuality brings them into conflict with religious ortho-doxy' (p.181). LGB Jews and Christians wanting to reconcile their sexuality and their faith can find significant support, which is not always available for Muslims. 'The most they can hope for, if not to be totally shunned and condemned, is to be told to change their ways and marry, or to spend their lives in celibacy' (Whitaker, 2006, p.181).

Whitaker points out that many LGB people would agree with the view that religion and homosexuality are fundamentally incompatible. Research carried out by Yip and Khaled (2010) of gay Muslims found a good deal of consistency in the notion of dissonance and the struggle to reconcile religion and their sexual identity (Yip, 2010). The struggle for some will mean taking the decision to withdraw from religion completely, a choice that in a secular society, they are free to make. However, as Whitaker points out, renouncing Islam can be as serious an offence as sodomy. He adds that within some families, coming out as a non-believer can be no less traumatic than coming out as gay or lesbian. He cites the case of an ex-Muslim living in the United States who avoided telling his parents in Pakistan that he was both atheist and gay; though of the two, he thought that confessing to atheism would be the worse: 'Even if I'm leading an immoral life and sleeping with boys, there's hope. . .But with this, I'm giving God the finger. It would hurt them that their son is going to hell' (Whitaker, 2006, p.182).

Traditional Muslim scholars may be unwilling to accept any alternative interpretations of the Qur'an and are harsh in their condemnation of those who seek to find alternative meanings. 'At the root of religious debate about sexuality is the willingness, or otherwise, of believers to adapt to changing circumstances and new understandings of human behaviour' (Whitaker, 2006, p.196). However, the absence of any specific reference to sexual di-versity in either the Qur'an or the Bible has given some the opportunity to approach an understanding of homosexuality and religion that is wider in scope, offering tolerance and to some extent, acceptance of their lifestyle.

Christianity

The Bible is a library of books in which hardline interpreters are in ongoing conflict with the more liberal. The canon of scripture might be closed but the ancient debates it preserves between the condemnatory moral rigorists and the humanitarians are still with us (Radcliffe, 2010).

The acceptance of LGB Christians is one of the most divisive issues in the Church today. Homosexuality's censure in Christianity appears to have its origins in the Bible, specifically in the Book of Genesis where we are first introduced to the word 'sodomy' and its associations with sinfulness and depravity. But the Bible, like most theological texts, is open to interpretation. It is an open book of 'conflicting viewpoints that opened the mind and heart to God. It did not close them' (Radcliff, 2010). It is such interpretations that some LGB people find useful in enabling them to lead 'good LGB Christian lives'. The various scholars contributing to *The Queer Bible Commentary* (Guest *et al.*, 2006) offer a subversive and transgressive analysis of Biblical text. The authors set out to de-stigmatise LGB lives and desires and offer an alternative interpretation of various texts within the Bible to those that censure and disapprove. Their collective work emphasises how reading text from different perspectives can affect interpretation[8].

There is no doubt, however, that the Bible is often relied on as being sufficient evidence to justify a generalised condemnation of homosexuality. But interpretation and meaning is important, and many Christians have grappled with their own understanding of texts within the Bible to make sense of the disapproval, as well as to shed light and deliberate on alternative interpretations that offer a different understanding and self-acceptance of their homosexuality. They are looking for what some have described as 'LGB affirming re-reading of texts'.

> Appropriating verses ... that turns them into statements of faith and ontology, underpinned by the unshakeable certainty that one's sexuality (and gender), no matter how despised and persecuted, is not just a choice of random genetic predisposition but divinely willed and planned (Yip, 2010, p.40).

The interest and, to an extent, beauty, of religion for believers and non-believers often lies in its incomprehensibility, in its obscureness, which allows religion to mean different things to each person and brings something unique to the individual experience. This could explain its perception as being above sexuality, something that transcends many boundaries, especially the physical. However, with this view also comes the suggestion of religion being sex-negative: inured from the banalities of pleasure, forming and transcending to a spiritual place.

In addressing the Abrahamic religions, Yip (2010) writes of the construct of the divine as the object of worship within which formulation, the understanding of sexuality is reduced to sex behaviour. In such a formulation the emphasis is on the 'mechanical aspect of sexuality' with the emotional side

---

[8] We would also refer the reader to Gross and Yip (2010) and Yip (1997).

to an extent 'downplayed'. This he says accounts for the recurrent 'gay' debates within Christianity which reveals how at odds it is with 'contemporary and social realities'.

Bisexuality and Christianity

In his essay, *Negotiating Identity - Life Narratives of Bisexual Christians*, Alex Toft (2009) addresses the issue of bisexuality and how bisexual Christians adapt and navigate their lives within a confining faith. Toft writes of bisexuals' ostracisation by both heterosexual and homosexual groups and argues that even the use of the term LGBT, while conferring some power to the overall 'plight of non-heterosexuals' (p.127), serves mostly to make bisexuality synonymous with homosexuality in terms of the challenges faced by both of living with spirituality. Toft goes on to say (p.128-129): 'The Christian faith has just two over-arching grounds for not fully accepting bisexual Christians into the Church . . . they "are seen as promiscuous and their resulting status being incompatible with the Christian concept of marriage".'

While there has been a good deal of research into bisexuality which has helped to lay bare what it means to be bisexual, much of this research, Toft asserts, fails to capture the range and diversity of the bisexual experience. Toft's research showed that bisexuals resisted attempts to understand their sexuality in terms of physical attraction alone with some preferring to reject any over-simplification of their sexuality. What the research revealed was the wide and varying self-definitions individuals used to interpret their bisexuality. He contends that it is this very scenario that bisexuals have to 'access religious space' (Toft, 2009, p.132). His research showed that many individuals coped with the dissonance of their spiritual and sexual lives by abandoning formal church attendance, with many 're-aligning their belief systems away from' church worship (p.132). Attendance by others was ad hoc, and for special occasions such as Christenings. Others who attended church 'practiced concealment', as one respondent put it, 'leaving one's sexuality at the door' (p.133).

Pertinently, the varying approaches bisexual Christians in Toft's research took to dealing with their faith and sexuality, led to their disenchantment with their religious identity rather than with their understanding of their sexuality, with sexuality becoming 'the core identity around which religious beliefs and practices are negotiated'(p.133). Yip similarly describes the process of 'turning externally-imposed shame to internally-generated pride': a sense of pride that stems from believing that despite what religious authority structures officially pronounce, God and Christ is on their side because they have learned to trust their own lived experiences of the goodness and mercy of God (2010, p.43).

The Bible will always sit at the centre of a dividing line between those who draw strength from it and those to whom it stands as an irrevocable treaty that speaks against homosexuality and LGB lives. Scholars will continue their re-examination of Biblical text and scripture, advancing theories that expose ambivalence where there was once absolutism. It is this that gives hope to those who continue to navigate the contextual dissonance of their faith and their sexuality.

Hinduism

Scholars of Hinduism generally suggest that 'homosexuality' as such, unlike in the Qur'an and Bible, is not directly referred to in Hindu religious texts. This is not surprising, considering that some scholars posit that:

> 'homosexuals' did not exist before the creation of the term 'homosexuality'; they claim that homosexual people, like the term 'homosexual' itself, are products of the peculiar conditions of modernity. This argument is the cornerstone of a political position that religious traditions have nothing to say about homosexuality or modern homosexuals, since their ancient scriptures have no term to describe them (Kugle, 2003, p.199).

This said, same-sex sexuality is documented in several Hindu texts, and is also evident in the paintings, poetry, murals and sculptures, some of which even grace holy temples throughout the Indian subcontinent, where Hinduism finds its origins, with some of these dating back to 1500 BCE. Furthermore, aspects of such sexuality are also celebrated in treatises such as the Kama Sutra. However, attempting to find evidence of 'homosexuality' within scripture in Hinduism for the purpose of claiming its rightful existence and indigenousness in Hindu culture, or for the purpose of exposing it as a Western abomination that has found a place in Hindu culture, is something of a moot point. Unlike in the Abrahamic religions, most Hindus are not in direct communion with Hindu scripture, but rather practices which are infused with myriad indigenous folk traditions, tantric and yogic ideas and rituals, philosophy, mythology, and theology. Therefore, we believe that the queering of Hindu texts, while an interesting (and perhaps useful) project, cannot be performed along the same lines as the queering of texts such as the Bible or the Qur'an. As Nayan Shah (1993) warns us:

While the project of reclaiming and reconstructing the past is critical for present political and cultural struggles, let us not read too much of 'us' today into the past. We may trap ourselves in the need of a history to sanction our existence (p.486).

The traditions of representing same-sex desire in several art forms continued well into the period covering medieval Hinduism as well as the introduction of Islam to the Indian subcontinent (Kidwai & Vanita, 2000). As mentioned earlier in the discussion on Islam and the idea of 'progress', again it was the European visitors who arrived on the subcontinent at the time who reported on such 'backward' practices (such as same-sex relationships) amongst the Hindus. It is interesting to note here that such Western ideology was instrumental in the framing of the Indian Penal Code's Section which criminalises 'carnal intercourse against the order of nature' (IPC 377)[9].

Hindus, particularly from the south Indian states, have recognised the fluid forms of gender and sexualities, as represented in one of their local deities, Lord Ayyappa. Ayyappa is believed to have been the offspring of a union between two male Gods, Shiva and Vishnu, with the latter taking on a feminine form. Similarly, in northern and eastern India, historical and religious texts refer to Bhagiratha, born to the widows of King Dilipa. Following the instruction of the family priest, the two women have intercourse, which results in one of them conceiving. The etymology of the name Bhagiratha itself suggests that the child was born of 'the *bhaga* (vulva) alone' (or in some other versions of the text, 'born of two vulvas') (Vanita, 2005). What is interesting is that these are not just historical mythologies or deities, but narratives of current significance to Hindus. Such narratives have the power to harness belief in the historical precedence of non-heterosexual sexualities, some even sanctioned by the Gods. The currency of such narratives, not just in the Indian subcontinent but also in the UK, is demonstrated by recent articles in newspapers such as *The Guardian,* in which people like Anil Bhanot, the General Secretary of the Hindu Council UK, has suggested that:

> The point here is that the [sic] homosexual nature is part of the natural law of God; it should be accepted for what it is, no more and no less. . .Homosexuals are full human beings, who in Hinduism even worship their own deity, the

---

[9] This Section has been the focus of controversy over the last many years, perhaps culminating in the Delhi High Court's landmark judgement in 2009 which decriminalised consensual homosexual relations.

Mother Goddess Bahuchara[10], for their spiritual link to the Absolute Brahm[11] (Bhanot, 2009).

Sri Sri Ravi Shankar (born 1956), a spiritual leader and founder of the international movement *Art of Living*, addressing the topic of homosexuality stated, 'Every individual has both male and female in them. Sometimes one dominates, sometimes other, it is all fluid' (Rupani, 2003, p.15). These statements by Sri Sri Ravi Shankar and Bhanot are important pronouncements. Non-heterosexual Hindus can look towards such leaders to help define and defend their identities and ways of being.

International Society for Krishna Consciousness (ISKCON), popularly known as the *Hare Krishna* movement, is a worldwide association which has attracted hundreds of thousands of devotees. ISKCON emerged in the UK in the late 1960s, and one of the Beatles (George Harrison) was instrumental in its popularity here. Recently, a small survey was conducted by Das (2005) on homosexuality and ISKCON, in which respondents (devotees) from eight different countries commented on their LGBT identity and how this was negotiated in ISKCON. While most of the participants were 'out' to some or all other devotees they knew, most of them did not live in the ashram for various reasons, one of which was homophobia from heterosexual ashram members. Interestingly, while half the respondents said that they would like to be in a same-sex marriage, only 36 per cent wanted homosexual marriage to be introduced in ISKCON. This, the author suggests, is in contradiction to the popular notion amongst (heterosexual) ISKCON devotees, who feel that all LGB people want marriage to be introduced in ISKCON. This said, more than half the LGB devotees felt that 'very few' ISKCON gurus had a 'proper attitude toward gay Vaishnavas[12]'. Perhaps it is because of this that half of the respondents felt that ISKCON did not offer them a fair opportunity for their spiritual advancement. But as many LGB devotees reported, the degree of acceptance they experienced was related to the local temple leadership and their attitudes towards non-heterosexual sexualities. When the leadership projected hostile attitudes, this led to some devotees abandoning their spiritual quest through ISKCON, most feeling

---

[10] It must be noted here that Bahuchara Mata is actually worshiped not by 'homosexuals', as Bhanot suggests, but by some *hijra* (trans) communities in India. Other deities are worshiped in other regions of India by hijras, for instance, Koothandavar (Aravan) in the South Indian state of Tamil Nadu.

[11] In Hinduism, Brahm is considered a state beyond bliss and God, and it is the ultimate aim of Hindu life to reach such a state.

[12] Vaishnavas are followers of Vaishnavism, a tradition of Hinduism, which recognises the Hindu God Vishnu as the supreme God.

isolated and with 29 per cent reporting having contemplated suicide (because of the conflict between their sexuality and their spiritual acceptance in their ISKCON community). Examining the qualitative data collected during Das's study (2005), it appears that LGB Krishna devotees at ISKCON want to emphasise that their sexuality is not a choice or a 'trend' but a god-given part of who they are. This active distancing from the notion of sexuality and sexual orientation being a 'preference' or a 'choice' is a rhetoric that is also seen in other religious discourse (e.g. Haider-Markel & Joslyn, 2008).

The specific literature around Hinduism and non-heterosexual sexualities is scant and the lived experience of practicing Hindus who also consider themselves LGB needs investigation. However, in the absence of such literature, some information about their experiences can be gleaned from exploring the race/sexuality nexus. Given that the majority of Muslims (and Hindus) in the UK tend to be of South Asian origin, some of these experiences and concerns reported may reflect a combination of racial and religious customs, beliefs, and attitudes, which cannot be disentangled from an individual's culture or cultural groupings (see Chapter 3 on Race and Ethnicity).

Working from a Position of Non-Belief

One of the biggest challenges non-religious people ('non-believers') face when dealing with conflictual issues related to sexuality and religion is dealing with their own prejudices both within the sexuality and belief arena. There has been considerable literature published which has exposed how *some* religious heterosexual therapists attempt to 'cure' or 'liberate' clients from their homosexuality/bisexuality *through* religion. Recently, media attention has brought to the fore such occurrence, for instance, through Patrick Strudwick's expose of 'gay-to-straight conversion' that some therapists in the UK are engaged in (Strudwick, 2010), and therapists' attitudes towards homosexuality and conversion therapies (e.g. Bartlett *et al.*, 2009). There is, however, far less published literature on how non-heterosexual, non-believer therapists deal with such issues in therapy. In an attempt to collect some stories which reflected such issues, we requested a few therapists (friends and acquaintances) we know to be LGB to send in their experiences by email. The following is a narrative offered by a therapist who struggles with his own prejudices against religion and the prejudices he has experienced because of his sexuality. These are real battles; battles related to identities and belief systems, which simply cannot be checked in at the door to the therapy room. While most of the stories in this book are narrated from a client's perspective, this is a therapist's story.

A Therapist's Reflection

I once had a client who had a rather rigid reading of the Bible related to aspects of sex and sexuality. He identified as heterosexual, but regularly engaged in sex with men and experienced sexual dysfunctions when having sex with women. He refused to entertain the possibility that he was anything but 'a regular straight bloke', who wanted to 'just have a regular life'. In therapy, we tried to explore his internalised and externalised homonegativity, and it appeared that this mainly stemmed from his religious beliefs that dictated that homosexuality was a sin. He said he abhorred homosexuals and 'pitied' them, for they had 'lost their way'. This kind of talk irritated me, because I was out to him, and I did not want the pity he was offering homosexuals. I found myself battling with a thought that kept coming back to me: 'if only he could get rid of his religion', knowing fully well that a more therapeutically acceptable reformulation of that thought would have been, 'if only he could be at peace with his sexuality and his religion'. I also found myself asking, 'why does he need this religious belief?'

This set the stage for me to question my own prejudices related to religion, and I attempted to draw parallels between religion and sexuality, and the prejudices associated with both. I wasn't offended by a rainbow flag lapel pin, but why was I offended by a pendant fashioned in the shape of a cross? I recalled that some Muslim anti-gay protesters were most offended by the fact that some parents brought their children along to the local Pride march. I also remembered getting annoyed when I saw churches advertise 'religious activities' for children. Amidst these thoughts was also the keen awareness that I have heard people say things like, 'Why do they have to flaunt it?' This could easily refer to LGB people who are open about their sexuality or to heterosexuals who have markers of their religious identities about their person (e.g. a hijab or a cross-shaped pendant). Would a butch lesbian sporting a short haircut and a denim jacket be 'flaunting' her sexuality as much as a Sikh man sporting a turban be 'flaunting' his religion? I wondered what the difference was? Was I being bigoted? My client was essentially asking me to cure him of his homosexuality, so I was mindful of not wanting to cure him of his religiosity! I recognise these are rather simplistic juxtapositions and comparisons, but sometimes your immediate thoughts are not lofty or sensible. They do, however, have the potential to spur further thought.

I found that my client belonged to a church which was anti-gay, and I enquired whether he would consider speaking to another priest who had another reading of the Bible, or whether he would like to meet with other gay Christians to see how they negotiated their religious and sexual identities, just to get a different point of view for him to consider. He was not interested. The Bible, he said, was unequivocal about issues related to homosexuality; he quoted passages from the Bible to support his claim. I dared to suggest that these could be open to interpretation. He was not having any of it. Reasoning, I reckoned, was not going to win the battle. But this is another problem I have with my understanding of religion: it defies reason and logic. But then again, it's not like I always operate with reason and logic as my allies. Then there are the patriarchal and male-dominant aspects of religion which I cannot swallow: God and the prophets are men. As a feminist, I struggle with this. My client decided to terminate our sessions together; he said he found a Christian counselling centre that was willing to cure him with prayer. I felt a sense of anger and relief when I heard this.

For this therapist, the battle is real, even if the battle lines are not precisely drawn out through reason and logic. This particular therapist went on to describe how he attempted to deal with this issue through supervision. Although there exists some literature on non-religious therapists and their religious clients, from a variety of psychological and therapeutic traditions (e.g. Lijtmaer, 2009, refers specifically to psychoanalysis; Ellis, 1992, on Rational Emotive Therapy), there is work to be done to explore how non-heterosexual and non-religious, agnostic, atheistic, or secular therapists negotiate their sexuality and non-religious stance with clients who are religious, and specifically with clients who view their non-heterosexuality as a problem related to their religion. The associations between therapist non-religious positions and LGB-affirmative therapies for religious clients, are tricky, and elude definitive answers or prescriptive ways of being (in therapy). Lijtmaer (2009), through her own introspections, reflects on these issues and concludes:

> It is important for therapists to be aware of their own personal associations to particular religious ideas in order to contain these countertransference

responses. The focus must be on understanding those emotional dynamics which characterize a patient's engagement in a particular religious behavior. Particularly, self-examination is crucial for a successful engagement in the treatment process (p.108).

Conclusions

Yip (2010) rightly suggests that religion/spirituality can also be an important 'resource for the construction of meaningful [LGB] lives' (p.43). This, however, can only be a resource for people who have been able to successfully negotiate the seeming contradictions between their religious beliefs and sexual desires/practices, and there is some acknowledgement, if not approval, from their religious communities of their sexual existence. For others who cannot reconcile their sexual and religious identities, resulting in a jarring of identities, this nexus can be a site of internal conflict, causing significant psychological distress. Therapists are well placed to help clients in their journey to resolving or minimising these conflicts. We also feel that therapists, because of their position in society, also have the power and privilege to encourage positive change in societies and communities that still view non-heterosexual sexualities as a disease, a curse, or a form of aberration. They can achieve this by engaging with these societies and communities, sharing their knowledge about sexualities and mental health and psychological wellbeing with community and religious leaders and by encouraging people to form or connect with peer support groups. Whether we are religious believers or not, we need to acknowledge that some of our clients are and that religion does play an important role in their lives.

Guidelines for Good Practice

In thinking about how religion and sexuality interact, therapists should be mindful:

- That some non-heterosexual clients are religious and their religion is important to them.
- That for some religious non-heterosexual clients, their psychological problems need not be related to a conflictual relationship between their sexuality and religion. For such clients, their religion and their religious affiliations may be a source of support for them, which therapists could harness.

- Not to ignore the affective components of the client's experience, when they are cognitively attempting to negotiate their sexuality with their religious beliefs.
- Of their own religious prejudices and how these can affect the therapeutic interaction and the manner in which support is offered.
- Of their own religious beliefs and how these relate to non-heterosexual sexualities. Therapists are reminded that it is not appropriate to attempt to modify the client's sexual orientation to bring it in line with the therapist's or client's understanding of their own religion(s).
- That many religious non-heterosexual clients may have felt some rejection or may still be experiencing rejection by the religious community to which they once belonged or belong.
- That religious non-heterosexual clients may be facing prejudice and discrimination from multiple areas of their life because of their religion *and* their sexuality, and this may affect the support they receive from their family, friends, and other social networks.
- That the client may feel more comfortable in discussing religious and sexual issues if the therapist has some basic understanding of their client's religion and its doctrines, particularly how they relate to non-heterosexuality. However, such information should not be used to essentialise the experience of *all* clients who come from the same religious background.

References

Balka, C. & Rose, A. (Eds.) (1989). *Twice blessed: On being lesbian or gay and Jewish.* Boston, MA: Beacon Press.

Bartlett, A., Smith, G. & King, M. (2009). The response of mental health professionals to clients seeking help to change or redirect same-sex sexual orientation. *BMC Psychiatry, 9,* 11doi:10.1186/1471-244X-9-11. Retrieved 13 February 2011 from http://www.biomedcentral.com/1471-244X/9/11/ABSTRACT%20/ PREPUB/ABSTRACT/PREPUB/COMMENTS/ABSTRACT/citation.

Beck, E.T. (Ed.) (1989). *Nice Jewish Girls: A lesbian anthology.* Boston, MA: Beacon Press.

Bhanot, A. (2009, 2 July). Hinduism does not condemn gay people. *The Guardian.* Retrieved 26 January 2011 from http://www.guardian.co.uk/commentisfree/ belief/2009/jul/02/gay-rights-india.

Browne, K., Munt, S.R. & Yip, A.T.K. (2010). *Queer spiritual spaces: Sexuality and sacred spaces.* Surrey: Ashgate.

Das, V. (2005). A Sociological Study of Homosexuality in ISKCON. Retrieved 26 January 2011 from http://www.galva108.org/homosexuality_ISKCON.pdf.

Ellis, A. (1992). My current views on Rational-Emotive Therapy (RET) and religiousness. *Journal of Rational-Emotive & Cognitive-Behavior Therapy, 10*(1), 37–40.

Gallup. (2009). *The Gallup Coexist Index 2009: A Global Study of Interfaith Relations.* Retrieved 5 May 2011 from http://www.abudhabigallupcenter.com/144575/gallup-coexist-index-2009.aspx.

Gross, M. & Yip, A.K.T. (2010). Living spirituality and sexuality: A comparison of lesbian, gay and bisexual Christians in France and Britain. *Social Compass, 57*(1), 40–59.

Guest, D., Goss, R., West, M. & Bohache, T. (Eds.) (2006). *The queer Bible commentary.* London: SCM Press.

Haider-Markel, D.P. & Joslyn, M.R. (2008). Beliefs about the origins of homosexuality and support for gay rights: An empirical test of attribution theory. *Public Opinion Quarterly, 72,* 291–310.

Helminiak, D.A. (2006). *Sex and the sacred: Gay identity and spiritual growth.* Binghampton, NY: Harrington Park Press.

Iser, W. (1974). *The implied reader.* Baltimore, MD: John Hopkins University Press.

Jillani, S. (2010). Imams help gay Muslims embrace new social identities. *BBC Online.* Retrieved 20 January 2011 from http://www.bbc.co.uk/news/10480987.

Jivraj, S., Tauqir, T. & de Jong, A. (2003). *Safra project: Initial findings.* Retrieved 11 May 2011 from http://www.safraproject.org/Reports/Safra_Project-Initial_findings-2002.pdf.

Kennedy, P.F. (1997). *The wine song in classical Arabic poetry.* Oxford: Clarendon Press.

Kidwai, S. & Vanita, R. (2000). *Same-sex love in India: Readings from literature and history.* New Delhi, India: Macmillan India Ltd.

Kugle, S.S.A. (2003). Sexuality, diversity and ethics in the agenda of progressive Muslims. In O. Safi (Ed.) *Progressive Muslims: On justice, gender, and pluralism.* Oxford: Oneworld Publications.

Lijtmaer, R.M. (2009). The patient who believes and the analyst who does not. *Journal of The American Academy of Psychoanalysis and Dynamic Psychiatry, 37*(1), 99–91.

Meghani, S. (2010). Islamicate cultures, sexual intersections. *Sexualities, 13*(6), 713–722.

Office for National Statistics (2005). *Focus on ethnicity and identity.* Retrieved 6 February 2011 from http://www.statistics.gov.uk/cci/nugget.asp?id=460.

Radcliff, A. (2010, 8 July). The Bible is an open book. *The Guardian.* Retrieved 11 February 2011 from http://www.guardian.co.uk/commentisfree/belief/2010/jul/08/bible-open-book-liberal-homosexuality?INTCMP=SRCH.

Rubin, G. (1984). Thinking sex: Notes for a radical theory of the politics of sexuality. In R. Parker and P. Aggleton (Eds.) (2007). *Culture, society and sexuality: A reader* (2nd edn). Oxon: Routledge.

Rupani, A. (2003). Sexuality and spirituality. *Trikone, 18*(4), 15.

Shah, N. (1993). Sexuality, identity, and the uses of history. In P.M. Nardi and B.E. Schneider (Eds). *Social perspective in lesbian and gay studies: A reader.* London: Routledge. pp. 481–490.

Shannahan, D.S. (2010). Some queer questions from a Muslim faith perspective. *Sexualities, 13*(6), 671–684.

Society of Friends (1964). *Towards a Quaker view of sex: An essay by a group of Friends.* London: Friends Home Service Committee, revised edition. Retrieved 1 September 2011 from http://www.worldpolicy.org/globalrights/sexorient/1964-quaker.html.

Strudwick, P. (2010, 1 February 2010). The ex-gay files: The bizarre world of gay-to-straight conversion. *The Independent on Sunday.* Retrieved 13 February 2011 from http://www.independent.co.uk/life-style/health-and-families/features/the-exgay-files-the-bizarre-world-of-gaytostraight-conversion-1884947.html.

Sweasey, P. (1997). *From queer to eternity: Spirituality in the lives of lesbian, gay, and bisexual people.* Washington DC: Cassell.

Timmerman, J. (1993). *Sexuality and spiritual growth.* New York, NY: Crossroads.

Toft, A. (2009). Negotiating identity – Life narratives of bisexual Christians. In *Narrative, memory and identities.* University of Huddersfield, Huddersfield, pp. 127–135. Retrieved 1 September 2011 from http://eprints.hud.ac.uk/4876/2/Chapter_13_Alex_Toft.pdf.

Vanita, R. (2005). *Gandhi's tiger and Sita's smile: Essays on gender, sexuality and culture.* New Delhi, India: Yoda Press.

Whitaker, B. (2006). Sex crimes. *New Humanist.* Retrieved 9 February 2011 from http://newhumanist.org.uk/971/sex-crimes.

Yip, A.K.T. (1997). *Gay male Christian couples: Life stories.* Westport: Praeger.

Yip, A.K.T. (2005). Queering religious texts: An exploration of British non-heterosexual Christians' and Muslims' strategy of constructing sexuality-affirming hermeneutics. *Sociology, 39*(1), 47–65.

Yip, A.K.T. (2010). Coming home from the wilderness: An overview of recent scholarship research on LGBTQI religiosity/spirituality in the West. In K. Browne, S.R. Munt & A.T.K. Yip (Eds.). *Queer spiritual spaces: Sexuality and sacred spaces.* Surrey, Ashgate.

Yip, A.T.K. & Khalid, A. (2010). Looking for Allah: Spiritual quests of queer Muslims. In K. Browne, S.R. Munt & A.T.K. Yip (Eds.). *Queer spiritual spaces: Sexuality and sacred spaces.* Surrey, Ashgate.

5

Refugees and Asylum Seekers

Stephen Higgins & Catherine Butler

There is a small but growing interest in lesbian, gay and bisexual (LGB) refugee and asylum issues from the human rights field (e.g. Human Rights Watch, 2009), asylum case law (e.g. de Jong, 2003) and more recently the news media (e.g. British Broadcasting Corporation [BBC] 2008, 2009a). However, little is known about the experiences of LGB and other non-heterosexual refugees and asylum seekers from a psychological perspective, as often their refugee status overshadows differences such as sexuality (Patel, 2003a). Some asylum seekers will not use the labels of LGB, which can be problematic when such identity labels may be an expected prerequisite to granting refugee status[1]. Such complexities mean the prevalence of LGB asylum cases is not known, though recent estimates suggest between 1200 and 1800 LGB asylum seekers arrived in the UK in 2008 (Metropolitan Support Trust [MST], 2009). This suggests LGB asylum seekers make up approximately 7 per cent of asylum cases nationally (Office of National Statistics, 2009) and as such represent a sizeable group that should be given consideration by asylum, health and social services.

LGB people persecuted for their sexual orientation are able to claim asylum on the basis that they constitute a 'particular social group' (Dauvergne & Millbank, 2003) under Article 1A(2) of the United Nations Convention Relating to the Status of Refugees (United Nations High Commissioner for Refugees, 2007), though advocates have sought to clarify this more explicitly through a framework for international human rights law relating to gender

---

[1] In this chapter we use the terms lesbian, gay, and bisexual (LGB) for parsimony but recognise that not all refugees and asylum seekers use these terms.

Intersectionality, Sexuality and Psychological Therapies: Working with Lesbian, Gay and Bisexual Diversity, First Edition. Edited by Roshan das Nair and Catherine Butler.
© 2012 John Wiley & Sons, Ltd. Published 2012 by John Wiley & Sons, Ltd. and the British Psychological Society.

identity and sexual orientation (Yogyakarta Principles, 2007). However, the Yogyakarta Principles remain aspirational and are not presently endorsed by the United Nations. The recent debates around the removal of 'sexual orientation' from the resolution condemning extrajudicial executions by the United Nations Social, Cultural and Humanitarian Committee [UNSHC] (UNSHC, 2010) and the United Nations General Assembly [UNGA] (UNGA, 2010) illustrates the ongoing controversy that LGB rights attract within the United Nations and the difficulties faced in developing international consensus.

In this chapter the phases of exile faced by LGB asylum seekers will be presented, followed by a focus on psychological issues including early life experiences, sexuality development and the consequences of trauma. Ways of supporting LGB asylum seekers/refugees are then discussed including issues for therapy. The chapter will draw on literature from psychology, the voluntary sector, human rights organisations, case law and the first author's (SH) doctoral research into the reported experiences of gay male asylum seekers from Iran and Iraq. No studies to date have specifically considered the issues for lesbian asylum seekers, this includes SH's research, as only gay men came forward as participants. It is likely that whilst there will be similarities between lesbians, bisexual men and women and gay male asylum seekers, there will also be a number of different issues raised with respect to gender, the status and treatment of women, and the life histories of lesbians compared with bisexual men and women and gay men. Further research focussing on lesbian and bisexual women's experiences is needed, as well as for bisexual men.

Literature on LGB Asylum Seekers

Refugees and asylum seekers are treated homogenously (Patel, 2003a) as if they all have the same needs and subgroup differences are overshadowed and unrecognised; they are thus assumed heterosexual unless they can prove otherwise. Psychological interest in refugees and those seeking asylum has been criticised for over-focussing on trauma symptoms, diagnosis and treatment within the narrower confines of Post Traumatic Stress Disorder (PTSD) focussed therapy (Patel, 2003a). Patel (2003a) argues that it is neither ethical nor possible for therapists to work with marginalised groups effectively, whilst ignoring the context of their clients' circumstances.

Literature on psychotherapeutic work with LGB migrants, asylum seekers or refugees is limited and, by necessity, has to be extrapolated from the general literature relating to gender, LGB, and (heterosexual) refugee and

Black and Minority Ethnic (BME) issues. Whilst such generalisations to LGB asylum seekers may help illuminate relevant issues, they should be made cautiously as most LGB and BME research relates to people living within, and who are from, a Western context. Similarly, the experiences of LGB refugees will not mirror that of heterosexual refugee groups.

The majority of the literature that specifically considers LGB asylum seekers comes from the human rights and legal fields and, although therapeutic and psychological factors are not their focus, reference will be made to these sources where appropriate. Their focus relates mainly to the asylum seeking process, reasons for exile and, to a lesser extent, the experiences LGB people face during their flight. Little consideration has been given to the early life and developmental experiences of LGB people, and nothing is known about the longer term resettlement of LGB people once refugee status has been attained. The steps towards refugee status will now be considered.

Phases of Exile

Phases of exile usually involve some pre-flight increase in persecution, a 'trigger to flight' where the individual personally becomes victimised, and subsequent experiences of exile.

Adult pre-flight experiences

LGB asylum seekers can individually experience lifelong, family, community and state sanctioned persecution, rather than the more 'typical' asylum seeker experience of increased conflict or political, ethnic or religious tension where their family or community group as a whole are oppressed by others. Adult pre-flight experiences of LGB people can be a continuation of childhood physical and sexual abuse, emerging homophobic experiences as individuals become involved in adult sexual and social relationships, a continued repression of their sexuality, or the development of a covert lifestyle to avoid persecution but with the constant fear of exposure (Pepper, 2005).

Pepper (2005) and Perez-Ramirez (2002) describe a wide range of on-going persecution from families, communities and the state including: violence, detention and intimidation by police including arrest, interrogation, imprisonment and torture, sexual assault, receiving death threats, being forced to become internal refugees[2], being kidnapped, and witnessing

---

[2]   Internal refugees refer to people who must give up their home and employment and move to another location within their home country because of fear for their safety, thus losing their livelihood and local support.

the torture and/or killing of other LGB people. Same-sex sexual relations for men are illegal in around 86 countries and for women in around 46 countries. Punishment for same-sex sexual relations varies widely from fines, flogging, and prison sentences (one year to life). The death penalty remains in force in seven countries for men and four countries for women (Amnesty International, 2008). Amnesty International (2008) suggests that more laws exist for men because women's sexuality is limited and policed by a raft of other legislation, as well as women often being absent from the public sphere, so there may be a lack of awareness of incidents of female same-sex relations. Such laws reflect the inherent sexism that restricts women's autonomy and sexual expression, as well as dividing the LGB community, as by joining campaigns to support gay men, women risk the extension of existing laws to include them. However, although not always criminalised in law, lesbians are subject to rape and violent attacks as they challenge the notion of male ownership of women's bodies and the reproductive function of sex (Amnesty International, 2008). In similar ways, gay men are viewed as transgressing traditional gender norms in their perceived adoption of 'feminine' roles and denial of male privilege (Amnesty International, 2008).

Violent oppression is supported by country law that either directly criminalises same-sex sexual acts (as immoral or against nature), indirectly criminalises it through not criminalising homophobic violence and persecution so no protection can be sought, or criminalising the 'promotion of homosexuality' for 'sanitation' or so as 'to protect children'. The framing of such laws 'to protect children' in fact places LGB children at greater risk because adults (including teachers) may be reluctant to support or protect them against violence and aggression at home and school, of which they are at greater risk than heterosexual students (Human Rights Watch, 2001). Avoidance of such oppression and violence can deny children the right to education, and such laws rob survivors of any age of any recourse to justice and chance of redress. In addition, they prevent community support by blocking the formation of organisations or campaigns to change these rights abuses (Amnesty International, 2008).

Trigger to flee

The trigger to flee involves the destabilisation of a personal situation rather than necessarily that of their family, community or state and is in response to the feared or actual responses of family, community and the state to the exposure of their sexuality. This can occur in otherwise stable situations, as an additional layer of persecution within conflict situations (BBC, 2009a), or where political and legal changes occur that increasingly target LGB people (BBC, 2009b). The destabilisation of the personal situation is varied and may include threat of exposure (Pepper, 2005), imminent or actual arrest and torture to self or partner, or increased concern about personal safety from either witnessing or hearing about the arrest or killing of LGB friends and acquaintances (Perez-Ramirez, 2002). The trigger to flight is as likely to be as a result of fleeing from their loved ones as it is from some outside force.

The decision to flee, therefore, is often unplanned and the individual may not be prepared with the required resources for the journey into exile. This lack of personal resources, coupled with difficulties LGB asylum seekers experience in finding support once they go into exile, may mean the exile journey is fraught with adversity. LGB asylum seekers may deliberately isolate themselves from these forms of support for fear that their sexuality will become known to those supporting them.

Journey into exile

The journey into exile is difficult for all asylum and refugee groups, with fears that the place of safety will not be reached, that they may be captured along the way, or refused entry into their desired destination (Tribe, 1999). For LGB asylum seekers the homophobic persecution that they are trying to escape is likely to continue with their journeys into exile marked by social isolation, risks of physical and sexual violence, financial abuse, and ongoing community as well as state homophobia (Organisation for Refuge, Asylum and Migration [ORAM], 2009). This homophobic hostility comes from all areas of society: local populations in reception countries, other asylum seekers, support services, state officials such as police and immigration personnel, and from the asylum application process (ORAM, 2009; MST, 2009; Buchan, 2002).

LGB asylum seekers fear and may experience physical and sexual violence, harassment and demands for sexual services in reception countries (ORAM, 2009). Sexual assault is commonly reported, ranging from 28–45 per cent for lesbians depending on the country where the asylum application is made (Berg & Millbank, 2009). Lesbians may especially fear for their safety if they are not accompanied by males when living in countries where women are expected to be escorted by men from their own family. Women breaking such cultural taboos and rules are likely to face open hostility and persecution from local populations (ORAM, 2009).

Police and asylum process

The retraumatising effect of the asylum process is well documented, with asylum seekers having to disclose traumatic experiences and provide accurate information at a pace that is far from therapeutic (Tribe, 1999). Intimidation and homophobia during the asylum application process is reported both within the UK and in other reception countries (ORAM, 2009). The application process in reception countries is likely to result in overt homophobia with reports of pejorative language, being mocked and shamed by police, asylum officials and interpreters during interviews, and being asked intimate sexual questions about their relationships and experiences of rape and sexual assault (Berg & Millbank, 2009; ORAM, 2009).

In the UK, the asylum application process reflects the adversarial nature of British law and places the burden of proof on the asylum seeker to demonstrate that they are 'gay'. Individuals fleeing persecution invariably have tried to hide their sexuality and therefore providing evidence of such (especially *sexual identity*) may be difficult. Homophobic and ignorant attitudes and beliefs amongst the United Kingdom Border Agency (UKBA) and judicial staff are prevalent (Miles, 2010), including intrusive and detailed cross-examination of one's sexual history including requests for detailed descriptions of sexual assaults that occurred both in childhood and adulthood (Berg & Millbank, 2009). This occurs despite clear UNHCR Guidelines on Gender-Related Persecution (UNHCR, 2002) that states 'it is unnecessary to establish precise details of the act of rape or sexual assault' (p.11). Such cross-examination can lead to 'secondary victimisation' in that it results in 'a spectacle of degradation visited upon the victim rather than the offender' (Lees, 1997, p.73). Berg and Millbank (2009) claim these guidelines, routinely used with women refugees, are almost completely ignored for LGB refugees. Berg and Millbank (2009) argue that this lack of sensitivity within the different asylum jurisdictions may explain the variation of reporting of sexual assault amongst gay male refugees from 2 per cent in the UK to 24 per cent in Canada.

Western models of sexual identity development (e.g. Cass, 1984) are commonly used to ascertain the authenticity of an LGB asylum application. There is an expectation that an individual will have a fixed LGB identity developing along prescribed lines and that this can be demonstrated in their testimony (Berg & Millbank, 2009). Those whose histories include relationships with all genders, who do not conform to an expected 'gay lifestyle', or those who do not present themselves stereotypically as an effeminate man or masculine woman, are less likely to have their testimony believed and gain asylum (Berg & Millbank, 2009). This is in direct contrast to possible reasons for persecution in the country of origin, in that violation of traditional gender norms in appearance and behaviour are policed against, regardless of sexuality (Amnesty International, 2008). More on the problems of using Western models of sexual identity development is described later (and in Chapter 3).

The time period between applying for refugee status and a decision being made can take years in the UK. This is a stressful and uncertain time for all asylum seekers, with frequent fears of detention or being returned to one's country of origin, making it impossible to plan for the future or begin to rebuild one's life (Tribe, 2002). This living in 'limbo' includes legislation not allowing asylum seekers in the UK to work, and so 'rebuild social capital and meaningful ways of life' (Summerfield, 2002, p.248). Eastmond (1998) found that those seeking asylum from Bosnian concentration camps did better psychologically when offered work training then when offered psychological services (cited in Summerfield, 2002). However, in those countries where asylum seekers can work (e.g. Turkey) there are reports of harassment and loss of employment once their sexuality is exposed to their employer and colleagues (ORAM, 2009). Language barriers can mean that the only employment available comes from within one's own ethnic or cultural community living in the reception country. Individuals may live a tenuous life with the constant fear of being 'outed' and potentially losing their employment. Some gay male refugees resort to sex work as a means of income, increasing the risk of sex-related health problems such as HIV and other sexually transmitted infections, risk of assault and arrest (ORAM, 2009).

An asylum seeker's priorities may therefore be to build security and access advocacy, rather than discuss their past and present difficulties with 'a stranger' in the form of a therapist. The Canadian Task Force on Mental Health Issues (1998) lists a number of predisposing factors to mental health problems for those in exile. These include: separation from community and family, an unwelcoming reception community, lacking knowledge of the reception language, prolonged or severe suffering prior to exile, loss of socio-economic status, and/or being elderly or adolescent. In addition, LGB asylum seekers also face issues around homophobia that exacerbate their difficulties when adjusting to living in the UK.

The UKBA and the National Asylum Support Service (NASS) provide dispersed accommodation for asylum seekers whilst their applications are being processed. People are dispersed throughout the UK and may be separated from partners or other LGB people they know. Accommodation is mostly cramped, sharing flats and rooms with other asylum seekers, many of whom may be homophobic. Isolation and fear of exposure of their sexuality and experiences of homophobic abuse, physical and sexual assault, and sexual harassment from fellow flatmates occurs (MST, 2009).

Neighbourhood racist harassment is commonly reported by refugees, but LGB refugees additionally report homophobic harassment occurring from local populations as well as from other asylum seekers (MST, 2009). Mahtani (2003) reports that for some clients the hardships they face in the reception country are more difficult to deal with than those in their country of origin. This is because in their country of origin the person will have expected ill-treatment and persecution because of their sexuality, and might have taken steps to try to protect themselves from this. However, they had expected greater human rights and better treatment in the UK.

LGB asylum seekers and refugees may not connect to UK LGB communities due to ambivalence because of ongoing struggles with their sexuality (Pepper, 2005), experiencing racist and anti-refugee attitudes (MST, 2009) in LGB venues, experiencing financial barriers to accessing the commercially based gay scene (MST, 2009), and holding conflicting social values to how they perceive a Western gay lifestyle to be (e.g. the centrality of drugs and alcohol) (also see Chapters 3, 4, and 6).

Many LGB refugees find support amongst themselves, becoming actively involved in supporting other refugees and socialising with other LGB people from a similar background and through this, reconnecting with their ethnic culture (MST, 2009). For some, political activity for LGB rights is a positive way to come to terms with what has happened to them. It gives meaning to their experiences by working to help others in the same situation and to improving the lives of future generations of LGB asylum seekers. But in order to take these steps, non-heterosexual refugees and asylum seekers will need to adopt a LGB identity and reconcile this with their own ethnic, religious, and cultural identities, which may not sit comfortably together.

There is an almost universal experience of bereavement in exile, with a sense of loss of culture and family (Perez-Ramirez, 2002). A feeling of loss and longing for family and culture, despite the traumas experienced, combine with a sense of alienation in the adopted country, where many feel they will never be accepted. van der Veer (1998) suggests that the loss of familiar cultural backing reduces a person's ability to integrate new experiences. Similarly, Summerfield (1998) highlights that 'those forced into exile experience a rupture in the narrative thread running through their lives and around which they have organised their actions and associations' (p.21). These losses can add to ongoing ambivalence with sexuality as the formation of a positive LGB self-identity may not be something that is desired or valued by the individual, particularly if they associate that very identity as the reason for their isolation from family, friends and culture (Pepper, 2005).

The following case study illustrates many of the issues discussed so far: pre-flight persecution by family and a lack of support or safety in wider society, unplanned flight and a consequential lack of resources, experiencing bereavement and symptoms of trauma in exile, isolation from potential support because of fear of sexuality disclosure, and finally inability to prove one's sexuality to authorities as part of an asylum claim.

Masani's Story

Masani woke up from a four week coma in a hospital bed in Northern Uganda. She had been badly beaten, raped and left for dead. Masani was informed that the woman she was with at the time of the beating had been killed. Masani was terrified and devastated, this woman had been her girlfriend and they had gone into hiding after she heard that her father had taken out a contract on her life. She was unable to tell the hospital staff the reason for her fear, but she paid a member of staff to help her leave the hospital and go into hiding again. She was introduced to someone who helped her leave the country and fly to Heathrow, costing her the remainder of her savings. Her guide left her at the airport; she had no money or possessions, knew no one in the UK, had never travelled outside Uganda, and did not know what to do next.

Masani was taken to Airport Security who contacted the police. She was again terrified as she did not understand if she was being arrested, offered help or if more violence would follow. She did not want to explain the reason for her arrival, but when officials started to talk about sending her back to Uganda she told one of them what had happened to her and so was placed in the asylum system.

Masani was housed by NASS in a women's hostel. She was befriended by other women but felt unable to share her story as she feared their reaction. She was allocated a lawyer who took her life history in a three hour session, then she was told to wait: this wait lasted 14 months. During this time Masani became depressed and suicidal. She was destitute, desperately missed home and deeply grieved for her girlfriend. She had nightmares about their attack and she feared going out after dark as she still felt constantly unsafe.

Masani's case was eventually heard in court: the verdict was disbelief of her story. The judge said that if her companion had been her girlfriend she would not have gone into hiding or fled, but would have wanted to go back to their locality to find out what had happened. Her lawyer told her that without any new evidence they would be unable to appeal this decision. Facing deportation and fearing for her life, Masani once more went into hiding, this time from the authorities in the UK.

Psychological Issues

The emotional consequences of life-long and ongoing adversity for LGB asylum seekers and refugees are unknown. However, the available literature suggests their experiences and consequential emotional distress may be different from heterosexual asylum seekers and refugees as it may involve a range of issues including self-identity, childhood abuse, family and community rejection, state-sanctioned persecution, social rejection, isolation and ongoing threats of homophobic physical and sexual violence.

Early life experiences

Experiences of childhood sexual, physical and verbal abuse are commonly reported within Western LGB literature, often relating to the emergence of a LGB identity or as a reaction to perceived gender atypical behaviour by others in the child's life (Rivers, 2002). However, it should be noted that not all LGB people have been abused as children and not all abused children practice same-sex sexual behaviour or identify as LGB as adults. Societies and families that advocate strong gender role identities are more likely to react negatively toward gender atypical behaviour (Pepper, 2005) and this may be the first experiences of persecution the LGB person experiences in their lives. The consequences of such childhood abuse and lack of support are well documented (e.g. Dhaliwal *et al.*, 1996; Dube *et al.*, 2005; Greenwald *et al.*, 1990) and result in a high prevalence of childhood and adult mental health problems.

Investigation of childhood abuse in the histories of LGB asylum seekers and refugees is rarely documented within refugee literature for a number of reasons. Legal testimonials tend to recount pre-flight and asylum process issues, rarely touching on the person's longer life history. In a small study with 18 gay male refugees from 12 different countries who had been tortured, Pepper (2005) found that half of the men reported being sexually abused as children and that all had experienced physical and emotional abuse throughout their childhood and that this often extended through to their adult lives. Perpetrators of verbal and physical violence were often close family members including parents and siblings.

Issues of sexuality

LGB asylum seekers and refugees have been found to internalise their experiences of abuse to form their identity: 'I was a river they washed their hands in' (Pepper, 2005, p.45); 'I was born to be fucked' (SH's doctoral research); as a way to understand the repeated sexual abuse they experienced throughout childhood and adolescence from members of their families and communities. These experiences of sexual assault in childhood and adolescence, along with a growing awareness of their sexuality, the fear this may engender and the disapproval experienced from family and their community may, unsurprisingly, affect an individual's sense of self. The juxtapositioning of religious or cultural identities against sexuality may lead to confusion, self-hatred and the development of beliefs of being abnormal, diseased and disordered (Pepper, 2005; Perez-Ramirez, 2002). These views may be reinforced by family, authority figures (such as local religious leaders) and by medical, psychiatric and mental health professionals whose help may be sought by the individual or their family as they become aware of their sexuality. Pepper (2005) reports that many men used selective inattention and other dissociative coping strategies to keep same-sex attraction thoughts out of their awareness. She felt some of the men were so traumatised by their experiences that the last thing they wanted to do on arriving in the USA was 'to be gay'. Being gay had been the reason they had been targeted and tortured and they actually wanted to be 'invisible'.

Pepper (2005) and Perez-Ramirez (2002) argue that though stage theories of sexual identity are problematic and there are cultural variations in the construction of sexuality, that the men in both studies did consistently articulate subjective experiences of a gay identity formation such as sensitisation and awareness of being different, identity confusion, gay identity assumption, and commitment or self-acceptance as a gay man. However, the experiences of the ongoing nature of persecution and the alienation from familial relations meant that the stages of gay identity formation extended well into adulthood and were marked by isolation, shame and a sense of personal 'wrongness' (Perez-Ramirez, 2002). SH found that while the men in his study appeared to accept their gay identity, they often remained conflicted about themselves and held an ongoing sense of being abnormal rather than a committed, positive gay self-identity. There may well be a wide range of perspectives that LGB refugees hold about their sexual identity, with some not even viewing it as an issue of identity but one of disease or disorder (Berg & Millbank, 2009).

Consequences of trauma

Individual psychological reactions to trauma tend to follow four general themes (Turner & Gorst-Unsworth, 1990). The first is incomplete emotional processing of what has happened; this can include flashbacks, nightmares, intrusive thoughts or memories. A person experiencing this may try to cope by avoiding internal or external triggers (e.g. active remembering or stimuli associated with memories). Such presentations are often diagnosed as PTSD. However, the consequences of trauma extend beyond this. The second common consequence is extensive loss, that is, of home, status, financial security, employment, friends, culture, and familiar surroundings. Thirdly, if a person has experienced physical violence, they may present with physical symptoms which have symbolic or associative meanings, for example, sexual problems. To describe such presentations as 'somatisation' would be to take them out of context. Finally, there will be a direct impact on personal meanings and values, for example, to remain hidden or find ways to fight for one's right for personal expression.

Pepper (2005) found that most of the gay men in her work met the diagnostic criteria for PTSD, dissociative and anxiety disorders, and major depression, and were also at risk of substance abuse (also see Shatan, 1973; van der Kolk, 1994). They also showed avoidance of trauma-related thoughts, experiences and situations and, similar to other torture survivors, reported feeling emotionally shut down and cut off from others (Basoglu *et al.*, 2001). Most did not want to take psychotropic medication due to cultural, religious and educational reasons (Pepper, 2005). Contrasting this, SH's research found that all the men reported concordance with prescribed psychotropic medication and some were also involved in counselling and psychotherapy.

While many of the symptoms a person can present with fall within the criteria for PTSD, this diagnosis has been criticised as being overly individualising and pathologising: 'a catch-all diagnosis and signifier, yet its criteria are frequently not what refugees consider significant about their predicament' (Summerfield, 2002, p.248), which might instead be for advocacy, safety and resources. In addition, the notion of a 'disorder' has been criticised (e.g. Marsella, 1994) as the criteria listed may be understandable, even adaptive, reactions to past and ongoing stress. The universalising nature of such criteria excludes important contextual differences between groups, such as those relevant to LGB asylum seekers and refugees. The concept of PTSD was developed based on reactions after exposure to fairly circumscribed traumatic events, Mezey (1997) therefore suggests the model is not relevant to prolonged and repeated trauma, such as ongoing homophobic persecution.

An alternate conceptualisation has been offered as 'cultural bereavement' (Eisenbruch, 1990), in that it is the lack of continuity of cultural practices, networks and contacts which is a key predictor of refugee mental health. Many cultural markers, and their loss, will be meaningful for LGB asylum seekers/refugees, even though some of the markers of heterosexual culture within their country of origin may not. However, an LGB person may never have established networks and contacts in their country of origin that relate to their sexuality, and so this model of loss also misses the complexities that living as a persecuted sexuality minority brings.

Supporting LGB Asylum Seekers and Refugees

LGB asylum seekers may require different types of support at different points in their journey. Grey and Young (2008) advocate a three phase clinical pathway for supporting traumatised asylum seekers and refugees:

 (i)   establishing a sense of safety,
 (ii) resolving symptoms and trauma-focussed psychotherapy, and
(iii) promoting social reintegration.

During asylum application processes, there is a great deal of uncertainty, insecurity and threat to wellbeing. This may be a time when supportive rather than restorative therapy may be more beneficial, such as connection to supportive networks, access to supportive counselling and material support. There is a real problem with the exacerbation and continuation of trauma and homophobia within the asylum application system and the services that are provided for asylum seekers (MST, 2009). That people should live in fear of others they live with or who are supposed to provide help and support is unacceptable and no form of psychotherapy should collude with abusive practices by services. Therapists have a role in working with refugee support services to raise awareness of LGB asylum and refugee issues to reduce homophobia in these settings (MST, 2009). There is also a remit to provide consultation in asylum application cases and advise the Home Office around the use of psychological models, such as stage models of sexual identity, when making judgements about the validity of an application for asylum (Berg & Millbank, 2009).

Summerfield (1995) emphasises that all work with asylum seekers and refugees must take place within a human rights framework, as 'posttraumatic symptoms are not just a private and individual problem but also an indictment of the social contexts which produced them' (p.7). Amnesty International (2010) reports the human rights represented in international human rights law that are violated by the criminalisation and persecution of homosexuality are:

- The right to be free from discrimination
- The right to privacy
- The right to liberty and security of person
- The right to freedom of expression
- The right to freedom of religion, thought and conscience
- The right to health
- The right to a fair trial

Jensen and Agger (1988) go as far as to say 'the commitment and the ideology of the therapist is a necessary precondition for a successful treatment outcome. It is an absurdity to maintain a neutral attitude' (cited in Turner, 2000). Patel (2003b) agrees that to be neutral as a therapist is to defend and legitimate 'the ideologies and practices that result in the continued exploitation, oppression and violation of marginalised people' (p.221). Instead, Herman (1992) invites the therapist to take a 'committed moral stance' (p.135) against injustice.

Community support

There is no literature on working with LGB refugees from a community psychology perspective[3], although there is discussion about how community psychology approaches can be of use to refugees generally (Webster & Robertson, 2007). Given the sense of isolation, community and family rejection and the lack of support within LGB society, it would seem that this approach could be beneficial in the resettlement process. Perez-Ramirez (2002) and SH both found that some LGB refugees were involved in LGB activism and had formed their own support, advocacy and campaigning groups that provided a sense of community for individuals. However, SH found that whilst the refugees attending these groups reported that they

---

[3]   Community Psychology is a social constructionist approach that argues psychological problems have social and interactional causes and attempts to redress social inequalities through prevention within everyday contexts by sharing psychotherapeutic skills with non-therapists. It seeks solutions that incorporate cultural understandings of mental health and enhance protective factors such as social support.

gave them a sense of purpose and support, they were still often unable to share their experiences of mental health difficulties with each other. It may be that stigma attached to mental illness remains high or that individuals are not sure how to support one another when suffering mental health difficulties. The use of community psychology approaches could have a role in working with these groups to develop their own expertise in providing emotional and mental health support for each other, based on their own cultural understanding of emotional distress.

Psychotherapy

Western models of psychotherapy focus on the individual as an independent entity, this being an indicator of psychological health and maturity (Arenas & Steen, 1994). However, this may be an oppositional view to that held by a non-western client, where the emphasis may instead by on connectivity, network and being a member of a group: the individual not existing without recognition of their contexts (Arenas & Steen, 1994). For LGB refugees, they may have already had a painful separation from the context of family and community in their country of origin because of their sexuality; in exile they have also lost the continuity of culture and country familiarity. To work in a culturally sensitive way, therapists need to consider their own cultural and professional biases and constructions and move beyond these to understand those of the client. Thus, 'symptoms of mental health problems' (e.g. nightmares, flashbacks) may have a different and significant cultural meeting to the client.

A client may not understand why therapy has been offered (as they may not see their difficulties as that of 'mental health'), understand the culture and expectations of therapy (e.g. weekly sessions at a set time, or that the therapist is not a friend), or why talking through their past or current difficulties is thought to be helpful. For example, Gong-Guy *et al.* (1991) found that clients who were unfamiliar with therapy thought the need for repeated visits were an indication that the therapy was not working. Patel (2003b) considers that for a client to make informed consent to treatment, they need to know 'the nature and purpose of therapy, the approach to be adopted, the procedure for making appointments, managing cancellations, making a complaint or providing feedback to the therapist, interpreter or an independent person about the service received' (p.232). It is also important for the therapist to be mindful of the sensitivity of information about a client's past, in that specific details or names may endanger others still living in the country of origin. A therapist does not need to know true names or specific locations to still be able to work with a client (Turner, 2000).

LGB refugees may present to any type of adult psychological service for help (e.g. adult mental health in primary or secondary care, sexual health, tier three trauma services, etc.). There are several useful roles therapists can have supporting this client group. An understanding of the issues and experiences facing LGB refugees is important when offering therapy, both of the history of the individual and their previous contexts (i.e. persecution in their home country and flight), and experiences since arriving in the UK (i.e. 'culture shock', homophobia, racism and anti-asylum discrimination, isolation, housing and financial concerns, etc.; Arenas & Steen, 1994). It is important to note the current stage of the asylum process that the client is in, as immediate needs may be more pressing than exploring past trauma (e.g. a report to help their appeal). The therapist must acknowledge their power as being a member of the reception country with knowledge of avenues of support and individual rights (e.g. LGB friendly support organisations for asylum seekers, letters to help improve living conditions, or access to language classes), in addition to potentially helpful therapeutic techniques (e.g. to help with sleep problems). A thorough assessment of the client's social contexts, as well as psychological presentation, is thus essential.

When working with refugees and asylum seekers, Turner (2000) proposes a general basis for psychotherapy is that of 'testimony', for the therapist to bear witness to past abuse, allow the client to emotionally process and reflect on what has happened to them, and find integration and hope for their future. He suggests that such an approach increases self-worth by 'making previous life history – political commitment, personal relationships, work and social connection – meaningful in the present and in the future' (p.188), to 'integrate the traumatic experiences into their lives by identifying its significance in the context of political and social events as well as the context of their personal history' (p.189). However, such work cannot be started until a trusting therapeutic relationship has been established as a client may fear open discussion of their sexuality when such disclosure has placed them in abusive and violent situations in the past. If the therapist works for the NHS, the client may have greater concerns about confidentiality as the NHS is perceived as a state institution and the state may be intrinsically involved in the client's previous persecution.

These concerns will be significantly increased if an interpreter is used, both in terms of another person knowing this information but especially if the interpreter is from the same community. The client may be expected to openly discuss their sexuality when the therapist's and interpreter's sexuality remains unknown. It is thus important for the therapist to be transparent, provide frequent explanations for why a line of exploration is being followed, and reassurances of confidentiality offered throughout the session if needed.

This might include being prepared to disclose their sexuality if asked directly, and then explore what the answer means to the client[4]. Prior to the session starting, a therapist can check with the interpreter their views and comfort in working with the issues that may be about to be discussed. This is important, and the second author (CB) uncovered anti-asylum and racist attitudes held by interpreters who worked in both the NHS and the Home Office (Butler, 2008), which impacted on the empathy and warmth that clients experienced in sessions and the gentleness and care taken in the translation. In addition, a client should be informed before the appointment that an interpreter will be present, what their role is and how the session will be conducted (Patel, 2003b). The client should be given an opportunity to speak to the interpreter directly at the start of a session to check out if they have common connections in their communities and if they feel they can work together. Turner (2000) suggests that when sensitive information, such as sexuality, is to be discussed, it might be appropriate to accept a friend as the interpreter if they already know of the client's history. However, Tribe and Morrissey (2004) insist that professional interpreters should always be used so as to insure confidentiality and accuracy in the work, with contracted clear guidelines provided by the employing agency.

Current psychological models of therapy do not adequately account for intersections in identity. For example, the stage model of sexual development offers a framework for understanding an individual's difficulties with their sense of self and their sexuality, but fails to account for cultural and religious influences. Intercultural therapy[5] can offer an alternative to the stage model framework but tends to focus on the development and understanding of the person's sexuality within their ongoing relationship with families and communities, presupposing these will be available to the person. Butler and Byrne (2008) advocate the use of social constructionist approaches in their work with sexuality and are especially vigilant about conflicts between therapists' personal views on sexuality and the views their clients bring to therapy. Brauner (2000) emphasises the different views that people may have about their sexuality, some viewing themselves as having an LGB identity or other such region-specific sexual identity labels, whilst others relate to sexual behaviours but not an LGB, or equivalent, identity, for example, Men who have Sex with Men (MSM). Those from a non-Western background, and

---

[4] Of course, in dealing with such sensitive issues related to sex, therapists are reminded of the guidance that Council for Healthcare Regulatory Excellence (CHRE) have on maintaining clear sexual boundaries. See www.chre.org.uk for details.

[5] Intercultural Therapy broadly refers to explicitly working with cultural diversity; it involves adapting Western theories to new contexts, such as race, with new meanings and beliefs.

particularly those from community-oriented cultures, may value familial and community connections and relationships over sexual self-expression and their relationship with their sexuality may only occur at the behavioural rather than identity level (Brauner, 2000).

Work focussed on sexuality should take a 'gay affirmative' approach (Davies, 1996). This approach can be used within any therapeutic modality and values a client's sexual, relationship and lifestyle choices as being equal to those of the dominant heterosexual group. This approach has been used with different therapeutic models including CBT, psychodynamic, Jungian and psychosynthesis therapies (Davies & Neil, 2000), as well as systemic (Butler, 2009), and existentialist (Langdridge, 2007) ways of working. However, once again, care should be taken not to impose the view that the goal is to accept a 'gay identity' and celebrate this. A careful investigation of the cultural, family, relationship and individual values of the client is needed to explore areas of conflict and support and to remain congruent with wider cultural and religious values, particularly as these connections may be weakened by living in exile. It should be noted, that a therapist should never agree to help a client change their sexual orientation. Such a goal has been deemed unethical, unprofessional, abusive and lacking in any evidence-base by the American (1998) and Australian (2000) Psychology Associations, as well as the United Kingdom Council for Psychotherapy (2010) and the British Association for Counselling and Psychotherapy (2009).

Without a secure base and feeling of safety, a therapist should not pursue work on past traumas until the client has found ways to manage in their current life to deal with their immediate pressures. However, if the client is not managing to cope because of interference of past traumas, work can address this. NICE guidelines (NICE, 2005) recommend trauma-focussed CBT and EMDR, but there have been no studies as to the effectiveness of these approaches when using interpreters or in cross-cultural work. A therapist must take time to explain their understanding of the client's presenting problems (e.g. 'depression'), explore how such an understanding fits into the client's cultural and personal view of their difficulties, and how the client's community might deal with it (Mahtani, 2003). A truly collaborative way of working can thus be negotiated, without such a stance the therapist repeats:

> ... the colonising process by imposing a therapeutic ideology rooted in the culture of the reception community, giving meaning to the survivor's experience in the language and symbols of that reception community and its professionals, and failing to recognise the rich sources of meaning and symbolism available to the survivor from his or her own culture (Blackwell, 1989; p.2; cited in Tribe, 1999).

Conclusion

Working with LGB asylum seekers/refugees is rich and rewarding, but therapists must tread carefully so as to not abuse their power and impose Western models of 'adjustment' and 'development' on clients. Therapists can instead use their power to provide practical assistance as well as a safe space to explore often confusing and painful memories from both past and current experiences of abuse and persecution.

Guidelines for Good Practice

Given the complexities and care needed in doing this work, there are a number of considerations therapists should bear in mind.

- It may take longer to build a therapeutic alliance and establish trust and purpose within the work. This time should be allowed so as to work at the client's pace and socialise them into therapy so that they can fully consent to all aspects of treatment.
- If interpreters are used, their attitude and understanding of LGB issues and the asylum process should be thoroughly investigated by the therapist in a pre-session meeting. The client should also be given the opportunity to talk to the interpreter at the start of the session to check out where they are from, their political/cultural allegiances, and if anyone is known in common. Care should be taken to allow the client to consent to using that interpreter in the work. The same interpreter should be used every time. During the session, time should be taken to check the subtly within interpretations including cultural meanings, values and hidden associations attached to words.
- Ensure that Western sexuality labels and identity markers or references are not forced upon the client if she/he does not relate to these. Explore whether they use any indigenous or area-specific identity labels to refer to themselves or their sexual behaviours, and attempt to understand these.
- Regular supervision and support is vital for the therapist to ensure they are not imposing their value system on the work and to help with the complex and emotional material discussed in sessions. A therapist should investigate a supervisor's level of knowledge/experience around working with asylum seekers/refugees and sexuality issues, and if found lacking, alternative arrangements for supervision should be made.

- In terms of therapy content, this should be led by the client. Helping clients with practical problems can be a way of establishing a relationship and gaining trust that will help with potential future therapeutic work.

References

American Psychological Association (1998). *Reparative therapy [Position statement].* Washington, DC: APA.

Amnesty International (2010). *Uganda: Anti-homosexuality bill is inherently discriminatory and threatens broader human rights.* London: Amnesty International.

Amnesty International (2008). *Love, hate and the law: Decriminalizing homosexuality.* London: Amnesty International.

Arenas, J.G. & Steen, P. (1994). Exile psychology and psychotherapy with refugees in a transcultural perspective. *Torture, 4*(2), 50–53.

Australian Psychological Association (2000). *APS position statement on the use of therapies that attempt to change sexual orientation.* Melbourne: Australian Psychological Association.

Basoglu, M., Jaranson, J., Mollica, R. & Kastrup, M. (2001). Torture and mental health: A research overview. In E. Gerrity, T. Keane & F. Tuma (Eds.) *The mental health consequences of torture.* New York, NY: Plenum.

Berg, L. & Millbank, J. (2009). Constructing the personal narratives of lesbian, gay and bisexual asylum claimants. *Journal of Refugee Studies, 22*(2), 195–223.

Blackwell, R.D. (1989). *The disruption and reconstitution of family, network and community systems following torture, organised violence and exile.* Paper presented at The Second International Conference of Centres, Institutions and Individuals Concerns with the Care of Victims of Organised Violence, Costa Rica.

Brauner, R. (2000). Embracing difference: Addressing race, culture and sexuality. In C. Neal and D. Davies (Eds.) *Pink therapy 3: Issues in therapy with lesbian, gay, bisexual and transgender clients.* Milton Keynes: Open University Press.

British Association for Counselling and Psychotherapy (2009). Retrieved 8 November 2010 from http://www.bacp.co.uk/media/index.php?newsId=1326&count=501&start=120&filter=&cat=&year=.

British Broadcasting Corporation (BBC) (2009a, 17 August). *Anti gay attacks on rise in Iraq.* Retrieved 30 October 2009 from http://news.bbc.co.uk/1/hi/world/middle_east/8204853.stm.

British Broadcasting Corporation (BBC) (2009b, 15 October). *Uganda MP urges death for gay sex.* Retrieved 8 December 2009 from http://news.bbc.co.uk/1/hi/8308912.stm.

British Broadcasting Corporation (BBC) (2008, 11 March). *Gay Iranian asylum seeker loses appeal.* Retrieved 30 October 2009 from http://news.bbc.co.uk/1/hi/world/europe/7290330.stm.

Buchan, S. (2002). A question of human rights. *In Exile,* September/October, 7–8.

Butler, C. (2009). Sexual and gender minority therapy and systemic practice. *Journal of Family Therapy, 31,* 338–358.

Butler, C. (2008). Speaking the unspeakable: Female interpreters' response to working with women who have been raped in war. *Clinical Psychology Forum, 192,* 22–26.

Butler, C. & Byrne, A. (2009). Culture, sex and sexuality. In C. Butler, A. O'Donovan & E. Shaw (Eds.) *Sex, sexuality and therapeutic practice.* London: Routledge.

Canadian Task Force on Mental Health Issues (1998). *After the door has been opened: Mental health issues affecting immigrants and refugees in Canada.* Ottawa: Health and Welfare.

Cass, V.C. (1984). Homosexuality: A concept in need of a definition. *Journal of Homosexuality, 9*(2/3), 105–126.

Dauvergne, C. & Millbank, J. (2003). Before the High Court: Applicants S396/2002 and S395/2002, a gay refugee couple from Bangladesh. *Sydney Law Review, 25,* 97–124.

Davies, D. (1996). Towards a model of gay affirmative therapy. In D. Davies and C. Neal (Eds.) *Pink therapy: A guide for counsellors and therapists working with lesbian, gay and bisexual clients.* Buckingham: Open University Press.

Davies, D. & Neil, C. (2000). Pink therapy 2: Therapeutic perspectives on working with lesbian, gay and bisexual clients. Buckingham: Open University Press.

de Jong, A. (2003). *Lesbian, gay, bisexual and transgender (LGB) refugees and asylum seekers: Navigation guide.* London: ICAR.

Dhaliwal, G.K., Gauzas, L., Antonowicz, D.H. & Ross, R.R.W. (1996). Adult male survivors of childhood sexual abuse: Prevalence, sexual abuse characteristics, and long-term effects. *Clinical Psychology Review, 16*(7), 619–639.

Dube, S.R., Anda, R.F., Whitfield, C.L., Brown, D.W., Felitti, V.J., Dong, M. & Giles, W.H. (2005). Long-term consequences of childhood sexual abuse by gender of victim. *Journal of Preventative Medicine, 28*(5), 430–438.

Eastmond, M. (1998). Nationalist discourses and the construction of difference: Bosnian Muslim refugees in Sweden. *Journal of Refugee Studies, 11,* 161–181.

Eisenbruch, M. (1990). Cultural bereavement and homesickness. In S. Fisher & C. Cooper (Eds.) *On the move: The psychology of change and transition.* Chichester: John Wiley & Sons, Ltd.

Greenwald, E., Leitenberg, H., Cado, S. & Tarran, M.J. (1990). Childhood sexual abuse: Long-term effects on psychological and sexual functioning in a non-clinical and nonstudent sample of adult women. *Child Abuse & Neglect, 14*(4), 503–513.

Grey, N. & Young, K. (2008). Cognitive behaviour therapy with refugees and asylum seekers experiencing traumatic stress symptoms. *Behavioural and Cognitive Psychotherapy, 36,* 3–19.

Gong-guy, E., Cravens, R.B. & Patterson, T.E. (1991). Clinical issues in mental health service delivery to refuges. *American Psychologist, 46*(6), 642–648.

Herman, J.L. (1992). *Trauma and recovery*. New York, NY: Basic Books.

Human Rights Watch (2009). *"They want us exterminated": Murder, torture, sexual orientation and gender in Iraq*. Retrieved 30 October 2009 from http://www.hrw.org/en/node/85049/section/1.

Human Rights Watch (2001). *Hatred in the hallways: Discrimination and violence against lesbian, gay, bisexual and transgender students in U.S. public schools*. New York: Human Rights Watch.

Jensen, S.B. & Agger, I. (1988). *The testimony method: The use of testimony as a psychotherapeutic tool in the treatment of traumatized refugees in Denmark*. Paper presented to the First European Conference on Traumatic Stress Studies (Lincoln, England).

Langdridge, D. (2007). Gay affirmative therapy: A theoretical framework and defence. *Journal of Gay and Lesbian Psychotherapy, 11*(1/2), 27–43.

Lees, S. (1997). *Ruling passions: Sexual violence, reputation and the law*. Buckingham: Open University Press.

Mahtani, A. (2003). The right of refugee clients to an appropriate and ethical psychology service. *International Journal of Human Rights, 7*(1), 40–57.

Marsella, A.J. (1994). Ethno-cultural diversity and international refugee. Challenges for the global community. In A.J. Marsella, T. Bornemann, S. Ekbald & J. Orley (Eds.) *Amidst peril and pain: The mental health and social well-being of the world's refugees*. Washington, DC: American Psychological Association.

Metropolitan Support Trust [MST] (2009). *Over not out: The housing and homelessness issues specific to lesbian, gay, bisexual and transgender asylum seekers*. London: Metropolitan Support Trust.

Mezey, G. (1997). Psychological responses to interpersonal violence: Adults. In D. Black, M. Newman, J. Harris-Hendriks & G. Mezey (Eds.) *Psychological trauma: A developmental approach*. London: Gaskell.

Miles, N. (2010). *No going back: Lesbian and gay people and the asylum system*. Stonewall: London.

NICE (2005). *Post-Traumatic Stress Disorder*. Trowbridge: Cromwell Press.

Office of National Statistics (2009). *Asylum seekers: Control of immigration*. Retrieved 7 November 2010 from http://www.statistics.gov.uk/cci/nugget.asp?id=261.

Organisation for Refuge, Asylum and Migration [ORAM] (2009). *Unsafe haven: The security challenges facing lesbian, gay, bisexual and transgender asylum seekers and refugees in Turkey*. Helsinki Citizen's Assembly-Turkey Refugee Advocacy and Support Program/Organisation for Refuge, Asylum and Migration.

Patel, N. (2003a). Clinical psychology: Reinforcing inequalities or facilitating empowerment. *The International Journal of Human Rights, 7*(1), 16–39.

Patel, N. (2003b). Speaking with the silent: Addressing issues of disempowerment when working with refugee people. In R. Tribe & H. Ravel (Eds.) *Working with interpreters in mental health*. Hove: Bruner-Routledge.

Pepper, C. (2005). Gay men tortured on the basis of homosexuality. *Contemporary Psychoanalysis, 41*(1), 35–54.

Perez-Ramirez, L.A. (2002). *Immigration and trauma: A study with latino-gay men asylum seekers*. Doctoral Dissertation. UMI Number: 3084485.

Rivers, I. (2002). Developmental issues for lesbian and gay youth. In A. Coyle & C. Kitzinger (Eds.) *Lesbian and gay psychology*. London: Blackwell.

Shatan, C. (1973). The grief of soldiers: Vietnam combat veterans' self-help movement. *American Journal of Orthopsychiatry, 43*, 640–653.

Summerfield, D. (2002). Commentary. *Advances in Psychiatric Treatment, 8*, 247–248.

Summerfield, D. (1998). The social experience of war and some issues for the humanitarian field. In P.J. Bracken & C. Petty (Eds.) *Rethinking the trauma of war*. London: Free Association Books.

Summerfield, D. (1995). Addressing human response to war and atrocity: Major challenges in research and practices and the limitations of Western psychiatric models. In R.J. Kleber, C.R. Figley & B.P.R. Gersons (Eds.) *Beyond trauma*. New York, NY: Plenum Press.

Tribe, R. (2002). Mental health of refugees and asylum-seekers. *Advances in Psychiatric Treatment, 8*, 240–247.

Tribe, R. (1999). Therapeutic work with refugees living in exile: Observations on clinical practice. *Counselling Psychology Quarterly, 12*(3), 233–243.

Tribe, R. & Morrissey, J. (2004). Good practice issues when working with interpreters in mental health. *Intervention: The International Journal of Mental Health, Psychosocial Work and Counselling in Areas of Armed Conflict, 2*(2), 129–142.

Turner, S. (2000). Therapeutic approaches with survivors of torture. In J. Kareem & R. Littlewood (Eds.) *Intercultural therapy* (2nd edn). Oxon: Blackwell Science.

Turner, S. & Gorst-Unsworth, C. (1990). Psychological sequelae of torture. *British Journal of Psychiatry, 157*, 475–480.

United Kingdom Council for Psychotherapy [UKCP] (2010). *UKCP statement on the 'reparative' therapy of members of sexual minorities*. Retrieved 8 November 2010 from http://www.psychotherapy.org.uk/article937.html.

United Nations General Assembly (2010). *Press release GA/11041*. Retrieved from 23 December 2010 http://www.un.org/News/Press/docs//2010/ga11041.doc.htm.

United Nations High Commissioner for Refugees [UNHCR] (2002). *Guidelines on international protection: Gender-related persecution within the context of article 1A(2) of the 1951 Convention and/or its 1967 Protocol relating to the status of refugees*. Retrieved 18 November 2010 from http://www.justice.gov/eoir/vll/benchbook/resources/UNHCR_Guidelines_Gender.pdf.

United Nations High Commissioner for Refugees [UNHCR] (2007). *Convention and Protocol relating to the status of refugees*. Retrieved 20 December 2010 from http://www.unhcr.org/3b66c2aa10.html.

United Nations Social, Humanitarian and Cultural Committee [UNSHCC] (2010). *Press release GA/SHC/3997*. Retrieved 16 December 2010 from http://www.un.org/News/Press/docs/2010/gashc3997.doc.htm.

van der Kolk, B. (1994). The body keeps the score: Memory and the evolving psychobiology of posttraumatic stress. *Harvard Review of Psychiatry, 1,* 253–265.

van der Veer, G. (1998). *Counselling and therapy with refugees and victims of trauma* (2nd edn). Chichester: John Wiley & Sons, Ltd.

Webster, A. & Robertson, M. (2007). Can community psychology meet the needs of refugees? *The Psychologist, 20*(3), 156–158.

Yogyakarta Principles (2007). *The Yogyakarta Principles: The Application of International Human Rights Law in Relation to Sexual Orientation and Gender Identity.* Retrieved 20 December 2010 from http://www.yogyakartaprinciples .org/principles_en.htm.

6

Social Class

Roshan das Nair & Susan Hansen

In this chapter, we consider the intersection of class and sexuality. We begin by exploring the relevance of class to sexuality, and note that much research in the area of sexuality – including the bulk of the research surveyed in this book – has an (unacknowledged) middle class subject. Thus, in this chapter we focus on the experiences of working class lesbian, gay and bisexual (LGB) people. Where possible we draw on British research, as the meaning and lived experience of class in the UK has a historical and cultural relevance that is arguably peculiar to the British cultural context.

What is Social Class?

Some politicians and theorists would have us believe that 'class' is a dated construct with no real currency in the era of globalisation and free-market economies, where it is believed that class distinctions have diminished, primarily because of the perceived plasticity and opportunities for 'self-fashioning' that democratic states afford. Such sentiments almost always suggest that there exist equal opportunities, and one only needs to reach out and make use of these opportunities to transcend one's classed position. In a meritocratic society, this then places the onus of such transcendence on the 'subjectivities of social actors' who are then 'marked as "wrong" or "right", "deficient" or "acceptable"' (Lawler, 2005, p.798), depending on whether or not they are able to surmount class barriers. In daily discourse, there is evidence of slippage where even well-meaning interlocutors move from talking about poverty to talking about 'taste', from lack of agency to 'lack of

Intersectionality, Sexuality and Psychological Therapies: Working with Lesbian, Gay and Bisexual Diversity,
First Edition. Edited by Roshan das Nair and Catherine Butler.
© 2012 John Wiley & Sons, Ltd. Published 2012 by John Wiley & Sons, Ltd. and the British Psychological Society.

will', or from the 'deserving poor' to the 'undeserving poor' (Bourdieu, 1998, p.43). As Lawler rightly points out, in defining class (and especially working class), it is middle class politics that 'homogenizes classes and hinges on the vilification of persons, communities and cultures' (p.803).

We follow Taylor (2010) who, in her work with working class lesbian women, asked them to self-define class on the basis of their own lived experience and knowledge. She found that the women's own categorisations corresponded with existing classifications based on 'objective' socioeconomic indicators. As Taylor (2004, p.11) asserts, 'class definitions are disputed and contested but . . . definitions are not so diffuse and "complex" that nothing can be said'. Thus, rather than defining social class according to its status as a macrosocial variable, to be determined by the application of socioeconomic categories alone, we instead approach class as being instantiated by daily practices:

> Ultimately, categories such as age, class, ethnicity, gender and sexuality are produced and reproduced in their differential forms of participation in communities of practice. And these categories are not produced separately, but are co-produced (Eckert, 2000, p.40).

That is, social class is intersubjectively produced as part and parcel of our daily lives.

Why is Class Relevant to Sexuality?

Riggs (2010) notes that class is an aspect of identity that is seldom examined in sexuality research. There are, however, a growing number of researchers (e.g. Keogh *et al.*, 2004; McDermott, 2006; 2011; Taylor, 2008; 2010) undertaking research on working class lesbians and gay men. These researchers point out that much existent research has an unstated focus on the experiences, aspirations and needs of middle class LGB people, and that working class LGB people are underrepresented in the literature. Riggs (2010) further points out that the privileged unmarked category of 'white middle class queer' is seldom critically examined.

Social class informs the ways in which LGBs make sense of, experience, and live their sexuality (Riggs, 2010). For instance, butch and femme identified lesbians tend to come more often from working class communities. Middle class lesbians have historically tended to regard butch and femme lesbians with suspicion: as 'aping' heterosexual gender roles. Similarly, older generations of (often middle class/educated) lesbian feminist separatists may dismiss butch and femme identified lesbians as passively reproducing patriarchal power relations. However, as Judith Butler (1990; 2004) has argued, rather than simply and unproblematically reproducing the heterosexual matrix, butch-femme identities draw critical attention to the constructed nature of both gender and sexuality.

Thus, in daily life, the lived experience of butch and femme lesbians may be challenging. The masculinity of butch lesbians is both a resource and a risk. This masculinity allows butches to be treated as 'one of the guys' in occupations where masculinity is a valued part of the work culture. However, it means that butches are more visibly queer in public spaces, which can lead to challenges with such mundane necessities as visiting a public toilet. Femmes may also experience a level of unwanted sexual attention from heterosexual men, and may face difficulties with their visibility as lesbian, and acceptance within middle class LGB venues.

Indeed, social class may affect the ways in which LGBs experience discrimination and harassment more generally. An experience sadly common to many LGBs, regardless of class background, is that of being subject to discrimination or prejudice and verbal or physical violence on the basis of their sexuality. The deleterious effects of discrimination and/or prejudice, or *perceived* discrimination, on mental and physical health have been documented (e.g. Burgess *et al.*, 2008; Mays & Cochran, 2001; Pascoe & Smart Richman, 2009; also, see Chapters 7 and 8 in this book).

While many LGBs face discrimination, Meyer (2010) notes that the ways in which working class and middle class LGB people deal with the experience of discrimination and violence may differ. He notes firstly that working class LGBs are more likely to experience physical violence than middle class LGBs. However, white middle class LGBs are more likely to regard their experiences of hate-motivated violence as more severe than are working class Black and Minority Ethnic (BME) LGBs. Meyer (2010) accounts for this difference by looking at the ways in which the friends and family members of LGB people responded to their experience of discrimination. While middle class LGB survivors of hate crime were encouraged to view their experiences as severe and to seek professional help from psychologists, and legal and medical assistance, working class LGBs were more often encouraged to minimize their experiences of violence, by comparing themselves with others who had survived more serious assaults:

Jasmine, a 44-year-old black lesbian woman who worked as a security guard, described her brother's response when she told him about being assaulted for revealing her sexuality: He told me that I was fortunate not to end up in the hospital like his friend Chris [who was stabbed in gang-related violence] . . . It made sense, what he said. It could have been worse. I could have ended up in the hospital. I guess I should feel lucky that I didn't (Meyer, 2010, p.987).

Thus, the forms of support and encouragement offered to LGB people by family and friends may differ according to class. Middle class LGBs are more likely to be actively encouraged to seek professional psychological assistance in the wake of such traumatic experiences. Therapy is regarded as a source of benign and trustworthy support, in a safe environment, to which middle class LGB people are likely to feel entitled. Working class LGB people may in contrast be more ambivalent about seeking psychological assistance. In fact, Meyer (2010) found that the forms of help offered by working class friends and family members tended to focus on providing direct emotional support and building resilience. Such support did not tend to suggest interacting with service providers and voluntarily accessing institutionalised forms of support. Indeed, working class LGB people and their families may have an established mistrust of professional sources of support and social services, which they regard as 'bureaucratic, dehumanising and oppressive' (Strier & Binyamin, 2010, p.1918). Therapeutic interactions may thus be regarded as a source of significant apprehension and mistrust.

Class and Psychological Therapies

Reviewing literature on counselling and social class, Ballinger and Wright (2007) observed that there has been little research on the relationship between therapy and class in the UK over the last 30 years. The intersections of class and sexuality in therapy are far less researched. The manner in which class affects the therapeutic encounter needs further interrogation, not only from the site of the therapy room, but also from the perspective of training of therapists. Anne Kearney notes that most trainers in counsellor training programmes occupy middle class positions, and 'training itself is influenced by middle class assumptions and values', and significantly, the 'emphasis on individualism, personal choice and personal responsibility are informed by (and in their turn form) an ethos of training which is class-based' (Kearney, 2010, p.117). Having worked on Clinical Psychology and Counselling programmes, we relate to these observations. Kearney goes on to critique the very idea of the construction of knowledge in our field, and how only certain types of knowledges are privileged over others. This is an important critique because it is such privileged knowledges that eventually form the hegemonic discourses that serve to regulate people, particularly those who deviate from the norms created by such discourses. Unfortunately, such discourses are rarely recognised as being hegemonic because they are elevated to a status of appearing 'obvious', 'natural' or 'spontaneous' and therefore go unnoticed, unquestioned or unchallenged. 'From the moment the client makes contact with us', Kearney says, 'our class differences or similarities are apparent – and significant' and '[t]elephone contact draws attention to accent, language use, the degree of warmth and/or formality and will mobilize a whole set of stereotypic assumptions on both sides which may facilitate or hinder further contact' (p.119). This observation is evidenced in the following reflective account of a recent telephone conversation one of us had with a client:

> Most of my clients appear to be well educated and often are from middleclass backgrounds. I recently had a referral to see a client who was having some issues about his gender. The referral letter was sketchy and did not give much indication of his background, except that he was from a 'council estate' in a rather rundown part of the city. I called him to arrange our first appointment. What struck me first when we spoke was the difference in our accents and the words we were using. I suddenly became conscious of how middleclass I was sounding. He was using words like 'mate' to refer to me. I cringed when the phrases such as 'presumably you would . . .' and 'should you not be able to . . .' slipped out of my mouth in the course of our little conversation. I do believe I was being warm, but I found myself wanting to lose my formal language (which I am so accustomed to in my clinical setting) but also worried about trying to sound like him (in case he thought I was imitating him).

For Kearney, accents and language can activate 'internalised classism' for both therapist and client, particularly before there has been an opportunity for a therapeutic relationship to be developed. While this can be a challenge for a short telephonic conversation, these are issues that can be discussed in therapy sessions, which can alleviate some of the (mis)apprehensions that both parties may have.

But as Foucault (1988, p.11) reminds us, 'power is always present', and this is all the more pertinent when we interrogate 'truth games' such as therapy, where we have 'relationships in which one wishes to direct the behavior of another' (p.11). Consider the power dynamics in therapeutic encounters: the rules and the costs of the game are explained, pre-formatted contracts are signed, rights and responsibilities are declared, the structure and etiquette are set: mostly all by the therapist. Furthermore, in therapeutic relationships, there are differences in the amount of knowledge both the client and therapist have about each other, with the therapist knowing more about the client, than the client knowing about the therapist. This can be particularly worrying for the client when he/she knows that their sexual orientation may already be disclosed to the therapist. Clients may not always know about their therapist's sexuality, and this could work as another rule of the game that feeds into the power differentials between both parties. Both Foucault and Gramsci recognised that power was not inherent in any single *apparatus*, but instead was vested in *relationships*. Indeed Taylor (2010) defines class itself as residing in the very practices of social interaction and this includes therapeutic settings. It is perhaps then, of no surprise that the (voluntary) uptake of psychological therapies by people from working class backgrounds is low, and the dropout rates are high (Sue & Lam, 2002). We also know from our own practice, that poor and working class clients have significant life events that do not permit them from fully engaging in therapy, because of more pressing and immediate needs, such as dealing with housing issues, debt, and so on.

Furthermore, the differing class background of therapists and their clients may result in therapists and clients making very different sense of the client's 'choices' and life experiences. Chalifoux (1996) asked working class women about their experiences with therapy and found that they described feeling that the therapist could not properly understand their experiences. Baker (1996) drew attention to particular potential problems that middle class therapists may encounter in therapy with working class clients; for instance, that of having little if any experience or understanding of the very different work-life realities and everyday constraints for working class people.

Unlike research on therapy and class differences, health inequalities discourse in the UK has had a tradition of focussing on class differences (Bailis *et al.*, 2001). The Strategic Review of Health Inequalities in England Post 2010 (The Marmot Review, 2010) acknowledged that health inequalities resulted from social inequalities, and reported that there was still a 'social gradient in health – the lower a person's social position, the worse his or her health' (p.9). In fact, ill-health was found to be related to both morbidity and mortality even in contemporary Britain: 'people in poorer areas not only die sooner but they will also spend more of their shorter lives with a disability' (p.9). Along with socio-economic status, the extent to which people experience a sense of autonomy and control in their daily lives, including their working and home lives, is a key factor in the social determinants of health and mental health. For Keogh *et al.* (2004, p.3), '[h]ealth inequality emanates from the breakdown of cohesive working class social structures as well as ingrained deprivation and is probably exacerbated by institutional inability to foster and develop the pre-existing social support networks within working class communities'.

When health inequalities are addressed in research, they often only focus on one aspect of an individual's identity (e.g. race or class), but rarely do they take an intersectional approach. Gay Men's Sex Surveys, including recent ones (Hickson *et al.*, 2010), do not directly refer to social class as a dimension by which sexual and health-related practices of gay men can be understood. But from such surveys, we do know that men who have sex with men (MSM) with less formal education have lower uptake of condom use when having anal intercourse, and higher prevalence of HIV compared to those educated up to A-level or above (in Keogh *et al.*, 2004). We also know that such men, and those who are unemployed, are less likely to attend gay social groups, bars and clubs (Keogh *et al.*, 2004), and are therefore less likely to receive targeted interventions which are normally delivered at such venues. Poverty and social inequality, as Murali and Oyebode (2004) rightly pointed out, 'have direct and indirect effects on the social, mental and physical well-being of an individual' (p.216).

The Class/Sexuality Nexus

Class is a loaded *moral signifier* (Sayer, 2005). Being poor and working class often subjects people to negative societal evaluation. However, as Taylor (2010) points out, the experience of being a working class sexual minority is complex and certainly not a matter of simply managing one's class as a negative aspect of a 'spoiled identity', from which people may seek to disidentify. Rather, Taylor, who has written extensively on the experiences of British working class lesbians (e.g. 2008; 2010), attends to the ways in which working class lesbians themselves define and experience class. She asserts that the women often described being working class as something 'which constituted, contained and even comforted; it was often a powerful refusal of middle-class normality, even "pretence", as something more "real", genuine and grounded' (Taylor, 2008, p.120).

Although LGB sexual identities transcend class distinctions, the manner in which these identities are played out may vary. There is little evidence to suggest that 'gay' identity is related to class identity or class mobility in the UK (Hickson *et al.*, 2003), and this may be more the case now than before, with people generally having more access to 'gay' identities, tropes, discourses, and brands, particularly via the internet. Indeed, the class/sexuality nexus has had minimal exposure in sexuality and/or psychological research, and as Brewis and Jack (2010) suggest, 'although class and consumption are well-trodden conceptual terrain, the intersection(s) of sexuality with class is much less well studied' (p.255).

'Chav' identity

Class subjectivity, it has been argued, can only be produced through interpellation (Kenway, 1990). Interpellation, from a Marxist perspective, refers to the formation of a subject by identifying, calling or 'hailing' the person into the subject position. The current use of the word 'chav' to delineate one type of working class subject is brought about by such interpellation, and has come to be regarded as a uniquely British classed identity category. Although stereotypically regarded as a category applying to particularly economically disadvantaged heterosexual working class youth, as we will see, this highly stigmatised and culturally evocative category is also relevant to the lived experience of working class LGBs.

The word chav itself is contested. Paul Johnson (2008) conceptualises chav as a 'phenomenon', the prevalence of which he traces to 2002 Britain. Tom Hampson, the Editorial Director at the Fabian Society (a think-tank affiliated to UK's Labour Party) urged people to 'stop using the word "chav"', because it is 'deeply offensive to a largely voiceless group and – especially when used in normal middle-class conversation or on national TV – it betrays a deep and revealing level of class hatred' (in Hampson & Olchawski, 2008). In this article, the authors equate chav with 'the white working class'. There are several issues we can unpick here: firstly, the assertion that this refers to 'a largely voiceless group' denies the people who are referred to as, or who self-refer as, chav the agency they have; secondly, the racial and class associations may also be problematic. As one commentator rightly pointed out, the word is not only in currency in 'normal middle-class conversation' but also used by members of other classes. Other commentators have suggested that 'chav' has less to do with class and socio-economic status, and more to do with a subculture, a way of dressing and behaving. Irrespective of the meanings attributed to this word, the frequency of its use suggests its currency in contemporary English lexicon.

The chav body is a marked construct and as such, is stylised to bear the insignia of class. Nayak (2006) constructs chavs as working class youth who have been 'priced out' (p.820) of establishments which other working class people have economic access to, thereby suggesting chav-ism as a subculture of a hegemonic working class, distinct with their own sense of style related to apparel, music, and talk. Nayak (2006) observed that there was a 'geographical contingency of subcultural identities which could be "toned down" or "played up" according to time, place and context' (p.821). This is relevant because some LGB establishments have a 'chav-free' policy, which restricts access to those who may claim (or appear to claim) both LGB and chav identities.

The figure of the 'chav' is most commonly presented as male; however, there is an equivalent female figure. Epitomised by fictional comedic characters like Vicky Pollard, a working class teenage mother of 12 on benefits (played by Matt Lucas in *Little Britain*), and claimed or ascribed as an identity category by contemporary British female celebrities including Cheryl Cole, Katie Price and Kerry Katona, the figure of the female chav connotes a hypersexualised 'trashy' femininity and feckless fecundity. The 'problem' of teenage pregnancy is often presented as residing with the irresponsible and precocious (hyper)sexuality of 'chav girls'. While teenage pregnancy may at first blush seem a social problem irrelevant to the issues more commonly faced by LGB people, as Saewyc *et al.* (2008) point out, for lesbian and bisexual youth, teenage pregnancies occur at between two and ten times higher a rate than for heterosexual young people. Thus, LGB youth are certainly not immune from the social problems and stigmatisation associated with chav 'hypersexuality', 'irresponsibility' and 'precocious fecundity'. There may be several reasons that lesbian and bisexual young people have a higher rate of pregnancy: firstly, they are more likely to have experimented sexually, and to have engaged in sexual activity at a younger age than heterosexual youth (Robin *et al.*, 2002). LGB youth are also more likely to have engaged in 'survival sex', or to have experienced sexual exploitation (Saewyc *et al.*, 2008). Indeed, young LGB people are at greater risk than heterosexual youth of becoming homeless, which may in turn place them at risk of becoming involved in coercive sexual activities (Smith *et al.*, 2007). Furthermore, the difficulties they experience when coming to terms with their sexuality may result in them engaging in heterosexual relationships in an attempt to avoid 'detection' and thus discrimination and harassment. Higher levels of problematic substance use among young LGBs may make them more likely to engage in risky, and unprotected, sexual behaviour (Marshal *et al.*, 2008). When this behaviour involves heterosexual intercourse, this may of course result in unintended pregnancy as well as risking transmission of STIs. Bridget's (2000) study with young LGBs explored the reasons young women had sexual intercourse with a man during their teenage years. Reasons included wanting to 'have a baby'; despite 'feeling sick' about it, and 'pressure' to engage in intercourse to prove that they were not a lesbian.

Marketing of 'chav' identity

Although embodying a stigmatized position in society, some people (who may or may not be chavs) have exploited chav identities to make their bodies desirable and economically marketable in a manner that is both unapologetic and perhaps, even, *uber-chav*. This is most ubiquitous in the pornography industry, which constructs for the pleasure of its viewers an opportunity to vicariously partake in sexual encounters with people they couldn't or wouldn't consider having sex with in 'real life'. However, gay consumption of 'chav' takes on a plethora of other activities also, from middle class people 'dressing down' in prototypical chav attire of (most often, counterfeit) Burberry-checked caps, tracksuits, and (white) trainers: for specific 'chav nights' at LGB venues; to seeking out actual sexual encounters with chavs, for instance via gay social networking sites, where people 'advertise' themselves as 'chavs' or 'chav-lovers'. Johnson (2008) in his exploration of the 'homosexual eroticization of class' argues that the 'chav remains an object – before, during and after his use – of disgust, filth and repudiation' (p.79). Johnson rightly asserts that 'there is violence in this. In attributing particular values to certain subject positions, representations simultaneously rob them [chav] of any worth' (p.79). However, the perceived unidirectionality of such subject positions, we feel, also robs the 'denigrated and impoverished' of agency. As one of our clients who identifies as a 'chav and proud' heterosexual claimed, 'if they [homosexual men] want a good dirty shag from a dirty council estate bloke, I'll give it to 'em rough and dirty . . . as long as they can pay for it'.

Such narratives clearly demonstrate the strategic deployment of cultural identity markers as currency that can at once perhaps empower, afford social control, and alienate people in cross-class sexual encounters. While such strategic deployment offers an alternative take on the politics of use/abuse of subcultural groups, we are sympathetic to Brewis and Jack's (2010) statement that 'any decision about the politics of anything depends on audience, context and timing, and no cultural complex is progressive or reactionary in its entirety' (p.253). In some instances, however, this 'symbolic violence' of *use* may take a more virulent turn, when the kinds of sexual activities (e.g. barebacking[1]) may determine the capital value of individuals. For instance, purchasing unsafe sex could be construed as *abuse*. Such consumption, however problematic it is, does go to some extent to trouble the notion of the 'pink pound thesis', which tends to universalize gay spending culture (e.g. fashion products) and creates a 'hegemonic homosexuality' (Brewis & Jack, 2010).

The production of hegemonic homosexuality is highly dependent on capital: for access to spaces and services, for education, and for the development, reshaping and dressing of the body. Working class LGBs may find that if they do not have the financial resources to be a part of this trope of homosexuality/bisexuality, that they may not be welcome in such spaces, unless they satisfy some fetishistic ideal of those who inhabit these hegemonic positions.

The significance of economic freedom cannot be discounted in many gay circles. As Brewis and Jack (2010) note, '[c]onsumption is seen to play an integral role in the coming-out experiences of many gay men, and in subsequent processes of socialization into the gay scene, such that these consumption rituals are said in part to create their sexual identities'

---

[1]   Anal intercourse without a condom.

(p.254). Therefore, for some men (and women) recourse to capital may be a prerequisite for carving out their gay identity and securing entry into gay circles and the spaces they inhabit. This was precisely one of the difficulties one of our clients had.

Clive's Story

Clive, a 21 year old white man, was referred for therapy to deal with his depression. The referral letter indicated that Clive thought that the depression was linked to his 'cross-dressing behaviour'. Clive described himself as heterosexual, and had been in a relationship with a woman until a year ago, when they split up. They had two children together. During therapy, it soon became apparent that his depression was mainly related to his sexuality and his ideas of masculinity. During his fourth session, Clive said that he had had sex with a few men in the past, and had enjoyed it. Clive lived with his 'straight mate' (who did not like 'fags') in a local council estate, and therefore did not dare disclose his sexual desires to anyone he knew. Exploring his sexual fantasies, Clive said he wanted to be anally penetrated by a man, while he was wearing women's clothing. He had previously met the men he had had sex with at a local nightclub. He had enjoyed the sex, although he described the first encounter as having been 'messy'. The man he was with did not use a condom, and Clive had not considered having a check up for sexually transmitted infections (STIs) following this encounter. There was inconsistent condom use on the three following sexual encounters.

During later sessions, Clive explored how he could meet other non-heterosexual men, which for him was proving to be a big hurdle. Because he had only recently quit his job (as a labourer in a factory) he had no state benefits yet. This therefore did not permit him to access gay spaces, such as the nightclub, because he did not have the money to pay the entrance fee. He also felt that he did not have any 'nice clothes' to wear if he went there. The internet was not an option for Clive, because the only places he could get on the internet were council libraries which did not charge to use their computing facilities, but which did not permit accessing popular gay social networking sites, because they were considered 'indecent'. Furthermore, not identifying as a 'gay' or 'bisexual' man, Clive did not feel comfortable accessing such sites in public spaces, in case someone he knew caught him doing this. Clive did not know of any cruising spots[2] in the city (many of them had ceased being cruising spots because people preferred to meet online or in saunas, which also charged an entrance fee). Clive was referred to a local gay social group with the hope of finding some support, and perchance, meet some men he could connect with emotionally/sexually. But following his first visit, he vowed never to go back because he felt alienated there. He said there was no one there who looked, dressed, and talked like him. The 'topic for the day' was 'gay hot spots in Berlin'. For Clive, who had not even visited London (an hour away from where he lived by train), there was just no common ground between himself and the others at the social group.

Negotiating LGB and Working Class Identities

There are real, practical difficulties for young, poor, non-heterosexual men in small cities to find other non-heterosexual men 'safely', even in a country where LGBT people have rights, and in an age where you can determine whether the person sitting across from you on the train is gay (and interested!) by solely using GPS technology on your iPhone or BlackBerry[3]. Some of the issues that Clive had to deal with have also been reported in other studies of working class gay and bisexual men.

One of the most authoritative British studies exploring the experiences of working class gay men is that by Keogh *et al.* (2004), which was a qualitative research project involving over a hundred interviews with working class men, and documented various aspects of their lives. The focus of this study appears to have been related to health promotion, but given the significance of this study, we offer a précis of some of their results from the first three categories here.[4] In order to extend this discussion, we also offer relevant findings from the emerging literature on British working class lesbians against these categories. Here, the work of Taylor (e.g. 2008; 2010), McDermott (e.g. 2006; 2011) and others allows us to consider the issues raised by Keogh and colleagues (2004) as they relate to both men and women.

---

[2] Public places where gay/bi men can find partners for casual sex
[3] Grindr (www.grindr.com) is one such location-based mobile network which can be downloaded to mobile phones.
[4] We do not report the findings related to HIV in this chapter, as we felt that while this is an important aspect of gay and bisexual men's lives, it is not the specific focus of this chapter.

The family and gay identity

Most working class gay men reported having experienced some form of early adversity within their families of origin, with many reporting that they had an unhappy relationship with their fathers, or step-fathers. There was also mention of the social services needing to be involved in some instances. These factors may have led to the development of 'psychological trauma (such as self-identified lack of esteem, difficulty in maintaining friends and relationships, and mental illness)' (Keogh *et al.*, 2004; p.9), and experiences of bullying, issues related to notions and self-perception of their own masculinity. However, it was perhaps these very early experiences which helped them develop a sense of independence and self-reliance, because they were thrust into adult roles and responsibilities before others in their age cohorts would have been required to.

An interesting finding was the constructed notions of the ideal family and/or relationship, which was modelled on traditional heterosexual models. While some had distanced themselves from their families of origin, they attempted to replicate it structurally, perhaps in an attempt to 'fix' the wrongs they had experienced. Perhaps not unlike non-heterosexual men from other social classes, Keogh *et al.*'s (2004) respondents varied in their awareness of their emerging sexuality, with most noticing some 'basic difference to other boys' (p.11), some beginning to experiment sexually at an early age, some adopting a gay identity thereafter, but others not coming out until much later, and yet others battling with their emerging sexual preferences.

Interestingly, the coming out stories of these men (mostly to their families of origin), seemed to cluster around: (i) those who decided to come out early in life, sometimes rather impulsively, and perhaps because they were autonomous in some respects, had a certain autonomy to be daring to come out; and (ii) those who decided to come out later in life, once they had consolidated their gay relationship and had been settled for some time. Again, not unlike some non-heterosexual men from other classes, some working class gay men did not articulate their sexuality in specific sexual identity terms, but allowed the family to read their lifestyles choices on their own terms and in their own time. This is not to suggest that the coming out stories were always received positively by the families; in fact, one-third of the participants suggested that there was a breakdown in their family relationships because of this disclosure, with some experiencing virulent forms of homonegativity.

Like working class gay men, working class lesbians are more likely than middle class lesbians to live close to their biological families (Taylor, 2008) within the communities where they grew up. They are less likely to be afforded the opportunity to relocate to large cities for educational or oc-cupational opportunities, which may also hold the concurrent promise of 'coming out' in a new environment and forming new links with other young LGB people in the (relatively) supportive environment of large universities, which are likely to have LGB societies and groups. However, close geograph-ical proximity and financial and caregiving obligations to biological family are often experienced positively, as Taylor (2009) asserts. Some working class lesbians are forced to relocate due to experiences of homophobia or to pursue relationships, but may find being distanced from their own working class communities difficult. Taylor (2004) interviewed Kelly, a young work-ing class lesbian, who relocated to a new working class area and describes her feelings of alienation:

> But see you're a lot different Lisa [her partner] 'cause you're still in your home environment, you come from Hull, you still hang around with your mum you know. I've, . . . sexuality has moved me, I belonged in that group em, and what my class identity means as a woman, and as a straight woman it would have been assumptions that I would have got married, live close to my mum and have some babies, live in each other's pockets. But I'm alienated from that because I've felt myself actually moving further and further away and I don't really fit in this area, that's obvious on some levels to me (Taylor, 2004, p.4).

The following client story describes the experience of a working class lesbian who continues to reside, with her partner and their child, in the working class community in which she grew up:

Abby's Story

Abby, 29 years old, reported that she and her partner and their child were 'perfectly happy' living in the small working class community where she grew up and that their neighbours treated them like 'any other family'. However, Abby's story also draws attention to other less positive aspects of the experience of being working class and lesbian. Neither she nor her partner currently works. Abby lost her job 12 months ago and has not found stable work since. Her partner did not complete high school, dropping out when she became pregnant, and has never worked. They deal with daily financial pressures and often run out of money at the end of the month. Abby described the constant stress of the threat of bailiffs knocking on their door as they are heavily in debt. They use an answering machine to screen their calls, so as to avoid calls from persistent debt collectors. Abby's partner claims a single parent benefit and although they are engaged, they cannot afford to enter a civil partnership as they would have to declare their relationship and would then lose these benefits. Thus, through necessity, they live a partially closeted life – they have separate bedrooms, even though in practice they share a bed.

Prior to the Civil Partnership Act (2005), same-sex couples were regarded as 'single' and did not come under scrutiny as families by the welfare state, and as yet, not all local councils responsible for administering benefits have explicitly sought to recognise the existence of same sex couples and families (Browne, 2011). The benefits of same sex 'marriage' do not extend to all same sex couples equally: and indeed some (e.g. Kandaswamy, 2008) have argued that these are 'privileges of a racially stratified welfare state' (p.706).

Education and work

Many working class gay men reported that their families of origin did not often have the financial, educational, or other resources to support them while at school, with low expectations from families and from school authorities. While at school, some experienced homophobic bullying for being seen as 'different', with parents and teachers not understanding the problem, or protecting or fighting for the bullied. The class differential here is related to how the bullied children are left to cope with the bullying and the effects of the bullying by themselves, with minimal or no support from their families or school. While homophobic bullying was not found to have had a direct impact on age at which these men left school, it did have an impact on the quality of their school life (Keogh *et al.*, 2004).

Nixon (2011) interviewed working class lesbian women about their experiences at school. The women described homophobic bullying as a reason to actively avoid being identified as gay:

Ahh I hated it. I didn't have, I didn't do no exams at all really (inhales deeply) well I was a loner (exhales deeply) and I just hated school... I was friends with a lad, we were always together, you know there was always me and him, but he got tortured, 'hey ya puff', and I think that's what kept me down (p.86).

McDermott (2011) reports that for young working class lesbians, coming out – which requires both material and emotional resources – may be a more difficult process than for young middle class lesbians. She asserts that whilst coming to identify as lesbian is likely to be a stressful process for both working class and middle class young lesbians, middle class lesbians may through their class advantage experience more protection from psychological and emotional stresses. Taylor (2006) reports that working class lesbians commonly reported a sense of being 'doubly disadvantaged': that both their sexuality and their class were experienced as intersecting sources of stress.

The age at which people leave school and the qualifications with which they leave school appear to be class-bound. We also know that pupils resident in the least deprived areas, as defined by the Income Deprivation Affecting Children Index, continue to outperform pupils in the most deprived areas (Department for Education, 2010). Most of the respondents in Keogh *et al.*'s (2004) study left full-time education at 16 or earlier, which was considered a social norm for them. The effects of the transition from school life to work/employment depended on the age of the respondents, generally with older cohorts having left education to enter into apprenticeships or the armed forces; but with younger men having had to traverse a more arduous trajectory in the Thatcherite era, with limited opportunities to find gainful employment; and even for younger men who left school in the mid-1990s, training of some form was considered important, and many appeared to have sought it.

With the changes in governmental priorities and economic restructuring, working class youth, the trajectory of whose lives once would have seen them through basic schooling to training and to apprenticeships, today find themselves considered 'unskilled, unemployable, redundant youth' (Nayak, 2006, p.816). These experiences cannot have been very different for heterosexual and non-heterosexual youth. School leaving should therefore be understood in terms of not only the so-called social 'norms' of the groups in question, but also in terms of how these norms were constructed and the (historical) socio-political environment in which people found themselves when approaching school-leaving age.

What is noteworthy here is the relationship between sexuality, sociality, and work. Keogh *et al.* (2004) found that a majority of their respondents did not consider their sexuality when choosing their job(s). Perhaps there were limited options to begin with in 'choosing' a job, and therefore sexuality was not a consideration, simply because it could not be. However, these authors report that their respondents had 'very few accounts of problems' at work because of their sexuality (p.23). There was however a high level of unemployment in their sample, and the adverse psychological effects that such a status can confer on the individual (especially if it is not their *choice* to be unemployed) cannot be discounted.

McDermott's research (2010; 2011) on young working class lesbians' post-compulsory schooling choices showed that these women were more likely than middle class lesbians to report having left school at 16–17. Stacey, a 22 year old working class lesbian interviewed by McDermott (2011), explains the combination of factors (her mother's health problems, her family's economic situation, her fear of unemployment) that led her to choose to leave school at 17, despite initially aspiring to gain further qualifications:

> So I just thought I may as well get a job, when this came up . . . it felt boss because I was bringing me own money in, as well as giving me mum money like as rent, 'cos it would help her, you see, whereas [brother and sister] I always say they couldn't give two shits, they do, but not the way I am with me mum, like if me mum said have you got any money? They'd say no, whereas I'd go out and find it for her and make sure she's got it (p.71).

Nixon (2011) has studied the experiences of working class lesbian mothers and their engagement with their own children's education. She notes that lesbian mothers are often regarded as belonging to the category of 'deviant' mother; along with single mothers, working class mothers and black mothers. Lesbian mothers may face particular difficulties in the school environment as their sexuality may be perceived as a 'sexual threat to children' (Richardson, 1996, p.280). Working class and middle class lesbian parents may have different expectations of their children at school. Whilst middle class parents are likely to focus on promoting their children's academic success, working class parents may place more emphasis on protecting their children from the possibility of homophobic bullying and strengthening their children's day-to-day resilience to the harsher challenges of life at school (Nixon, 2011). Working class lesbian parents may be anxious about the possibility that they are the 'cause' of any bullying their child might experience. As Taylor (2004) has pointed out, through their own earlier negative experiences at school, working class lesbian mothers may not feel at ease in the school environment. Working class parents are often regarded by teachers as being disengaged with, and passive about their children's life at school. However, as Nixon (2011) argues, choosing not to be visibly involved with one's child's education may rather be a strategy in encouraging children to become autonomous and to 'find their own way'.

Sociality

For Keogh *et al.*'s (2004) respondents, the formation of a 'gay identity', although challenging, was not without its benefits, which included a sense of freedom from dominant heterosexual male scripts and norms, access to families or choice and gay communities, and alliances with heterosexual women. However, a gay identity also came at the cost of 'familial, social and romantic security' (p.26) for over a quarter of the respondents.

A significant finding of the Keogh *et al.* (2004) study, in our opinion, is the manner in which these men negotiated and lived out their gay identity. This is particularly relevant when viewing their experiences from an intersectional perspective. The 'gay community' [sic], for these men was seen as an *adjunct* to their social network, and as such, they distanced themselves from certain aspects of gay lifestyles, including a rejection of 'commodified or politicised gay cultures' (p.26). The financial restrictions these men faced when accessing the gay commercial scene was highlighted in their discussions, and they asserted a sense of control over the scene by frequenting their 'local' gay venues. While this may be a possibility in larger cities, in smaller cities, where such a choice is often restricted and where the 'local' gay venue is perhaps the only one, working class gay men with meagre finances may find such spaces difficult to access (see Clive's story).

Similar sentiments were expressed by working class lesbians, who often dismissed the commercial scenes as 'pretentious' and expensive (Taylor, 2008). Taylor's respondents preferred working class LGB venues, which are often located in less cosmopolitan areas of the city and may provide for a broader range of patrons than middle class venues. However, such working class LGB spaces are increasingly vulnerable to being 'upmarketed' and 'rebranded' as more cosmopolitan LGB venues, as part of the process of 'urban renewal'; effectively excluding their existing working class customer base. Working class lesbians are also often unable to reside in and socialise within the more cosmopolitan and LGB-friendly areas of cities as these areas tend to be prohibitively expensive. Indeed the housing 'choices' available to working class lesbians may be limited. Thus, for example, it may be difficult to simply relocate to a more 'tolerant' area for those experiencing homophobia from neighbours. However, working class areas are not necessarily intolerant of LGB community members.

Working class lesbians may have a complicated relationship with working class community spaces (Taylor, 2008). Whilst simultaneously describing working class LGB pub culture as being more 'real' than middle class scene culture, Taylor's participants to some extent also 'pathologised' working class LGB culture, by describing the typical patrons of such venues as being excessively 'hedonistic' and problematically invested in the banal pursuits of getting drunk, popping pills and having fun. Keogh *et al.* (2004) also problematise the idea of 'gay values', by suggesting how working class gay values may be different from the values of gay men from other classes. The question they pose is: 'can we meaningfully talk about 'gay' values?' (p.43). The dialectics posed by this question takes the form of another question:

> If a significant group of gay men embrace a set of values which prizes their position within their biological family and local community rather than a sense of being an individual self-actualised gay man; are these values not also 'gay' values? (p.43).

They go on to explain:

> That is, whatever a *significant group* of gay men aspire to, and identify as, become their gay aspirations and gay identities. The lives of the men in this sample render our traditional understandings of the social distinctions between gay and straight redundant (p.43; emphasis added).

In taking this problematic further, there is an interesting point here: there is a suggestion of a critical mass ('significant group') being required to garner some form of validation of an aspiration or identity. Such groupings may be of more significance to public health discussions, than to therapeutic ones, because for the latter, what would be more instructive would be the manner in which the individual carves out their own aspirations and version(s) of gay identities, and how they fit with larger group (or subgroup) identities. A case in point is Martin, one of our clients, describing his 'gay' identity:

> I'm fed up of going to them places [referring to gay venues], you know. I ain't like em fellas [other working-class gay men] there, you know. I don't wanna be like em. All that swearing and shit . . . and being so man [manly] – but I don't wanna be like them poncy gays also. You know what I mean? Jus showing off and screaming. I just don't fit in no gang. May be that's my problem. But I just don't wanna have to force myself to be one of em.

For Martin, one of the challenges he faces is how to negotiate his id-iosyncratic social class and sexual identity positions which defines him as 'Martin'. There are cultural signifiers which foster group cohesion, whether we are referring to groups related to class, creed, sexuality, etc. Sport, for instance, particularly football in Britain, has been recognised as a means of cementing class (and geographical) identities and fraternity (Nayak, 2006) for men[5]. For some working class men, who are 'camp', however, playing football (or even being near where it is played) may not be a source of bonding or cohesion, but an alienating and 'outing' experience. As Cameron, one of our clients reported:

> ...watching the lads play footie was a mixed experience for me. It was sexy and scary...sexy because I could see em all muddied and sweaty...and I knew I was gonna think of em when I, you know...but also, I was scared to go near em; cos if that ball come anywhere near me, there's no chance I'm gonna kick it back to em, or worse, throw it...that would be the end of me...I'd be a right show up (laughs).

Cameron's apprehension was related to his inability to throw and kick the football 'like a man'. For his local peer group, this inability immediately placed him not only as an outsider, but also as 'the local puff'. While there are several activities that many of us cannot engage in with any degree of proficiency, for a young working class man, there may be restrictions placed in terms of what he has access to in the first place. Football, 'the working man's ballet', can be a cultural adhesive for many working class folk, and not participating in this activity, or not being able to participate, can be variously construed as 'not being man enough' or 'not proud to be working class', questioning the authenticity of gender (and implicitly, sexuality) and class.

This is in no way to perpetuate the myth that gay men do not like or play football. Groups such as The Gay Football Supporters Network (GFSN) was founded in 1989 by dedicated group of football enthusiasts 'who happened to be gay' (see www.gfsn.org.uk). This said, homophobia is rife in football and terraces. Even in 2010, *The Independent* newspaper reported that professional footballers 'refused to appear in a campaign video against homophobia because they fear being ridiculed for taking a stand against one of the sport's most stubborn taboos' (Herbert, 2010). However, other groups, such as Kick It Out (www.kickitout.org) have been attempting to tackle this problem head-on. The Justin Campaign[6] (www.thejustincampaign.com) is

---

[5] We direct readers interested in tracking the changes related to class, capitalism, and football to Imlach (2006), *My Father and Other Working Class Football Heroes*.

[6] Justin Fashanu is considered the world's first openly gay professional footballer. It is thought that his identity as a black gay man living and working in a hostile, homophobic environment was a contributing factor that led to his suicide. The Justin Campaign launched *Football v Homophobia – An International Day* (February 29th) opposing homophobia in football.

another movement that seeks to challenge the stereotypes and misconceptions that exist around LGB people in football.

The Impact of Sexuality on Socio-Economic Status

Thus far, we have discussed the experiences of gay men and lesbians who have grown up with a particular class background or identity. However, it is also important to consider the ways in which one's sexuality can – sometimes dramatically – impact upon one's socio-economic status, financial security and life choices.

As noted in Chapter 10 (on *Age and Ageing*), a significant proportion of older lesbians have previously been in heterosexual marriages, during which they had children. Often such women did not leave their male partner until later in life, once their children were older. This can seriously affect the socio-economic status and financial security of many older lesbian women (Cronin & King, 2010). Coming out as lesbian later in life can mean that women have to adjust to a far less secure existence, which can be a source of significant anxiety as they approach the age of retirement.

Younger LGB people may also be vulnerable to a dramatic loss of socioeconomic status and to housing difficulties; especially when coming out to their family and friends for the first time. Studies have found that LGB young people are significantly over-represented amongst homeless young people. Some 25–40% of homeless young people identify as LGBT, versus approximately 5 per cent of the population (Kruks, 1991). More recently, Stonewall Housing (2001) showed that young British LGBT people were at high risk of becoming homeless; contributing factors include prejudice, discrimination, intolerance, bullying and harassment from peers, the emotional distress and extreme isolation associated with being rejected by family and friends, and mental health problems associated with 'difficulties coming to terms with sexual or gender identity'. Homeless people, of whatever sexuality, are also subject to pernicious highly negative societal attitudes and may be vulnerable to dehumanising hate-motivated crimes (including murder). Stonewall Housing (in London) provides vital support for LGBT people faced with housing crises, whether due to harassment from homophobic neighbours, eviction, or rejection by one's biological family.

In this chapter, we have considered the often neglected intersection of class and sexuality. We have explored the relevance of class to sexuality, with a focus on the experiences of working class LGB people in Britain. Given the omission of class from much of the literature on sexuality, we hope that this chapter has attuned the reader to some issues, challenges and rewards peculiar to the experiences of working class LGB people; and more particularly, that it has brought into relief the already implicitly classed status of what we think we know about LGB people's lives.

Guidelines for Good Practice

Embracing a social justice agenda, we take the lead from Smith (2008, p.912–919), who reminds us that the 'social, economic, political, and cultural implications of classism are far-reaching, and scholars throughout the social sciences have unique contributions to make to its exploration' (p.912). Therapists are also reminded to:

- Take into consideration how social class influences the client's perceptions, attitudes, and beliefs about their own gender and sexuality, how they embody these, and how others in their social groups view these also.
- Consider their own social locations, and how these might impact on their perception of the client, and how the client perceives them. The therapist's own privileged class position should be acknowledged. Therapists should also be mindful of the classism that may be embedded in the theories and practices which they employ in therapy.
- Be aware of the socio-political landscape that their client comes from, and to keep abreast the socio-political changes and trends in this sphere, by acquiring a deep understanding of the lived experiences of their clients, related to their classed positions. This includes being familiar not only with the pressures, threats, and challenges people from disadvantaged social backgrounds come from, but also the support services, opportunities, and avenues that clients can access to deal with these challenges.
- Be aware of their own negative assumptions and stereotypic characterisation of people from disadvantaged social classes and the cultural discourses that support these, and not make an implicit assumptions, for instance that 'people are poor because they are lazy'.
- Be cognisant of the different ways in which the therapist's social class is conveyed to the client, and how some of these 'codes' of class (such as wearing designer 'labels') can deter the client from developing a good therapeutic relationship.
- Consider their own motivations to help clients and be careful not to reproduce the existing power differentials that disenfranchise clients in

society, by imposing the therapist's values and attitudes on to the client; and to decode the meanings of help-seeking and help-providing.

- Pay attention to the possibility of disadvantage and oppression that being a metaminority entails, and to investigate the intersections of the client's minority/disadvantaged identities to explore how these can be used to foster resilience and growth.
- Consider how they can work with their poor and underprivileged clients and their communities to act as agents for social change.

References

Bailis, D., Segall, A., Mahon, M.J., Chipperfield, J.G. & Dunn, E.M. (2001). Perceived control in relation to socioeconomic and behavioural resources for health. *Social Science and Medicine, 52*(11), 1661–1676.

Baker, N. (1996). Class as a construct in a "classless" society. In M. Hill & E.D. Rothblum (Eds.). *Classism and feminist therapy* (pp. 13–24). New York, NY: Harrington Park.

Ballinger, L. & Wright, J. (2007). Does class count? Social class and counselling. *Counselling and Psychotherapy Research, 7*(3), 157–163.

Bourdieu, P. (1998). *Acts of resistance: Against the new myths of our time.* (Trans. R. Nice). Cambridge: Polity.

Brewis, J. & Jack, G. (2010). Consuming chavs: The ambiguous politics of gay chavinism. *Sociology, 44*(2), 251–268.

Bridget, J. (2000). *ACTION for lesbian, gay and bisexual young people in Calderdale,* Research Report, Lesbian Information Service. Retrieved 30 May 2011 from http://www.lesbianinformationservice.org/action98.htm.

Browne, K. (2011). 'By partner we mean . . .': Alternative geographies of 'gay marriage'. *Sexualities, 14*(1), 100–122.

Burgess, D., Ding, Y., Hargreaves, M., van Ryn, M. & Phelan, S. (2008). The Association between perceived discrimination and underutilization of needed medical and mental health care in a multi-ethnic community sample. *Journal of Health Care for the Poor and Underserved, 19*(3), 894–911.

Butler, J. (1990). *Gender trouble: Feminism and the subversion of identity.* New York, NY: Routledge.

Butler, J. (2004). *Undoing gender.* London: Routledge.

Chalifoux, B. (1996). Speaking up: White working class women in therapy. In M. Hill & E.D. Rothblum (Eds.). *Classism and feminist therapy: Counting costs.* New York, NY: The Haworth Press.

Cronin, A. & King, A. (2010). Power, inequality and identification: Exploring diversity and intersectionality amongst older LGB adults. *Sociology, 44*(5), 876–892.

Department for Education (2010). *Statistical first release: GCSE and equivalent attainment by pupil characteristics in England, 2009/10.* London, UK:

Department for Education. Retrieved 9 January 2011 from http://www
.education.gov.uk/rsgateway/DB/SFR/s000977/index.shtml.

Eckert, P. (2000). *Linguistic variation as social practice.* Oxford: Blackwell.

Foucault, M. (1988). The ethic of care for the self as a practice of freedom. In
J. Bernaeur and D. Rasmussen (Eds.). *The final Foucault.* Cambridge, Mass.:
MIT Press, pp. 1–20.

Hampson, T. & Olchawski, J. (2008, 17 July). Ban the word 'chav'. *The Guardian.*
Retrieved 7 January 2011 from http://www.guardian.co.uk/commentisfree/
2008/jul/15/equality.language.

Herbert, I. (2010, 12 February). Football accused in homophobia row. *The Independent on Sunday.* Retrieved 30 January 2011 from http://www.independent
.co.uk/sport/football/news-and-comment/football-accused-in-homophobia-
row-1897128.html.

Hickson, F., Bourne, A., Weatherburn, P., Reid, D., Jessup, K. & Hammond, G.
(2010). *Tactical dangers: Findings from the United Kingdom Gay Men's Sex
Survey 2008.* London: Sigma Research.

Hickson, F., Weatherburn, P., Reid, D. & Stephens, M. (2003). *Out and about:
Findings from the United Kingdom Gay Men's Sex Survey, 2002.* London: Sigma
Research.

Imlach, G. (2006). *My father and other working class football heroes.* London: Yellow
Jersey Press.

Johnson, P. (2008). 'Rude boys': The homosexual eroticization on class. *Sociology,*
42(1), 65–82.

Kandaswamy, P. (2008). State austerity and the racial politics of same-sex marriage
in the US. *Sexualities, 11*(6), 706–725.

Kearney, A. (2010). Class and counselling. In C. Lago & B. Smith (Eds.). *Anti-
discriminatory practice in counselling & psychotherapy: Professional skills for
counsellors.* London: Sage.

Kenway, J. (1990). Education and the Right's discursive politics: private versus state
schooling. In S. Ball (Ed.). *Foucault and education: Disciplines and knowledge.*
London: Routledge.

Keogh, P., Dodds, C. & Henderson, L. (2004). *Working class gay men: Redefining
community, restoring identity.* London: Sigma Research.

Kruks, G. (1991). Gay and lesbian homeless/street youth: Special issues and concerns, *Journal of Adolescent Health, 12,* 515–518.

Lawler, S. (2005). Introduction: Class, culture and identity. *Sociology, 39*(5),
797–806.

Marmot Review, The (2010). *Fair society, healthy lives: Strategic review of
health inequalities in England post 2010.* Retrieved 30 May 2011 from
www.ucl.ac.uk/marmotreview.

Marshal, M.P., Friedman, M.S., Stall, R., King, K.M., Miles, J. & Gold, M.A. (2008).
Sexual orientation and adolescent substance use: A meta-analysis and methodological review. *Addiction, 103,* 546–556.

Mays, V.M. & Cochran, S.D. (2001). Mental health correlates of perceived discrimination among lesbian, gay, and bisexual adults in the United States. *American Journal of Public Health, 91,* 1869–1876.

McDermott, E. (2011). The world some have won: Sexuality, class and inequality. *Sexualities: Special Issue on Class, 14*(1), 63–78.

McDermott, E. (2010). 'I just want to be totally true to myself': Class and the making of the sexual self. In Y. Taylor (Ed.), *Classed intersections: Spaces, selves, knowledges.* Farnham: Ashgate.

McDermott, E. (2006). Surviving in dangerous places: Lesbian identity performances in the workplace, social class and psychological health. *Feminism and Psychology, 16*(2), 193–211.

Meyer, D. (2010). Evaluating the severity of hate-motivated violence: Intersectional differences among LGBT hate crime victims. *Sociology, 44*(5), 980–995.

Murali, V. & Oyebode, F. (2004). Poverty, social inequality and mental health. *Advances in Psychiatric Treatment, 10,* 216–224.

Nayak, A. (2006). Displaced masculinities: Chavs, youth and class in the post-industrial city. *Sociology, 40*(5), 813–831.

Nixon, C. (2011). Working class lesbian parents' emotional engagement with their children's education: Intersections of class and sexuality. *Sexualities, 14*(1), 79–99.

Pascoe, E.A. & Smart Richman, L. (2009). Perceived discrimination and health: A meta-analytic review. *Psychological Bulletin, 135*(4), 531–554.

Richardson, D. (1996). Constructing lesbian sexualities. In S. Jackson and S. Scott (Eds.). *Feminism and sexuality: A reader.* Edinburgh: Edinburgh University Press. pp. 276–286.

Riggs, D.W. (2010). On accountability: Towards a white middle-class queer 'post identity politics identity politics'. *Ethnicities, 10*(3), 344–357.

Robin, L., Brener, N., Donahue, S., Hack, T., Hale, K. & Goodenow, C. (2002). Associations between health risk behaviors and opposite-, same-, and both-sex sexual partners in representative samples of Vermont and Massachusetts high school students. *Archives of Pediatric and Adolescent Medicine, 156,* 349–355.

Saewyc, E., Poon, C., Homma, Y. & Skay, C. (2008). Stigma management? The links between enacted stigma and teen pregnancy trends among gay, lesbian, and bisexual students in British Columbia. *Canadian Journal of Human Sexuality, 17*(3), 123–139.

Sayer, A. (2005). Class, moral worth and recognition. *Sociology, 39*(5), 947–963.

Smith, L. (2008). Positioning classism within counseling psychology's social justice agenda. *The Counseling Psychologist, 36*(6), 895–924.

Smith, A., Saewyc, E., Albert, M., MacKay, L. & Northcott, M. (2007). *A profile of marginalized and street-involved youth in BC.* Vancouver, BC: McCreary Centre Society.

Stonewall Housing and National Centre for Social Research (2001). *Meeting the needs of homeless lesbian and gay youth.* Retrieved 30 May 2011 from http://www.stonewallhousing.org/research.html.

Strier, R. & Binyamin, S. (2010). Developing anti-oppressive services for the poor: A theoretical and organisational rationale. *British Journal of Social Work, 40*(6), 1908–1926.

Sue, S. & Lam, A.G. (2002). Cultural and demographic diversity. In J.C. Norcross (Ed.). *Psychotherapy relationships that work: Therapist contributions and responsiveness to patients* (pp. 401–422). New York, NY: Oxford University Press.

Taylor, Y. (2004). Negotiation and navigation – an exploration of the spaces/places of working-class lesbians. *Sociological Research Online, 9*(1). Retrieved 30 June 2006 from http://www.socresonline.org.uk/9/1/taylor.html.

Taylor, Y. (2006). Interactions of class and sexuality in the classroom. *Gender and education, 18*(4), 447–452.

Taylor, Y. (2008). That's not really my theme: Working class lesbians in (and out of) place. *Sexualities, 11*, 523–546.

Taylor, Y. (2009). Complexities and complications: Intersections of class and sexuality. *Journal of Lesbian Studies, 13*(2), 189–203.

Taylor Y. (2010). Complexities and complications: Intersections of class and sexuality. In: Y. Taylor, S. Hines, M. Casey (Eds.) *Theorizing Intersectionality and Sexuality* (pp. 37–55). Basingstoke: Palgrave Macmillan.

7

Physical Health

Adam Jowett & Elizabeth Peel

In recent decades the roles of clinical, health and counselling psychologists have become increasingly important in healthcare. Psychological practice in relation to physical health ranges widely from the development of health promotion initiatives, preparing patients for medical procedures, helping people modify health behaviours, to counselling those diagnosed with chronic or life threatening medical conditions. Although the work of clinical and counselling psychologists is primarily focused on mental health (see Chapter 6), mental health concerns, and psychosocial issues more broadly, can be the cause or result of our state of physical health. As such, physical health issues are relevant for therapists when working with clients (Karademas, 2009).

With the exception of HIV and sexual health, psychologists may rarely consider sexual identity in relation to physical health (cf. Peel & Thomson, 2009). This is perhaps due to the individualistic approaches psychologists tend to adopt when thinking about health and illness. Furthermore, what is considered 'relevant' to an individual's health is often determined by biomedical considerations (Fish, 2006). Despite this, *critical health psychologists* (Murray, 2004) have pointed out that such individualistic approaches are ill equipped to explain health inequalities between social groups and neglect the diverse ways in which people may experience ill health. In this chapter, we outline some of the empirical data of interest to therapists on the health of non-heterosexuals. We provide a brief overview of some disparities in the physical health of heterosexuals and non-heterosexuals. We then outline some psychological implications of living with a chronic health condition, before considering how such

Intersectionality, Sexuality and Psychological Therapies: Working with Lesbian, Gay and Bisexual Diversity,
First Edition. Edited by Roshan das Nair and Catherine Butler.
© 2012 John Wiley & Sons, Ltd. Published 2012 by John Wiley & Sons, Ltd. and the British Psychological Society.

experiences may intersect with sexual identity with reference to research about non-heterosexual experiences of chronic illness. In doing so, we will explore how health inequalities affect lesbian, gay and bisexual (LGB) lives and how marginalisation based on sexual identity intersect with experiences of ill health.

Health Disparities Between LGB People and the General Population

With the advent of HIV/AIDS, gay and bisexual men have come under intense public health surveillance. Originally referred to as Gay Related Immune Deficiency (GRID) and dubbed a 'gay cancer' or 'gay plague' by tabloid media (Watney, 1987), it was apparent that gay men were disproportionately affected by the disease early on in the AIDS crisis. However, it took much political activism by LGB communities for gay men's health to be placed firmly on the public health agendas of national governments (Epstein, 2003). Ever since, HIV (and sexual health more broadly) has widely come to be considered a 'gay health issue' (Kitzinger & Peel, 2005) and understandably has dominated the gay men's health agenda. Not only has the dominance of this disease led to what Eric Rofes (2007) has referred to as a HIV-centric view of gay men's health, but the health needs of lesbian and bisexual women have been marginalised.

While HIV is certainly an important health concern within gay and bisexual men's communities, there are also a range of other health issues that affect them. There is a danger that the importance placed on HIV as a 'gay health issue' may result in the relative risk of other health conditions for LGB people being underestimated and overlooked. Much has been written on the subject of HIV/AIDS (see for example, Frederick, 2004; Kanellakis, 2000) and on sexual health generally, so in this chapter we focus on health behaviours such as substance use, diet and physical activity as well as chronic health conditions other than HIV/AIDS. It should be noted, however, that chronic health conditions can often lead to sexual health problems, such as sexual dysfunction. In addition, those living with HIV/AIDS may have similar experiences as those with other chronic health concerns, and HIV (or its treatment) may actually increase the likelihood of developing other conditions such as cancer and diabetes.

Since the 1970s, research has been conducted which examined the disparities in health between LGB people and the general population. Much of this research was conducted on shoe-string budgets either by LGBT (LGB and

Transsexual) community groups or by LGB academics. Questions about sexual identity have rarely been included in large public health surveys, resulting in only a small number of studies that can claim to be representative of the population. Furthermore, most population-based studies have examined disparities in mental or sexual health, with only a handful reporting disparities in physical health behaviours and/or conditions. Thus, much of the information we have about the physical health of LGB people comes from studies which have used non-probability sampling and has compared findings from among the LGB community with large surveys of the 'general' population.

Smoking, alcohol use and obesity

It is widely recognised that the use of substances such as tobacco and excessive alcohol consumption are leading causes of chronic health conditions. For instance, smoking significantly increases the risk of developing cardiovascular disease, chronic obstructive pulmonary disease, stroke, emphysema and various forms of cancer (particularly lung cancer, pancreatic cancer and cancers of the mouth and larynx). Similarly, excessive alcohol consumption is associated with an elevated risk of liver disease, dementia, stroke and cancers of the mouth, larynx, liver, breast and bowel. From a review of the literature regarding smoking among LGB people (1987–2000), Ryan *et al.* (2001) found that smoking rates among non-heterosexuals were consistently higher than those reported nationally, in some cases almost double. This finding has more recently been replicated in population-based studies in the US and Canada (Conron *et al.*, 2010; Gruskin *et al.*, 2007; Steele *et al.*, 2009). Similarly, early research suggested that lesbians and gay men were at an alarmingly higher risk of problem drinking than their heterosexual counterparts (e.g. Fifield *et al.*, 1977). However such studies were often methodologically flawed, typically recruiting participants directly from gay and lesbian bars. A review of the literature (1973-1993) by Bux (1996), suggested that evidence for higher levels of alcohol problems has been more robust for lesbians than for gay men, although both appear to be less likely to abstain from alcohol completely and less likely to reduce their alcohol consumption as they age. Again, this trend has been found more recently with a large sample of Californians in which lesbians were found to be significantly more likely than heterosexual women to be heavy drinkers, while gay men had a borderline significant increased risk for heavy drinking compared to heterosexual men (Gruskin & Gordon, 2006). Lesbians and gay men have also been found to be more likely to use illicit drugs than the heterosexual population (Skinner & Otis, 1996; Conron *et al.*, 2010). A nationwide UK survey of lesbian and bisexual women's health found that two thirds of lesbian and bisexual women have smoked compared to a quarter of women in general and that lesbian and bisexual women were five times more likely to have taken drugs (Hunt & Fish, 2008).[1]

Much less research has explored other aspects of LGB people's health such as diet, exercise and weight. This is despite the fact that obesity is often cited as a leading cause of conditions such as cardiovascular disease, type 2 diabetes and certain forms of cancer. There is some evidence that lesbians may be at a higher risk of being overweight or obese. For instance, in a population-based study conducted in the US, Boehmer *et al.* (2007) reported that more than twice as many lesbians were overweight or obese than heterosexual women. Interestingly, women who identified either as bisexual or 'something else', were no more likely to be overweight/obese than heterosexual women. Conron *et al.* (2010) also reported this trend in their US study, as well as finding that gay men were less likely to be overweight/obese than heterosexual men. Again, bisexual men did not differ from heterosexual men in this regard. In fact, gay men have been reported to be at a higher risk of developing eating disorders such as anorexia nervosa (Russel & Keel, 2002; Williamson & Hartley, 1998).

Pathways between sexual identity and health

The evidence regarding disparities in the precursors of ill health between LGB people and heterosexuals are striking, yet the 'causal pathways' between sexual identity and health behaviours are not yet fully understood. A number of suggestions have been put forward. The limited social networking opportunities available for LGB people to meet, socialise or find a partner has been theorised as shaping the use of substances such as alcohol, tobacco and other recreational drugs (Weinberg, 1994). As gay bars represent a rare social space in which non-heterosexuality is the norm, many LGB people may choose to socialise more in these settings where alcohol consumption is normalised. Socialising in such venues and taking part in what may be seen as cultural activities may also be used to reaffirm a gay identity. In a recent qualitative study in Britain, Keogh *et al.* (2009) found that gay and bisexual men reported using drugs and alcohol as a 'social lubricant' to hide low self-esteem and to gain confidence so as to approach potential sexual partners.

---

[1]   With a sample size of 6178, this is the largest UK study of lesbian and bisexual women's health and social care needs.

The men also reported that alcohol was deeply embedded in gay culture and that this made it difficult for them to control their alcohol consumption, even once they had identified it as a problem. To address these issues some therapists have worked with clients to improve their self-confidence and widen their social networks beyond substance-based meeting places (Butler & Bryne, 2008), for example, joining a gay sports group. Another factor to consider is the possibility of protective factors which heterosexuals are more likely to benefit from. For example, the responsibilities of parenthood may deter some people from behaviours such as smoking and provide motivation for adopting healthier lifestyles. Merline *et al.* (2004) found that heterosexual parents were significantly less likely to be substance users than those without children. Similarly, Skinner and Otis (1996) found significantly lower levels of alcohol consumption among lesbians with children, than childless lesbians. Although substantial numbers of LGB people are parents, they remain less likely to have children than heterosexuals.

The concepts of 'internalised homophobia' and 'minority stress' have also been widely used to explain the increased use of health damaging substances among LGB people (Williamson, 2000). Internalised homophobia has been defined as a non-heterosexual's 'direction of negative social attitudes toward the self, leading to a devaluation of the self and resultant internal conflicts and poor self-regard' (Meyer & Dean, 1998, p.161). This 'poor self-regard' is widely believed to undermine LGB people's concern with their own health, interfering with health behaviour decision making. Williamson (2000) suggests that the concept of internalised homophobia has been widely used as it is 'easily understood by clients within the therapeutic milieu' and 'strikes a chord with almost all gay men and lesbians' (p.98). Hammelman (1993), for instance, found that 59 per cent of young lesbians and gay men with a substance abuse problem directly attributed this as to coping with heterosexism. The gay and bisexual participants in Keogh *et al.*'s (2009) study also suggested that alcohol and drugs were used as a form of self-medication in order to deal with conflicting feelings about their sexuality. Meyer (1995) has conceptualised internalised homophobia as a component of 'minority stress' arising 'from the totality of the minority person's experience in dominant society' (p.35). From this perspective, internalised homophobia represents one dimension of minority stress, together with perceived stigma and actual experiences of discrimination. LGB youth may be particularly vulnerable, often experiencing stressors such as homophobic school bullying, concerns about being 'different' and coming out at a time when they are susceptible to peer pressure and prone to experimenting with substance use. Furthermore, internalised homophobia and minority stress have also been suggested as a possible reason for higher rates of eating disorders among gay men (Williamson & Hartley, 1998; Reilly & Rudd, 2006) and obesity among lesbian women (Roberts *et al.*, 2010).

Some, however, have been critical about the concept of internalised homophobia, for example Kitzinger (1997) has argued that it risks repathologising LGB people: 'instead of going to a heterosexual therapist to be cured of our homosexuality, now lesbians and gay men are supposed to seek out lesbian and gay therapists to be cured of our internalized homophobia' (p.211). These individual-level solutions arguably do little to change the social and structural determinants of ill health (see also Aguinaldo, 2008). Critical health psychologists have argued for more public health and community-level interventions such as creating substance-free LGB community events and venues, and challenging the targeted advertising of alcohol to LGB consumers (Adams *et al.*, 2007). Another problem with the minority stress hypothesis is that it fails to explain the gendered pattern in some of the health disparities found. For instance, why are lesbians more likely to be obese than gay men and why are gay men more likely to suffer from anorexia than lesbians? Siever (1994) proposed that this may be a result of cultural gender differences in the importance that men and women place on the weight of their sexual partners. According to this theory, men place greater emphasis on the slenderness of their partners and, consequently, gay men and heterosexual women may be under greater pressure to be thin than heterosexual men or lesbian women. Lesbians for instance have been found to have less negative attitudes towards being overweight than their heterosexual counterparts (Roberts *et al.*, 2010).

While Williamson (2000) cautions against internalised homophobia being uncritically adopted as a catch-all explanation for health differences between LGB people and heterosexuals, he has argued that it is important to recognise that many LGB people do benefit from therapeutic interventions which attend to this issue. He emphasises the need for therapists to address problems as their clients see them, using the client's own language. The challenge of the therapist may be to actively affirm their client's non-heterosexual identity (Langdridge, 2007) and support LGB clients in consciousness-raising about the socio-political nature of heterosexism, in a way which minimises a pathologising of the client (Russell & Bohan, 2007).

Prevalence of chronic illnesses among the LGB community

Currently, there is very little data about the prevalence of chronic health conditions among the LGB population as data on sexual identity is not routinely collected in epidemiological studies. From large scale, population-based health surveys which have included questions about sexual identity (conducted largely in North America), non-heterosexuals have been found to be more likely to report a diagnosis of asthma, which the researchers suggested may be related to increased rates of smoking and urbanicity (Cochran & Mays, 2007; Conron *et al.*, 2010). Items regarding other health conditions such as diabetes and cardiovascular disease were included in studies by Mays *et al.* (2002) and Conron *et al.* (2010); however, no differences were found despite higher rates of risk factors such as smoking and obesity among lesbians. This was partly attributed to the relative young age of the studies' samples as well as under-detection among LGB people. Lesbians have also been found to be at greater risk of developing breast cancer than heterosexuals (Dibble *et al.*, 2004). This may be due to risk factors such as higher rates of smoking and obesity, but also due to a higher rate of nulliparity (not bearing children), thus being less likely to breastfeed[2]. Evidence suggests that breastfeeding offers significant protection against breast cancer and may also protect against endometrial cancer (Newcomb *et al.*, 1994; Newcomb & Trentham-Dietz, 2000). In addition, a higher rate of polycystic ovary syndrome (PCOS) has been found among lesbians than heterosexual women (Agrawal *et al.*, 2004), a condition which is associated with a higher risk of endometrial cancer, cardiovascular disease and type 2 diabetes.

A note of caution

Although it is important to be aware of health inequalities between heterosexuals and non-heterosexuals, there is also a need for caution about the framing of certain health problems as 'LGB health issues'. Treating LGB people as having a distinct health profile is problematic for a number of reasons (Epstein, 2003): to do so may overemphasise the risk of developing certain conditions (e.g. HIV), while downplaying the threat posed by conditions such as cardiovascular disease, which may be substantially larger for LGB people. There is also a danger that conceptualisations of 'risk' may conflate identity and behaviour. For instance, Fish (2006) argued that it is important to stress that it is childlessness, smoking and being overweight that are risk factors for breast cancer, not being a lesbian. However, health

---

[2] Although estimates suggest that about a third of British lesbians are mothers (Golombok *et al.*, 2003), many lesbians are not birth (or biological) mothers but social (or non-biological) mothers and therefore breastfeeding rates for lesbians are further lowered (see also Zizzo, 2009). It is also important to acknowledge the increase in planned lesbian (and gay male) parented families in recent decades, which brings with it culturally specific health issues (see, for example, Peel, 2010).

issues that are the same for heterosexuals and LGB people require culturally sensitive interventions. For example, there is a growing subculture of gay and bisexual men who describe themselves as 'bears' and celebrate being physically large as more masculine (Gough & Flanders, 2009). Although obesity may not be more prevalent among gay men than heterosexual men, obesity is rising among the population in general and this will likely include gay men. Interventions designed to tackle obesity, therefore should also consider the culturally specific ways in which health issues may be understood within LGB communities.

In addition, health heterogeneity *within* LGB communities needs acknowledgement. Little is known about bisexual health specifically, as few studies have examined bisexual people separately. However, there may be important differences between bisexuals when compared to lesbians and gay men (Boehmer *et al.*, 2007; Conron *et al.*, 2010). Several recent studies have found that bisexual women report poorer physical health than lesbians and heterosexual women and are more likely to smoke and drink heavily (Conron *et al.*, 2010; Steele *et al.*, 2009). One possible reason for this is that bisexuals may experience greater levels of minority stress due to stigma from both heterosexuals and the lesbian and gay community (Dobinson *et al.*, 2005).

We should not assume, however, that LGB people's sexual identities are more consequential for their physical health, than other social categories such as race/ethnicity, social class, gender, ability, religion and so on. We know little about health disparities between racial/ethnic minority LGB people compared to heterosexuals from the same racial/ethnic group or to white LGB people (although see Mays *et al.*, 2002; and Chapter 3). Moreover, while such aggregate differences in health are vitally important for public health, practitioners working with individual clients should treat them as such and not assume that their client's health behaviours or concerns are attributable to their sexual identity.

Living with Chronic Illness as an LGB Person

Chronic illness refers to long term health conditions which are rarely completely cured (Dowrick *et al.*, 2005), the most common of which include cardiovascular disease, arthritis, respiratory problems, diabetes, epilepsy and cancer. In just over a century there has been a dramatic shift in the leading causes of mortality from acute to chronic diseases. This has largely been the result of improved sanitation and public health surveillance together with advances in medicine. More effective medications have also seen diseases such as HIV transformed from terminal to chronic conditions (Frederick, 2004). Chronic conditions may lead to loss of physical and/or mental functioning and may result in reduced life expectancy and quality of life. Chronic diseases are often understood within a biomedical model of biology, physiological pathology and medical treatment. Yet the psychosocial factors involved in living with illness are important in order to provide holistic care (Engel, 1977). The term 'illness' is often used by psychologists over the more medical term 'disease', to incorporate the psychosocial experience of living with a chronic condition (Radley, 1994). However, the term 'illness' in some ways is problematic as many people with chronic conditions may effectively be 'well' but will never be cured. For this reason, clients may not consider themselves to be 'ill' and may prefer the term 'health condition'.

Receiving a medical diagnosis may come as a shock and can be difficult to come to terms with. Illness disrupts our taken-for-granted assumptions about life, gives rise to questions like 'why me?' and requires a re-working of one's sense of self (Bury, 1982). Uncertainty is a key aspect of living with many chronic conditions (Shuman, 1996) and considerable psychological adjustment may be required. Many chronic illnesses require life-long treatment, sometimes in the form of complex medical regimens which demand difficult lifestyle adjustments. There is often a negative impact on a person's quality of life, for instance people with chronic illness are more likely to experience stress, depression, disability, sexual dysfunction and disrupted personal relationships (Smith & Nicassio, 1995). The challenges posed by illness require social support from others and it can be helpful to discuss feelings of fear, loss or sadness that accompany living with illness. However, people may feel unable to discuss such feelings with their friends and families. For instance, they may not wish to upset others as illness not only affects the individual diagnosed but also those close to them. Well intentioned friends and family may also refuse to engage with such emotions and insist that they 'think positive' (Turner & Kelly, 2000). A diagnosis of chronic illness also often confers a level of stigma as the individual is viewed by others and/or themselves as being 'different' (Goffman, 1963). The level of stigma attached to different illnesses will be culturally specific, although those which are transmittable (e.g. HIV) or viewed as the result of unhealthy lifestyles (e.g. type 2 diabetes, lung cancer, HIV) are likely to be particularly stigmatising. As many chronic conditions are not noticeable, people may choose to conceal their illness in order to avoid discrimination and awkward social interactions (Joachim & Acorn, 2000).

Experiences of illness are as diverse as those who live with them. The importance of 'cultural competence' is increasingly being recognised within health care in relation to race/ethnicity (Tseng & Streltzer, 2008), yet sexual orientation is often not considered (cf. Garnero, 2010). An exception to this is sexual health and HIV services which are often aware and inclusive of their gay male service-users. One possible reason why sexual identity is often not considered in relation to other conditions is that, unlike HIV, many illnesses are not considered 'gay health issues'. Thus sexuality is often not deemed to be of relevance. Lipton (2004) has suggested that gay men living with illnesses other than HIV may feel they are living with the 'wrong' illness to receive support from within their communities and that mainstream healthcare may be poorly equipped to provide support sensitive to non-heterosexual individuals.

Many of the concerns of LGB people with chronic health conditions are likely to be similar to those of heterosexuals. There may, however, be some important differences and understanding these may be vital in order to provide adequate and sensitive support (Wilkinson, 2002). Unfortunately, there is a currently a lack of research which considers LGB people's experiences of chronic illnesses (other than HIV). We do know that in addition to problems of living with a long-term condition, those who identify as LGB are likely to experience disruptive life events associated with their sexuality. For instance, coming out (Clarke, 2007) and incidents of homophobia (Peel, 1999) may cause considerable stress. Some LGB people may also receive less social support from their relatives due to family members' non-acceptance of their sexuality. Alternatively, illness might heal rifts within families resulting from coming out.

Elsewhere we have reported the findings from a qualitative online survey of LGB people's experiences of chronic illness(es) (Jowett & Peel, 2009). Data was collected from 190 people living with chronic health conditions mainly from the USA and the UK. Respondents were living with a wide variety of chronic illnesses, approximately half of whom had more than one. The most common conditions represented within the study were arthritis (20%), hypertension (20%), diabetes (15%), asthma (14%) and chronic fatigue syndrome (8%). HIV/AIDS and cancer were jointly the eighth most prevalent illnesses in the sample (6%). The analysis focused on four themes within the respondents' comments: stigma within LGB communities, social isolation, heteronormative forms of support and homophobia from health care professionals.

Stigma

Many respondents reported feeling that LGB communities failed to provide support or display awareness of those with chronic conditions other than HIV. Many experienced stigma from within LGB communities because of their health condition. LGB people with chronic health conditions may be viewed as experiencing multiple forms of stigmatisation based on both their sexual identity and their illness. In a follow up interview study, we also found that diabetic gay men reported a concern that others might mistake diabetes medication for signs of a positive HIV status (Jowett *et al.*, in press). This highlights that gay men's experience of health problems may further be shaped by the association of illness with HIV within gay male communities and HIV-related stigma. Lipton (2004) has argued that gay men (and we would add lesbians and bisexuals) living with chronic health conditions 'must negotiate a complex and at times chaotic web of stigmatized identities' (p.9). However, other survey respondents provided accounts of LGB communities being supportive and found their LGB friends to be more accepting of their differences than they found elsewhere. Bisexual respondents in particular described their own communities in this way, while gay men reported that a youth and fitness orientated gay male culture not only excluded and stigmatised older gay men but also young gay men with health problems.

Isolation

Respondents also reported experiencing various forms of isolation. Those with more disabling illnesses who relied on the assistance of others described difficulties in accessing LGB venues. For instance one woman commented that she could not get to the gay area of her city and could not get a volunteer to pick her up a gay magazine (see further examples in Chapter 9). Others reported avoiding LGB venues which are often bars or nightclubs, believing them not to be conducive to good health. Many described feeling like a minority within a minority (cf. Bennett & Coyle, 2007) and expressed a desire to meet other LGB people living with their health condition. As a result, several had tried to connect with others by creating their own online support groups. While such groups were felt to be beneficial, they were rarely as active as they had hoped for. Unlike HIV/AIDS which has many organisations, support groups and publications which specialise in helping gay men, only a few exist for LGB people living with other chronic health conditions. Walden (2009) conducted a study of one such group in the US which provides social care services for lesbians living with chronic illness. She explored the motivating factors that led women to contact the organisation and found that loneliness was often the primary reason for women using the service. A number of clients were either not out to family members or had a strained or non-existent relationship with their families of origin. This rare form of support thus fulfilled needs unmet by health services and family members as well as relieved social isolation by acting as a point of contact with the lesbian community.

Heteronormative support

As Lipton (2004) notes, those services and sources of support aimed at the general population are rarely sensitive to the needs of LGB people. This was also reported by our survey respondents who suggested that support groups did not address their concerns and that written forms of support (e.g. websites, self-help books) assumed that the reader was heterosexual. This can be seen in the titles of self-help books such as *Prostate Cancer: a guide for women and the men they love* (Wainrib *et al.*, 1996). Support groups for illnesses which predominantly affect either men (e.g. prostate and testicular cancer) or women (breast cancer, polycystic ovary syndrome) were also described as being dominated by the concerns of heterosexuals (see the following client story, and Perlman, 2005).

Michelle's Story

Michelle is a lesbian with polycystic ovary syndrome (PCOS). Due to her condition Michelle began to experience facial hair growth and found it difficult to lose weight. After several strangers had made unkind comments to her in public, she decided to join a support group for women with PCOS. At her first meeting Michelle described these experiences to the group. In response, another group member shared her own 'humiliating' experience of being called a lesbian by a teenager in her neighbourhood. Feeling uncomfortable in this situation, Michelle chose not to come out within the support group. While other group members discussed their husbands openly, Michelle was careful not to refer to the gender of her partner. Furthermore, many of the group discussions were dominated by concerns about fertility which was not a concern shared by Michelle. Over the following months she began to feel increasingly alienated within the group and soon stopped attending.

Homophobia within health care contexts

Therapists should also be aware that experiences, and fear, of heterosexism may chequer LGB people's interactions with health services. Respondents reported homophobic incidents within health and social care contexts, which took on many different forms. For instance, one respondent reported that nurses had made judgemental comments about his sexuality. Another reported that a fellow patient had told her that she would go to hell while in a doctor's waiting room. Such experiences also extended beyond the traditional healthcare contexts of doctor's surgeries and hospital wards. For example, one respondent reported experiencing homophobia within her own home from a home help worker. What makes heterosexism different within health or social care contexts is that the LGB person often feels a heightened state of vulnerability as their care lies in the hands of those very professionals. For instance, the same respondent also stated that she was too frightened to make a complaint in case she got someone who was worse. Even when respondents had no experience of homophobia, some reported concealing their sexual identity from health professionals for fear that it might negatively affect their care.

Research has shown that despite being out in most other contexts (e.g. to family and at work), many people do not disclose their sexual identity to their healthcare professionals (Eliason & Schope, 2001). In many cases, LGB people will report that their sexuality does not appear relevant to the treatment of their condition (Fish, 2006). While it may not be necessary for health professionals to know the details of each patient's personal relationship, it is important that LGB people feel comfortable enough to share personal information freely and discuss their home situation or sexual behaviour should it become relevant. In the study we conducted with LGB people with diabetes (Jowett *et al.*, in press), one gay man described how he was not out to health professionals responsible for the care of his diabetes and would visit a gay men's sexual health clinic for his sexual health. This compartmentalisation of his health, however, began to cause difficulties when he developed sexual dysfunction related to his diabetes and had to contemplate discussing his sexual behaviour with his diabetes clinician.

Irrespective of how widespread (or not) homophobia is within healthcare today, many LGB people will have heard horror stories and it is understandable that they may have some trepidation about being out in such contexts. Even those who are out may fear that should they be admitted to hospital, health professionals may not acknowledge their partner or deny them hospital visits. It is widely believed that the introduction of civil partnerships solved this problem by giving registered partners next-of-kin status. However, as guidelines by the Royal College of Nursing and Unison (2004) point out, the term 'next-of-kin' has never had much legal meaning in healthcare and health professionals should always respect who their clients wish to have around and who they wish to have information given to, irrespective of the legal status of the relationship. The Civil Partnership Act (2004) may however have brought such issues to widespread attention and sent a signal to health professionals that same-sex relationships should be treated equally. Furthermore, subsequent equality legislation in the UK has outlawed discriminatory behaviour in the provision of goods and services on the basis of sexual orientation and this includes the delivery of health services. Despite this, legal prohibition of discrimination alone is unlikely to eradicate heterosexism altogether due to underreporting of homophobic incidents (Peel, 1999) as well as the insidious and mundane nature of some forms of heterosexism (Peel, 2001). Therefore, health professionals and therapists should actively seek to make LGB people feel safe (see Garnero, 2010; McNair & Hegarty, 2010).

Heterosexist assumptions and stereotypes

In addition to unacknowledged differences between heterosexual and non-heterosexual experiences of illness, there may also be heterosexist assumptions of differences where in fact there are similarities. For instance, Wilkinson (2002) found that lesbians with breast cancer experienced heterosexist assumptions that lesbians are not concerned about their physical appearance or do not 'need' their breasts. In contrast to this, the women emphasised that their breasts played an important role in their sex lives, their appearance and in some cases motherhood. Clinicians should not assume that someone in a same-sex relationship will not be concerned about the effect an illness or its treatment might have on their fertility. In such cases, clients should always be offered the same options (e.g. freezing sperm or eggs before treatment) and support that would be offered to heterosexual individuals and couples.

Conversely, there is often an assumption that gay men will be more concerned about changes in their physical appearance either as a result of a health condition or as a result of its treatment. Although there may be cultural differences which predispose gay men to body image concerns (as described previously) that may be exacerbated by medical conditions (Hanjorgiris et al., 2004), such assumptions risk perpetuating stereotypes of gay men as narcissistic. Their primary concern, instead, is likely to be their future health rather than their physical appearance. Mitteldorf (2005) notes that, despite much concern pre-surgery, none of his gay male clients who had undergone prostate cancer surgery expressed concerns about their abdominal scars. In fact, he suggests that those who do raise their scars in therapy often describe them in positive ways such as 'badges of honour' or as 'war wounds'.

Sexual dysfunction

Changes in sexual functioning associated with chronic illness may also need to be addressed. Sexual dysfunction may even be the first sign of a chronic health condition which is yet to be diagnosed. LGB people are often notably absent from the clinical and therapeutic literature on sexual dysfunction and, as noted previously, heteronormativity is pervasive within the self-help literature surrounding this topic. The very definition of erectile dysfunction is often framed in terms which are inappropriate for gay men with references to vaginal intercourse. For instance Roszler and Rice's (2007) self-help text *Sex and Diabetes* asks; 'have you been experiencing difficulty recently in achieving erections that you and your partner consider adequate for vaginal intercourse?' (p.8). Moreover, conceptualising erectile dysfunction in terms of a failure to 'perform' intercourse fails to acknowledge erectile problems in the context of other sexual activities and the wider sexual repertoires of LGB people (Jowett *et al.*, in press; Cove & Boyle, 2002). The experiences of a single gay man may be very different from that of a heterosexual man in a monogamous relationship (see the following client story). Nichols and Shernoff (2000) and Campbell and Whiteley (2006) provide broad discussions about working with lesbian and gay clients with sexual problems, however, the way in which particular health conditions may complicate these problems should also be considered (Goldstone, 2005). Such concerns may extend beyond sexual 'dysfunction' *per se*, for instance our interviews with diabetic gay men revealed that hypoglycaemia during or after sex with a new or casual partner was also a concern (Jowett *et al.*, in press).

Colin's Story

Colin is a single gay man with type 1 diabetes. He has suffered from erectile dysfunction, a complication of his condition, since a relatively young age. He does not feel like a 'typical' gay man and has had few sexual or romantic relationships throughout his life. Colin believes gay culture to be highly sexualised and is anxious that potential partners will expect to engage in sex very shortly after meeting. He fears he will be rejected once other gay men discover his sexual difficulties and that if someone were to find out about his erectile problems, gossip might spread throughout his small local gay community. He believes this problem to have had a severe impact on his self-esteem, affecting not only his ability to seek a partner but also his ability to form new friendships.

Much less has been written about women's sexual dysfunction in general and lesbian and bisexual women in particular. Vascular and endocrine complications of chronic conditions such as diabetes may cause reduced desire for sex, decreased arousal, and difficulties in achieving orgasm. In addition, women may experience reduced vaginal lubrication and recurrent thrush. For further discussion of sexual problems arising from chronic illness and disability see Chapter 9.

Summary

In this chapter we have highlighted some of relationships between sexual orientation and physical health. While HIV is commonly understood to be a gay men's health issue, a range of health inequalities between LGB people and the general population may result in a higher prevalence of some of the most common chronic health conditions. More epidemiological data on chronic health conditions which include information on sexual orientation is needed, as is more research which examines health disparities within LGB communities. Heterosexism and minority stress are widely understood to contribute to health inequalities, and although therapy for individuals with health problems or concerns is important, as critical health psychologists we also advocate more community-level public health interventions. LGB people living with chronic illness experience the same concerns as heterosexuals living with such conditions, however, LGB people also face stigmatisation, isolation, discrimination and heterosexist assumptions based on their sexual identity. Future research in this area could usefully use qualitative methods to explore LGB experiences of a range of illnesses not usually considered 'LGB health issues' and practitioners should endeavour to provide culturally sensitive support for their LGB clients.

Guidelines for Good Practice

- Consider the impact that heterosexism and homophobia may have on the physical health of clients.

- However, with this in mind, avoid making assumptions. Treat the client as an individual and focus on their unique concerns and their own interpretations of their problems.
- Educate yourself about the cultural stereotypes that are in circulation about LGB communities (e.g. see Peel 2002, 2005, 2009) in order to enhance understanding about how they may impact on LGB clients with physical health problems.
- Make yourself aware of any LGB health-related support groups or services (virtual or otherwise) and consider referring clients to these where appropriate.
- Visit www.healthwithpride.nhs.uk: this website has been developed by NHS Barking and Dagenham as part of their effort to better serve their LGB service-users and staff. It provides a wealth of information about LGB health inequalities, working with LGB patients, the rights of LGB service-users, ideas for LGB health promotion and many useful links to other relevant websites.

References

Adams, J., McCreanor, T. & Braun, V. (2007). Alcohol and gay men: Consumption, promotion and policy responses. In V. Clarke & E. Peel (Eds.), *Out in psychology: Lesbian, gay, bisexual, trans and queer perspectives*. Chichester: John Wiley & Sons, Ltd.

Agrawal, R., Sharma, S., Bekir, J., Conway, G., Bailey, J., Balen, A.H. & Prelevic, G. (2004). Prevalence of polycystic ovaries and polycystic ovary syndrome in lesbian women compared with heterosexual women. *Fertility and Sterility*, *82*(5), 1352–1357.

Aguinaldo, J.P. (2008). The social construction of gay oppression as a determinant of gay men's health: 'Homophobia is killing us'. *Critical Public Health, 18*(1), 87–96.

Bennett, C. & Coyle, A. (2007). A minority within a minority: Experiences of gay men with intellectual disabilities. In V. Clarke & E. Peel (Eds.), *Out in psychology: Lesbian, gay, bisexual, trans and queer perspectives*. Chichester: John Wiley & Sons, Ltd.

Boehmer, U., Bowen, D.J. & Bauer, G.R. (2007). Overweight and obesity in sexual-minority women: Evidence from population-based data. *American Journal of Public Health, 97*(6), 1134–1140.

Bury, M. (1982). Chronic illness as biographical disruption. *Sociology of Health and Illness, 4*(2), 167–182.

Butler, C. & Byrne, A. (2008). Queer in practice. In L. Moon (Ed.) *Feeling queer or queer feelings?* London: Routledge.

Bux, D.A. (1996). The epidemiology of problem drinking in gay men and lesbians: A critical review. *Clinical Psychology Review, 16*(4), 277–298.

Campbell, T. & Whiteley, C. (2006). Working clinically with gay men with sexual performance problems. *Sexual and Relationship Therapy, 21*(4), 419–428.

Clarke, C. (2007). Facilitating gay men's coming out: An existential phenomeno- logical exploration. In E. Peel, V. Clarke & J. Drescher (Eds.), *British lesbian, gay and bisexual psychologies: Theory, research and practice.* New York, NY: The Haworth Medical Press.

Cochran, S.D. & Mays, V.M. (2007). Physical health complaints among lesbians, gay men and bisexual and homosexually experienced heterosexual individuals: Results from the California Quality of Life survey. *American Journal of Public Health, 97*(11), 2048–2055.

Conron, K.J., Mimiaga, M.J. & Landers, S.J. (2010). A population-based study of sexual orientation identity and gender differences in adult health. *American Journal of Public Health, 100,* 1953–1960.

Cove, J. & Boyle, M. (2002). Gay men's self-defined sexual problems, perceived causes and factors in remission. *Sexual and Relationship Therapy, 17*(2), 137–147.

Dibble, S., Roberts, S.A. & Nussey, B. (2004). Breast cancer risk profiles between lesbians and their heterosexual sisters. *Women's Health Issues, 14,* 60–68.

Dobinson, C., MacDonell, J., Hampson, E., Clipsham, J. & Chow, C. (2005). Im- proving access and quality of public health services for bisexuals. *Journal of Bisexuality, 5*(1), 39–78.

Dowrick, C., Dixon Woods, M., Holman, H. & Weinman, J. (2005). What is chronic illness? *Chronic Illness, 1*(1), 1–6.

Eliason, M.J. & Schope, R. (2001). Does 'don't ask don't tell' apply to health care? Lesbian, gay and bisexual people's disclosure to health care providers. *Journal of the Gay and Lesbian Medical Association, 5*(4), 125–134.

Engel, G.L. (1977). The need for a new medical model. *Science, 196,* 129–136.

Epstein, S. (2003). Sexualizing governance and medicalizing identities: The emer- gence of 'State-centered' LGBT health politics in the United States. *Sexualities, 6*(2), 131–171.

Fifield, L.H., Lathan, J.D. & Phillips, C. (1977). *Alcoholism in the gay community: The price of alienation, isolation and oppression.* Los Angeles, CA: Gay Community Services Center.

Fish, J. (2006). *Heterosexism in health and social care.* Basingstoke: Palgrave Macmillan.

Frederick, R.J. (2004). The multidimensional challenge of psychotherapy with HIV positive gay men. In B. Lipton (Ed.) *Gay men living with chronic illnesses and disability: From crisis to crossroads.* Binghamton, NY: Harrington Park Press.

Garnero, T.L. (2010). Providing culturally sensitive diabetes care and education for the lesbian, gay, bisexual and transgender (LGBT) community. *Diabetes Spectrum, 23*(3), 178–182.

Goffman, E. (1963). *Stigma: Notes on the management of a spoiled identity.* Engle- wood Cliffs, NJ: Prentice Hall.

Goldstone, S.E. (2005). The ups and downs of gay sex after prostate cancer treatment. In G. Perlman & J. Drescher (Eds.), *A gay man's guide to prostate cancer.* New York, NY: Harrington Park Press.

Golombok, S., Perry, B., Burston, A., Murray, C., Mooney-Somers, J., Stevens, M. & Golding, J. (2003). Children with lesbian parents: A community study. *Developmental Psychology, 39*(1), 20–33.

Gough, B. & Flanders, G. (2009). Celebrating 'obese' bodies: Gay 'bears' talk about weight, body image and health. *International Journal of Men's Health, 8*(3), 235–253.

Gruskin, E.P. & Gordon, N. (2006). Gay/Lesbian sexual orientation increases risk for cigarette smoking and heavy drinking among members of a large Northern Californian health plan. *BMC Public Health, 6,* 241.

Gruskin, E.P., Greenwood, G.L., Matevia, M., Pollack, L.M. & Bye, L.L. (2007). Disparities in smoking between the lesbian, gay and bisexual population and the general population in California. *American Journal of Public Health, 97,* 1496–1502.

Hammelman, T. (1993). Gay and lesbian youth: Contributing factors to serious attempts or considerations of suicide. *Journal of Gay and Lesbian Mental Health, 2*(1), 77–89.

Hanjorgiris, W.F., Rath, J.F. & O'Neill, J.H. (2004). Gay men living with chronic illness or disability: A sociocultural, minority group perspective on mental health. In B. Lipton (Ed.), *Gay men living with chronic illnesses and disability: From crisis to crossroads.* Binghamton, NY: Harrington Park Press.

Hunt, R. & Fish, J. (2008). *Prescription for change: Lesbian and bisexual women's health check.* Retrieved 20 May 2011 from www.stonewall.org.uk/documents/prescription'for'change.pdf.

Joachim, G. & Acorn, S. (2000). Stigma of visible and invisible chronic conditions. *Journal of Advanced Nursing, 32*(1), 243–248.

Jowett, A. & Peel, E. (2009). Chronic illness in non-heterosexual contexts: An online survey of experiences. *Feminism & Psychology, 19*(4), 454–474.

Jowett, A., Peel, E. & Shaw, R. (in press). Sex and diabetes: A thematic analysis of gay and bisexual men's accounts *Journal of Health Psychology.*

Kanellakis, P. (2000). Issues in HIV/AIDS counselling. In C. Neal & D. Davies (Eds.), *Issues in therapy with lesbian, gay, bisexual and transgender clients.* Buckingham: Open University Press.

Karademas, E.C. (2009). Counselling psychology in medical settings: The promising role of counselling health psychology. *European Journal of Counselling Psychology, 1*(1), 18–37.

Keogh, P., Reid, D., Bourne, A., Weatherburn, P., Hickson, F., Jessup, K. & Hammond, G. (2009). *Wasted opportunities: Problematic alcohol and drug use among gay men and bisexual men.* London: Sigma Research.

Kitzinger, C. (1997). Lesbian and gay psychology. In D. Fox & I. Prilleltensky (Eds.), *Critical psychology: An introduction.* London: Sage.

Kitzinger, C. & Peel, E. (2005). The de-gaying and re-gaying of AIDS: Contested homophobias in lesbian and gay awareness training. *Discourse & Society, 16*(2), 173–197.

Langdridge, D. (2007). Gay affirmative therapy: A theoretical framework and defence. In E. Peel, V. Clarke & J. Drescher (Eds.), *British lesbian, gay and bisexual psychologies: Theory, research and practice.* New York, NY: The Haworth Medical Press.

Lipton, B. (2004). Gay men living with non-HIV chronic illness. In B. Lipton (Ed.), *Gay men living with chronic illnesses and disabilities: From crisis to crossroads.* Binghamton, NY: Harrington Park Press.

Mays, V.M., Yancey, A.K., Cochran, S.D., Weber, M. & Fielding, J.E. (2002). Heterogeneity of health disparities among African American, Hispanic, and Asian American women: Unrecognised influences of sexual orientation. *American Journal of Public Health, 92*(4), 632–639.

McNair, R.P. & Hegarty, K. (2010). Guidelines for the primary care of lesbian, gay and bisexual people: A systematic review. *Annals of Family Medicine, 8*(6), 533–541.

Merline, A.C., O'Malley, P.M., Schulenberg, J.E., Bachman, J.G. & Johnston, L.D. (2004). Substance use among adults 35 years of age: Prevelance, adulthood predictors, and impact of adolescent substance use. *American Journal of Public Health, 94*(1), 96–102.

Meyer, I.H. (1995). Minority stress and mental health in gay men. *The Journal of Health and Social Behaviour, 36*(1), 38–56.

Meyer, I. H. & Dean, L. (1998). Internalized homophobia, intimacy and sexual behaviour among gay and bisexual men. In G. Herek (Ed.), *Stigma and sexual orientation.* Thousand Oaks, CA: Sage.

Mitteldorf, D. (2005). Psychotherapy with gay prostate cancer patients. In G. Perlman & J. Drescher (Eds.) *A gay man's guide to prostate cancer.* New York, NY: Harrington Park Press.

Murray, M. (2004). Criticizing health psychology. In M. Murray (Ed.) *Critical health psychology.* Basingstoke: Palgrave Macmillan.

Newcomb, P.A., Storer, B.E., Longnecker, M.P., Mittendorf, R., Greenberg, R., Clapp, R.W., Burke, K.P., Willett, W.C. & MacMahon, B. (1994). Lactation and a reduced risk of premenopausal breast cancer. *The New England Journal of Medicine, 330*(2), 81–87.

Newcomb, P.A. & Trentham-Deitz, A. (2000). Breast feeding practices in relation to endometrial cancer risk, USA, *Cancer Causes Control, 11*(7), 663–667.

Nichols, M. & Shernoff, M. (2000). Therapy with sexual minorities: Queering practice. In S.R. Leiblum (Eds.) *Principles and practice of sex therapy* (4th edn). New York, NY: The Guilford Press.

Peel, E. (1999). Violence against lesbians and gay men: Decision making in reporting and not reporting crime. *Feminism & Psychology, 9*(2), 161–167.

Peel, E. (2001). Mundane heterosexism: Understanding incidents of the everyday. *Women's Studies International Forum, 24*(5), 541–554.

Peel, E. (2002). Lesbian and gay awareness training: Homophobia, liberalism, and managing stereotypes. In A. Coyle & C. Kitzinger (Eds.), *Lesbian and gay psychology: New perspectives*. Oxford: BPS Blackwell Publishing Ltd.

Peel, E. (2005). Effeminate 'fudge nudgers' and tomboyish 'lettuce lickers': language and the construction of sexualities in diversity training. *Psychology of Women Section Review, 7*(2), 22–34.

Peel, E. (2009). Intergroup relations in action: Questions asked about lesbian, gay and bisexual issues in diversity training. *Journal of Community & Applied Social Psychology, 19*, 271–285.

Peel, E. (2010). Pregnancy loss in lesbian and bisexual women: An online survey of experiences. *Human Reproduction, 25*(3), 721–727.

Peel, E. & Thomson, M. (2009). Lesbian, gay, bisexual, trans and queer health psychology: Historical development and future possibilities. *Feminism & Psychology, 19*(4), 427–436.

Perlman, G. (2005). Prostate cancer, the group, and me. In G. Perlman & J. Drescher (Eds.) *A gay man's guide to prostate cancer*. New York, NY: Harrington Park Press.

Radley, A. (1994). *Making sense of illness: The social psychology of health and disease*. London: Sage.

Reilly, A. & Rudd, N.A. (2006). Is internalized homonegativity related to body image? *Family & Consumer Sciences Research Journal, 35*(1), 58–73.

Roberts, S.J., Stuart-Shor, E.M. and Oppenheimer, R.A. (2010). Lesbians' attitudes and beliefs towards overweight and weight reduction. *Journal of Clinical Nursing, 19*(13–14), 1986–1994.

Rofes, E. (2007). *Thriving: Gay men's health in the 21ˢᵗ century*. Retrieved 13 June 2010 from: http://www.ericrofes.com/pdf/THRIVING.pdf.

Roszler, J. & Rice, D. (2007). *Sex and diabetes: For him and for her*. New York, NY: American Diabetes Association.

Royal College of Nursing & Unison (2004). *Not 'just' a friend: Best practice guidelines on health care for lesbian, gay and bisexual service users and their families*. London: Royal College of Nursing and Unison.

Russell, C.J. & Keel, P.K. (2002). Homosexuality as a specific risk factor for eating disorders in men. *International Journal of Eating Disorders, 31*, 300–306.

Russell, G.M. & Bohan, J.S. (2007). Liberating psychotherapy: Liberation psychology and psychotherapy with LGBT clients. *Journal of Gay and Lesbian Psychotherapy, 11*(3/4), 59–79.

Ryan, H., Wortley, P.M., Easton, A., Pederson, L. & Greenwood, G. (2001). Smoking among lesbians, gays, and bisexuals: A review of the literature. *American Journal of Preventive Medicine, 21*(2), 142–149.

Siever, M.D. (1994). Sexual orientation and gender as factors in socioculturally acquired vulnerability to body dissatisfaction and eating disorders. *Journal of Consulting and Clinical Psychology, 62*(2), 252–260.

Shuman, R. (1996). *The psychology of chronic illness*. New York, NY: Basic Books.

Skinner, W.F. & Otis, M.D. (1996). Drug and alcohol use among lesbian and gay people in a southern U.S. sample: Epidemiological, comparative, and methodological findings from the Trilogy Project. *Journal of Homosexuality, 30*(3), 59–92.

Smith, T.W. & Nicassio, P.M. (1995). Psychological practice: Clinical application of the biopsychosocial model. In P.M. Nicassio and T.W. Smith (Eds.), *Managing chronic illness: A biopsychosocial perspective.* Washington, DC: American Psychological Association.

Steele, L.S., Ross, L.E., Dobinson, C., Veldhuizen, S. & Tinmouth, J.M. (2009). Women's sexual orientation and health: Results from a Canadian population-based survey. *Women & Health, 49*(5), 353–364.

Tseng, W. & Streltzer, J. (2008). *Cultural competence in health care: A guide for professionals.* New York, NY: Springer.

Turner, J. & Kelly, B. (2000). Emotional dimensions of chronic disease. *Western Journal of Medicine, 172*(2), 124–128.

Wainrib, B., Haber, S. & Droller, M. (1996). *Prostate cancer: A guide for women and the men they love.* New York, NY: Dell Publishing Group.

Walden, E.L. (2009). An exploration of the experience of lesbians with chronic illness. *Journal of Homosexuality, 56*(5), 548–574.

Watney, S. (1987). *Policing desire: Pornography, AIDS and the media.* London: Methuen.

Weinberg, T.S. (1994). *Gay men, drinking, and alcoholism.* Carbondale, IL: Southern Illinois University Press.

Wilkinson, S. (2002). *Lesbian health.* In A. Coyle & C. Kitzinger (Eds.) *Lesbian and gay psychology: New perspectives.* Oxford: BPS Blackwell Publishing Ltd.

Williamson, I.R. (2000). Internalized homophobia and health issues affecting lesbians and gay men. *Health Education Research, 15*(1), 97–107.

Williamson, I.R. & Hartley, P. (1998). British research into the increased vulnerability of young gay men to eating disorders and body dissatisfaction. *European Eating Disorders Review, 6*(3), 160–170.

Zizzo, G. (2009). Lesbian families and the negotiation of maternal identity through the unconventional use of breast milk. *Gay & Lesbian Issues and Psychology Review, 5*(2), 96–109.

8

Mental Health
Roshan das Nair & Sarah Fairbank

Individuals are not just their culture, their sexual orientation, their age, their nationality, or any other single identifier; they are all of the above, and much more. Although it is very, very useful to know and be appreciative of the panoply of different ways people live their lives, ultimately you can only know what is important to a person by asking her the right questions and listening to the answers (Cook-Daniels, 2007, p.11).

Lesbian, gay, bisexual (LGB) and other non-heterosexual folk have historically had a tenuous association with healthcare professionals, particularly mental health professionals. This is hardly surprising given that mental health professionals served as agents of the state to identify, categorise (or codify), diagnose, cure, discipline and/or incarcerate non-heterosexual and 'deviant' sexual practices (depending on which period of history and geographical space we are referring to) that did not conform to the prescribed norms surrounding reproductive heteronormativity (Foucault, 1978). This relationship between non-heterosexuals and mental health professionals has undergone considerable repair over the decades, but it is far from being anything more than cordial at best, as non-heterosexuals still face prejudice from some healthcare staff (Bartlett *et al.*, 2009). It must also be remembered that although the Test Revision of the Diagnostic and Statistical Manual of Mental Disorders (DSM-IV-TR; American Psychiatric Association [APA], 2000) does not include homosexuality (or bisexuality) as a diagnostic category, and the latest edition of the World Health Organization's International Classification of Diseases (ICD-10; WHO, 1994) clearly states that sexual orientation is not to be regarded as a disorder, there are many non-heterosexuals who lived in times when these diagnostic systems

Intersectionality, Sexuality and Psychological Therapies: Working with Lesbian, Gay and Bisexual Diversity,
First Edition. Edited by Roshan das Nair and Catherine Butler.

codified homosexuality as a mental disorder. This legacy has had a severe and enduring effect on some LGB people who may have been diagnosed and 'treated' on the basis of these categories. It must also be noted that there are still associations and organisations which purport to 'cure' people of their homosexuality, which although distanced from many medical and mental health professional organisations, still practice their craft unchecked by governments and health protection agencies (e.g. NARTH). Therefore, although the idea that homosexuality (and bisexuality) *per se* not being a mental illness has been clarified by professional bodies, in practice there still exists considerable leeway to disregard this position, and actively engage in the project of 'converting' or 'repairing' non-heterosexual people.

In this chapter, we focus on six aspects of mental health and sexual preference. We begin with a summary of the mental health and psychological wellbeing of LGB people; examine how discrimination, disadvantage, and disenfranchisement play a role in causing psychological distress; explore LGB people's access to mental health services, and the factors that may prevent them from accessing such services; the experiences of LGB people with severe and enduring mental health problems; how staff and services can work towards ensuring inclusion and appropriate service provision for non-heterosexuals under their care; and finally, we end with a first-person account of dealing with sexuality and mental health issues, and accessing services. While the focus of this chapter is on sexual preference, we feel that it is also important to touch upon some broader aspects of sexuality, as this encompasses sexual preference but also covers sexual ability and practices: all of which are sometimes neglected in mental health settings. This permits us to take not only an intersectional approach to understanding individuals, but also a more holistic view of the individual in his/her social context. As Loree Cook-Daniels cautions, instead of 'summing up an individual with one identity label and calling up a stereotype about that group . . . think about each new individual as a multi-dimensional collection of experiences and influences' (2007, p.1).

Mental Health and Psychological Wellbeing of LGB People

Research has shown that LGB people in the UK experience greater 'psychological distress' (King *et al.*, 2003) and 'mental disorder' (Warner *et al.*, 2004) than their heterosexual counterparts. These findings were further confirmed in a recent systematic review (King *et al.*, 2008). In this review (and meta-analysis) that contained data from 214 344 heterosexual and 11 971 non-heterosexual people, across 25 studies, King *et al.* found increased risk of suicidal behaviour, mental disorder (such as anxiety and depression) and substance misuse and dependence in LGB people than heterosexual people. Findings were similar in men and women, but women were more at risk of substance dependence, while lifetime risk of suicide attempts was especially high in men.

There are several reasons suggested for these high rates of mental health problems, but one that is often cited in literature is the notion of 'minority stress' (Lindquist & Hirabayashi, 1979), conceptualised as any 'excess stress individuals from stigmatized minority groups experience as a result of being part of that group' (Vanden Berghe *et al.*, 2010, p.154). These authors suggest that the specific stressors for LGB minorities include; (i) stressful events and conditions in the environment (such as workplace discrimination), (ii) the expectation of such stressful events, and (iii) *internalised homophobia* or *homonegativity*[1] (the internalisation of negative societal attitudes towards non-heterosexuals: for a critique of this construct see Chapter 7). We add to this list a fourth category of stressors (related to the second), which is, *perceived* discrimination that non-heterosexuals feel they will face. The King *et al.* (2008) review also comments on the role that discrimination, stigma, and social hostility plays in contributing to these adverse psychological states in sexual minorities.

While these aspects have been conceptualised as general factors related to mental distress, there may be other more nuanced reasons that could have a role to play in the increased incidence of specific mental health problems in non-heterosexuals. Researchers, for instance, have suggested that the reasons for significantly high rates of substance mis/use include: (i) limited social environments where non-hetersexual people can meet, with the usual places being bars, pubs, nightclubs, and other venues where alcohol is served and where there is access to other illicit substances; and (ii) internalised homonegativity (Amadio & Chung, 2004; Weber, 2008). While most of these findings are based on studies which have examined the mental health of LGB adults, other research has also found similar problems in LGB adolescents (e.g. Vanden Berghe *et al.*, 2010).

Speaking mainly from a Black and Minority Ethnic (BME) non-heterosexual perspective, das Nair (2006) suggested that models that focus on the psychosocial aspects of vulnerability to developing mental health problems should consider: (i) the internal (individual and intrapsychic)

---

[1] We prefer the term homonegativity to homophobia, as the latter almost absolves the person with the prejudicial attitudes and behaviours against non-heterosexuals of any blame, because it can be misunderstood as a specific form of 'phobia'. In such instances those with homonegative attitudes can be seen as hapless victims of a psychological condition. We do however use the term homophobia (and variants of this term) when referring to studies which have specifically employed this term.

vulnerabilities, (ii) the psychological manifestation of this vulnerability, and (iii) the external (social) contributors to such vulnerabilities. As we have already discussed some of the psychological issues related to being a non-heterosexual, we will focus on the internal and external vulnerabilities here.

Coming Out and Homonegativity

Coming out is related to identity development and consolidation. Herek and Glunt (1995) demonstrated the psychological benefits of such identity consolidation, particularly when belonging to a minority group. While coming out has largely been recognised as a rite of passage that brings along with it many advantages, it must be recognised that not only is this a potentially stressful process in itself, but also that some people experience greater stress *as a result* of their coming out (e.g. Chan, 1987). The coming out process can be protracted in some instances, particularly when there is no supportive environment to come out into, and can result in non-heterosexuals experiencing isolation caused because of a sense of not belonging, and/or because of rejection from others. This too can have adverse psychological consequences, particularly for young LGB people (Uribe & Harbeck, 1992). Healthcare staff can facilitate coming out if the individual feels that that is what is right for them. This was the experience of one of our clients:

> One of the nurses helped me tell my family that I was gay. It was so difficult but I am so glad I did it. They still don't like it but at least I don't have to pretend. It is such a relief and that makes me feel better as it is one less thing I have to worry about.

Rejection from family and friends because of sexual orientation can be a significant stressor for non-heterosexual people, particularly for teenagers and young adults. One study (Ryan *et al.*, 2009), which interviewed over 200 young LGB adults (under 25 years of age), found that higher levels of family rejection resulted in an 8.4 times higher risk of attempted suicide, 5.9 times higher risk of depression, 3.4 times higher risk of substance misuse, and high-risk sexual behaviours, compared to peers from no or low levels of family rejection.

Mental health problems and internalised homonegativity

Many of the stressors non-heterosexuals face have the potential to cause low self-esteem in individuals. This has further been linked to problems such as eating disorders (Williamson & Hartley, 1998), high-risk sexual activities (Stokes & Peterson, 1998), amongst other mental health problems (Taylor & Robertson, 1994). Conversely, high levels of self-esteem and social supports may act as a buffer to 'gay-identified stressors' (Grossman & Kerner, 1998). Low self-esteem may also be linked to internalised homonegativity and the lack of positive role models, especially for young LGB people.

The effect of internalised homophobia (or internalised homonegativity) on 'internalising' mental health problems (such as anxiety and depression; Herek *et al.*, 1998) has also been documented in several independent pieces of research (for reviews see Szymanski & Kashubeck-West, 2008; Williamson, 2000). A recent meta-analytic study (Newcomb & Mustanski, 2010) found a small to moderate correlation between internalised homophobia and symptoms of depression and anxiety, with internalised homophobia having a higher impact on depression. Another interesting finding was that there was no moderating effect of the year of data collection (cohort effects) on the relationship between internalised homophobia and mental health problems. Newcomb and Mustanski (2010) hypothesise that this could be because although there is an assumption that societies have become more tolerant towards sexual minorities over the years, and new legislation prohibits overt acts of discrimination, these changes do not tap the subtler forms of homophobia, which may still go unchallenged. Furthermore, even some changes to legislation which create tiered systems of rights and privileges may also actually contribute towards internalising this homonegativity. For instance, same-sex couples are only permitted to have civil partnerships and are not 'married' as heterosexuals are in the UK, while in other countries there is no recognition of same-sex unions, and in yet other countries, same-sex sexual activities are completely outlawed/ criminalised (see Chapter 5 for more on this). These laws are likely to have an effect on the psychological make-up of non-heterosexuals, particularly in relation to their sense of self and identity. This idea has been supported by a US study by Hatzenbuehler *et al.* (2010) who examined the relation between living in states that banned same-sex marriage during the 2004 and 2005 elections and the prevalence of psychiatric morbidity among LGB people. Using a large non-institutionalised adult sample of over 34 000 people, they found a significant increase in mental health problems (mood disorders, generalised anxiety disorder, increased alcohol use, and other psychiatric comorbidity) amongst LGB people in these states compared to other states that had more gay-affirmative legislation. There was no similar increase in mental ill-health observed in the heterosexual cohort. This study also found certain age effects of internalised homophobia, which the authors suggest is indicative of an additive mechanism that ultimately may lead to mental ill-health. While Hatzenbuehler *et al.* (2010) acknowledge that there are some limitations to their meta-analysis, their findings are still important because they establish the validity of the internalised homophobia construct, and its detrimental effects on mental health. They also apply a caveat:

> Clinicians should evaluate the relative importance of IH [internalised homophobia] and other stressors related to sexual minority status with each client rather than making assumptions about the detrimental effects of these variables. Clinicians and other mental health workers should also be aware that the effects of IH on mental health may vary between LGB subgroups, such as those of race/ethnicity (p.1028).

The Effects of Discrimination, Disadvantage, and Disenfranchisement

There are at least two ways in which discrimination, disadvantage and disenfranchisement can cause and worsen psychological distress:

(i)   through stress related to being a prejudiced minority, and
(ii) through non-heterosexual people not engaging with health services, which some may feel are complicit with and responsible for the perpetuation of discrimination.

The latter point may in fact have an adverse effect on how non-heterosexuals relate to healthcare providers and their own care. The relationship between mental health (and other healthcare) providers and non-heterosexuals with mental health difficulties is vital in many respects, not least of which includes ensuring that a clear case history is obtained (including a good sexual history if relevant). Furthermore, positive relationships offer opportunities to promote health behaviours, safer sexual practices (Quinn & Browne, 2009), and to discuss other general health concerns. This is particularly important for people with mental health problems, as they are more likely to engage in high-risk sexual behaviours, including poor condom use (Higgins *et al.*, 2006), and more vulnerable to sexual abuse. Sexual dysfunctions may also be a common side-effect of some of the medications that people with mental health issues are prescribed; these problems can have devastating consequences for the client and their sexual partner(s).

Issues Across the Lifespan

A major problem that many young non-heterosexual people go through is bullying in schools because they are LGB or *assumed* to be by other pupils. A recent Stonewall report (*The Teachers' Report*, Stonewall, 2009) found that '[n]ine in ten secondary school teachers and more than two in five primary school teachers (44%) say children and young people, regardless of their sexual orientation, currently experience homophobic bullying, name calling or harassment in their schools' (p.3). A similar report (*The School Report*, Stonewall, 2007) found that two thirds of LGB pupils experienced homophobic bullying at school. Therefore, both from teachers' and pupils' perspectives, homophobic bullying is rife. Research has pointed out that homophobic bullying at schools was also likely to have long-term negative consequences on the psychological wellbeing of LGB youth (Card & Hodges, 2008; Rivers, 1995). Such bullying can include myriad presentations and diverse outcomes, not least of which include underachievement, truancy, dropping out from school, to more severe forms of mental health problems and risks, such as suicide, in youth and sometimes this can extend into adulthood.

Some local councils have taken positive steps towards targeting and stamping out homophobic bullying in schools, and offer some guidance to staff in education on how to deal with such issues (e.g. the Anti Homophobic bullying strategy 2009–2012 for the Liverpool City Council: http://www.liverpool.gov.uk/). Therapists may want to consult such guides from their own local councils and may also direct parents (if appropriate) to such guidance, and suggest that they hold schools accountable for the safety of pupils, and that schools endorse such guidance or have explicit policies on dealing with homophobic bullying. Therapists may also want to highlight this problem to schools by writing to the board of Governors at the school where their client is from; as such issues cannot only be dealt with in therapy sessions but also in the communities where clients live. Therapists must remember that their word on such matters can have a powerful influence on shaping local school policies, which can go a long way to protecting vulnerable pupils.

The role of social support as a buffer to the development of mental ill-health has been long established (e.g. Cohen & Wills, 1985). We also know that lack of social support or *perceived* lower levels of support are risk factors for the development of depression (Meyer, 2003; Yang & Clum, 1994). Vanden Berghe *et al.* (2010), in their Belgian survey of LGB youth, found a positive effect of having 'confidant support' in reducing their stress levels. They also found that 'stigma consciousness' (i.e. being conscious of the stigma attached to being part of LGB minorities) and 'internalized homonegativity' were substantial predictors of depression. Given that for some youth, realising that they are not heterosexual and being non-heterosexual can be an alienating experience, therapists can be 'confidants' and should seek to provide a safe environment for such youngsters to share their concerns, hopes and aspirations.

Just as there are specific mental health issues that affect non-heterosexuals in youth, there are particular issues that older non-heterosexuals face (see Chapter 10). When seeing older non-heterosexuals[2] in therapy, Cook-Daniels (2007, p.3–5) suggests thinking of the following questions: Who did this person grow up around? (think about the culture in which this individual was brought up); What did this person grow up as? (think about the 'us' and 'them' binaries which map onto 'stigmatised' and 'normal' groups); Where did this person grow up? (think about geographical space(s)); When did this person grow up? (think about the zeitgeist that predominated various age cohorts); How much money and options did this person have? (think about social class, and what challenges and opportunities such a position would have entailed); Why have things happened, according to this person? (the perception of an individual's reality is crucial to understanding the person; therefore, think in terms of his/her view of their locus of control, agency, etc.).

Sexual Issues of People with Severe and Enduring Mental Health Problems

There is a paucity of published research investigating sexuality issues faced by those with mental health problems (McCann, 2010a; Volman & Landeen, 2007), in homosexual, bisexual, and heterosexual groups. This is surprising given that issues pertaining to sexuality are commonplace in mental health settings, with some patients voluntarily bringing up such issues. In a US survey, for instance, 78 per cent of the psychologists reported being asked about sexual issues that were of concern to the clients (Di Giulio & Reissing, 2005). There are several possible reasons why healthcare professionals are reluctant to talk about sex and sexuality with their patients. Haboubi and Lincoln (2003) found that in a rehabilitation setting healthcare professionals did not have adequate training to talk about sex. This is hardly startling, as a recent survey of the Doctorate in Clinical Psychology training programmes

---

[2]   Some of these questions have relevance for other age groups also.

in the UK found that teaching on sex and sexuality on these courses was varied, with some courses having little teaching on this subject (Shaw *et al.*, 2008). Other reasons for not wanting to talk about sex could include broader societal attitudes towards sexuality; it being considered an intensely private subject, which therefore has led to a paucity of readily available language to talk about sex, particularly in formal settings. Some clinicians may also fear personal or patient sexual arousal while talking about sex, or a sudden awareness of the clinician's own sexual concerns, or even a worry about having his/her moral repugnance show to the patient whose sexuality (and/or sexual practices) are different from that of the clinicians. Kautz *et al.* (1990), in their study of why nurses did not meet sexuality-related nursing care standards, found that those nurses who were brought up in families where sex was a taboo subject had the most difficulty in addressing issues related to sexuality in clinical practice.

Some staff may harbour the idea that people with mental health problems are asexual (McCann, 2003), which is another major problem in dealing with issues of sexuality. A recent UK study (McCann, 2010a; 2010b) found that there were significant differences between staff and service-user perspectives of needs related to intimate relationships and sexual expression, with the staff significantly underplaying these needs. While 90 per cent of service-users identified sexual expression as an important need, only 10 per cent of the staff acknowledged this as a need. In a qualitative study by McCann (2010a), which investigated mental health service-user views on sexual and relationship issues, one respondent said:

> I like the very fact you've made me think of the issues. I didn't come looking for it . . . I'm open to the CPN [Community Psychiatric Nurse] enquiring about my partnership. I'm open to them asking me about it. If you asked me 20 years ago I'd probably be closeted. I'm proud to be lesbian. I thought your questions were about sexual positions and the like . . . like the Kinsey report. The questions are actually fine (p.255).

Participants in this study not only discussed issues related to intimacy, but also the challenges they faced in establishing and maintaining relationships, sexual concerns and issues (e.g. AIDS/HIV, safer sex issues, etc.), sexual knowledge and understanding, stigma and self-esteem, family planning and parenting, the effects of medication on sexual functions, and forms of formal and informal support they received (McCann, 2010a). This clearly shows that not only are heterosexuals and non-heterosexuals with mental health problems capable of having such discussions, but that they are also willing to engage in such discussions, provided that there is clarity as to what it is that the therapist is keen to know and understand.

There is no doubt that talking about sexuality may be quite uncomfortable for some service-users[3]. However, therapists can help people talk about sex by bringing it up during sessions, thereby legitimising sex and sexuality as a valid topic of discussion, and more importantly, one that is permitted to be discussed in therapy. Some therapists find it useful to factor sex and sexuality in when taking a clinical case history, along with other history (e.g. family history, educational and occupational history, etc.). Furthermore, when taking a history, a competent therapist will be mindful of differences in family systems that some LGB people may have, which may not be similar to 'traditional' heterosexual family systems. 'Families of choice'[4] may need to be consulted in care arrangements in certain cases.

What are the Issues that Non-Heterosexuals Face in Mental Health Services?

Social exclusion

Adults with long term mental health problems are one of the most excluded groups in society (Office of Deputy Prime Minister [ODPM], 2004) and therefore lack a number of opportunities that people without mental health difficulties would take for granted. Social networks and social support are reduced for those with a mental health diagnosis. Fewer than four in ten employers would consider employing someone who has experienced mental health problems, and a third of people with mental health problems report having being dismissed or forced to resign from their jobs (ODPM, 2004). Social isolation is identified as an important risk factor for deteriorating mental health and suicide (ODPM, 2004). Social exclusion may be a consequence of, and a contributory factor to, being diagnosed with a mental health problem (ODPM, 2004). This means that clients who have mental health difficulties and identify as LGB could potentially face more stigma from both labels, and an increased risk of discrimination, prejudice and social exclusion.

---

[3] We suggest interested therapists consult Butler, O'Donovan & Shaw (2010) *Sex, sexuality and therapeutic practice: A manual for therapists and trainers*, for practical exercises and suggestions on how to raise the topic of sex in therapy.

[4] Families of choice are a 'flexible, informal and varied, but strong and supportive network of friends and lovers, often including members of families of origin [who] provide the framework for the development of mutual care, responsibility and commitment for many non-heterosexual people' (Weeks *et al.*, 2001, p.4).

Mental Health NHS Trusts have recently begun to address social exclusion and to focus on holistic care with the implementation of the recovery strategy (Repper & Perkins, 2003). Research has shown the positive impact of spirituality, family and community support as coping mechanisms for people experiencing severe and enduring mental health difficulties. However, such resources may not always be accessible for some LGB people who may have been ostracised from these networks because of their sexuality. Also, some cultures perceive mental health problems to be a form of punishment (e.g. Agara *et al.*, 2008) and sexuality remains a taboo subject not to be discussed (Lister, 1986). For some individuals such ostracisation may play a significant part in exacerbating problems and increasing feelings of guilt, shame and isolation.

Repper (2000) argues that tackling issues of exclusion has the potential to make the most significant impact on the lives of individuals experiencing mental distress. A lot of work has recently gone into mental health services in raising awareness of mental health problems and trying to reduce the discrimination through anti-stigma campaigns such as *Time to Change* (www.time-to-change.org.uk).

Being 'gay and mad'

Some people draw parallels and comparisons between the discrimination and isolation they experience as being a non-heterosexual and being a person with mental health problems. There are interesting stories on how people 'come out' as having a mental health problem. One writer, BriB, on the *Time to Change* website talks of his '"coming out" as a loony'. BriB writes:

> . . . with the help of my partner and the staff at the local psychiatric day hospital (which I attended daily for twelve months), I "Came Out" to my family and dearest friends, making them aware of other breakdowns, suicide attempts, etc, that they had been unaware of. Now, the reason I have borrowed the term "coming out" from the Gay Community is because from that day I no longer fear the stigma, the insults or the patronisation. This is me, I am now officially a loony . . .

Statements such as this suggest that for *some* clients, this kind of coming out can have an emancipatory function, not unlike that which some LGB people experience when coming out. Another parallel that can be drawn between the two groups is the phenomenon of reclaiming words which were once used as pejorative ways to distinguish an out-group and label them. From the LGB perspective, words such as 'queer' and 'gay' have been reappropriated in a counter-hegemonic move to minimise or negate the negative valence of such terms. In a similar way, though perhaps to a lesser extent, some people who have/have had mental health problems have reappropriated words like 'mad', 'psycho', and 'loony'. Another point of commonality, along with the reappropriation of terms once used to oppress those who did not conform to the norms dictated by society, is the incorporation of such terms as self-identity markers. This has been taken a step forward in some instances, whereby these identities are celebrated, for instance through Pride marches. The first known event specifically organised by people who identified as 'psychiatric survivors' was in Canada in 1993, and initially called 'Psychiatric Survivor Pride Day'. By the late 1990s similar events were being organised in London, and were named 'Mad Pride'. These events served to educate the general public about mental health problems, the common nature of these problems, to dispel associated stigma, and to show others that their conditions did not preclude them from living productive and meaningful lives, and contributing to society.

In drawing parallels, however, there is the risk of ignoring intersections. Gay pride marches do not always have 'mad' floats or sections, and mad pride marches do not always recognise 'gay' factions. And yet, there are many people who subscribe to both identities, experiencing the prejudice from straight and gay 'non-mad' quarters. For some, coming out may not be a one off event, with difficult decisions needing to be made as to when, where, who and how to come out, but also to come out as what: mad *or* gay, or mad *and* gay?[5]

Accessing Mental Health Services

We know that there can be 'no health without mental health' (Prince *et al.*, 2007). Research has also demonstrated the psychological ill-effects of having a physical health condition, particularly chronic health conditions (see Chapter 7). This indicates the interplay between physical and mental (ill) health. Prince *et al.* (2007), in emphasising the ubiquitous nature of mental health in influencing our general health, go on to suggest that '[m]ental health awareness needs to be integrated into all aspects of health and social policy, health-system planning, and delivery of primary and secondary general health care' (p.859).

Despite the high levels of mental health problems reported in LGB communities, research has shown that a significant number of LGB people with

---

[5]   Interested readers may find Kitzinger & Perkins' (1993) book *Changing our minds: Lesbian feminism and psychology*, an instructive read on this topic.

psychological difficulties do not access mental health services (Noret *et al.*, 2006). Some of the reasons why non-heterosexual people do not access services include clients' own experiences of prejudice when accessing services previously (e.g. Wintrip, 2009), or the stories they have heard about the experiences of others. It must be acknowledged that sometimes it is 'fear' of the negative consequences that disclosure of sexual preference would bring, and other times it is the worry of professionals attributing the mental health problems to the client's sexual preference (Golding, 1997). Some clients who are not 'out' to their families may have fears about confidentiality or repercussions of the disclosure. Another reason is related to clients' experience or perception that the staff at such places do not *understand* LGB issues (Taylor, 2004), and that there is a heterosexist approach to their care (Heaphy *et al.*, 2003). King *et al.* (2003) found that LGB people experienced overt homophobia and lack of empathy from some mental health professionals. Such sentiments were also echoed by Douglas-Scott *et al.* (2004).

These studies illustrate the alienating effects of homonegativity and heterosexism, but are in no way the only experience that service-users have when attending hospitals or healthcare facilities. For instance, one of our service-users was 'surprised' by the level of understanding related to same-sex relationships that was demonstrated at the service her partner was at:

> My partner was in hospital under a section. When I went to visit her all of the staff were really friendly. They explained everything to me and told me how to tell the kids. It surprised me as I didn't think many nurses understood same-sex relationships as most people assume that as I have kids I must be straight.

The fact that this carer was 'surprised' is telling. This suggests that service-users and carers have now come to expect the worst from healthcare services. It is worth remembering that not all service-users will have the agency to challenge homonegativity and heterosexism, therefore, staff need to take responsibility for doing this, when they can. Therefore, the responsibility of correcting the services' image is mainly that of the service itself and the staff within such services.

While almost all non-heterosexual people have to negotiate heterosexism in daily life, non-heterosexuals with mental health problems also have to contend with 'sanism' or 'mentalism'. Sanism and mentalism are terms that describe discrimination on the basis of mental (ill) health which is characterised by complex social inequalities in terms of power and agency. This may be another factor which determines whether or not non-heterosexuals with mental health problems will disclose their problems to others, and further, access services to help them deal with their problems.

Perhaps partially as a result of these experiences of discrimination or fear of prejudice, some larger cities in the UK have seen the mushrooming of 'specialist services' that cater to the needs of LGB people. While this is essential in some instances, it can also be seen as a 'catchall' service for *any* issues that LGB people face. This has the potential for ghettoising LGB issues to specific services, leaving mainstream services out of touch with, and unskilled to work with, the problems faced by non-heterosexuals.

One interesting issue related to access and evaluation of service provision is that data are not routinely solicited or collected on service-users' sexual orientation. This then makes it difficult to determine whether there are differences in experiences of accessing mental health services based on service-user feedback. Anecdotally, mental health workers admit to making assumptions about a client's sexual orientation, primarily assuming that they are heterosexual unless the service-user states otherwise or some marker of same-sex sexuality is observed in clinical practice. Often, services are overly cautious not to ask about sexual identity for fear of it causing upset to or anger from service-users. However, a study by Noret *et al.* (2006) showed that 80 per cent of their lesbian and gay sample reported that they would feel comfortable disclosing their sexual orientation to service providers. This figure was lower (50%) for bisexuals, which is not surprising, given that bisexuals often face a more virulent form of discrimination sometimes from both heterosexual and homosexual quarters. Ross *et al.* (2010) confirmed this assertion when they found that bisexual experiences of accessing mental health services were even worse than lesbian and gay experiences. The experience of having to respond to questions related to sexual identity/orientation can be made better for service-users by having sensible options for people to select from and by having sensitive means of collecting this information.

People will only access services if they feel that their identities will not be the subject of criticism or consternation. One study found that only about 22 per cent of their sample felt that the service providers acknowledged the needs of LGB people (Noret *et al.*, 2006). While services can acknowledge such needs in various ways, including having explicit policies to this effect, ultimately, it is service delivery which will determine whether or not people feel comfortable to disclose their sexual identity, problems or concerns. As one participant from the Noret *et al.* (2006, p.24) study astutely articulated:

> I also think that while services may have good policies it is individual staff who need training and educating regarding their own attitudes and prejudices – the policy is only as good as the individuals who support it!

Direct interventions

With the recent push to increase access to psychological therapies through IAPT[6] services, many non-heterosexual clients may be offered cognitive behavioural therapy (CBT) aimed at addressing mental health difficulties such as anxiety or depression. For a number of clients their mental health difficulties may be unrelated to their sexuality and so therapists should not assume that the individual's orientation is a problem for them. Sessions should focus on the client's goals and coping with mental health difficulties that may be the result of discrimination or stigma regarding their sexual orientation or mental health diagnosis, but may be unrelated[7].

In addition to one to one therapy, mental health services can set up groups for LGB clients. The recorded benefits of groups overwhelmingly seem to be that of reducing isolation and increasing feelings of 'universality'. For many clients who find that the main difficulty they experience is stigma and discrimination regarding their mental health, sexual orientation, or both, group work may be an appropriate intervention (or used as an adjunct). The problem with these groups is that clients need to be out and comfortable about being out in order to attend them. Our experience of setting up such a group has shown that it is not only feasible but is also found to be extremely useful for service-users.

Improving access to mental health services

Richards (2010, p.20–21) makes excellent recommendations for mental health services to improve inclusion of marginalised groups. Although these pertain mainly to addressing self-harm, suicidal ideation and suicide, they are applicable to any issue dealt with in mental health services, and perhaps, even other healthcare facilities. Similarly, the *Out but not Left Out* report (Noret *et al.*, 2006, p.28) makes similar recommendations. These reports recommend that mental health services should:

- Increase awareness of the specific needs of the LGB communities amongst service commissioners and providers.
- Be mindful of heteronormative cultures or environments within the service and its practices, and discuss these with staff.

---

[6] Improved Access to Psychological Therapies.
[7] We direct the interested reader to the Pink Therapy trilogy edited by Dominic Davies and Charles Neal, particularly Volume 2 which covers the use of various types of therapies with LGBT clients: http://www.pinktherapy.com/pagesource/resources/recommended.for.therapists.htm.

- Ensure that all staff have the opportunity to receive periodic training in LGB issues. This should include senior management to facilitate discussion of these issues at a strategic level.
- Increase awareness of services available to LGB communities. This can be achieved by many mechanisms, for example, advertising in LGB venues and the gay press, participating in Pride events, and disseminating LGB-affirmative literature related to mental health.
- Display LGB-affirmative material at the service. Even a simple rainbow flag in the window will help some LGB people identify that this is an LGB-friendly service.
- Endeavour to 'reach out' to all sections of the LGB population.
- Ask for feedback and consult with LGB clients where feasible.
- Seek support and liaise with LGB organisations.
- Appoint a member of staff to lead or 'champion' for the service to ensure the needs of the LGB people are addressed.
- Use appropriate equal-opportunities monitoring forms that explicitly ask about sexual identity, but also offer a 'do not wish to disclose' option.

We would like to add to these points by suggesting that direct targeting of 'LGB' groups in itself may alienate some non-heterosexuals who do not see themselves as LGB. Furthermore, direct targeting of services for non-heterosexuals at designated LGB 'scenes' may also miss those who do not or cannot use such spaces. In such instances, sometimes, simple visuals would suffice without having to spell out sexual identity labels. Such advertising, again, should not be restricted to centres that already have LGB services, but should be seen in more generic healthcare settings, such as GP surgeries and acute and community hospitals. Such materials will serve not only as a sign that non-heterosexuals are welcome to the service and that they can be who they are, but will also serve to remind staff (and other patients) that non-heterosexuals also use their service. Such simple acknowledgement of acceptance is sometimes all service-users need to get them through the door of the service. However, service-users will need to feel affirmed about their sexuality, or else all the other signs and images would be nothing more than a tokenistic gesture, which will soon lose all symbolic meaning and worth. As an interesting activity, therapists could look around their own service environs and examine whether the materials (posters, leaflets, etc.) represent non-heterosexual populations.

One of the first steps to ensuring that mental health services provide a quality and accessible service for LGB and other non-heterosexual individuals is to address the attitudes of the staff within that service. Although recent legislation (i.e. Equalities Act, 2010) has afforded some protection against discrimination from services, this does not altogether eliminate the subtler forms of homonegativity. Furthermore, given the history of prejudice that LGB people have faced from mental health services in the past, services need to go the extra mile to assuage the fear and distrust that may still reside in some of these individuals and communities. Therefore, good services have to; (i) work towards providing an inclusive service, (ii) be proactive in preventing mental health problems, and (iii) be seen as gay affirmative. Such activities need to be made at both a policy level and in everyday practice.

The first step to this is increasing staff awareness and understanding of the issues non-heterosexual clients' face that can either impact upon or can exacerbate their mental health difficulties. As mentioned earlier, a number of staff would assume that clients are heterosexual unless otherwise stated which highlights the importance of asking the service-user about their sexuality, where appropriate. Surveying staff from our own services, most staff felt that it was beneficial to ask this question because it demonstrated to the service-user that the service believes their sexual orientation is an important aspect of their life.

Interestingly, in Enhanced Care Programme Approach (CPA) documentation (e.g. CPA documentation used by Nottinghamshire Care coordinators[8]), sexuality is mentioned once in a three-inch space to record any issues relating to 'Culture, gender and sexuality' (p.4). It is one of the last categories to be completed in the documentation, and sometimes this category is left blank or marked 'not applicable'. For the majority of the time the client is simply described in categorical terms ('white, heterosexual, Christian female') without a more comprehensive explanation or consideration of what these identities mean to the client and how they may impact on their personal identity, mental health, and life generally. This highlights a need for staff training to increase awareness and understanding of sexuality, and to validate this as an important topic to be addressed by all staff working in mental health services not just those working in specific gender/sexuality services.

Some service-users benefit from working with members of staff who identify as LGB. One of our clients, for instance, reported: 'When I was in hospital I had a nurse who was openly gay. It was amazing: I felt surprisingly normal and all the staff treated me well'. These kinds of experiences, however, have led to a tendency in some services whereby if a client discloses their LGB status then they are referred to work with a LGB staff member who is out. However, this allows staff who are unfamiliar or inexperienced working

---

[8] Enhanced Care Programme Approach documentation (2010). Nottinghamshire Healthcare NHS Trust.

with LGB clients to continue to avoid this topic under the guise of offering the 'best service to the client' to meet *their* needs.

There has been a recent push for NHS Trusts to address a number of areas that come under the umbrella of diversity, with sexuality and sexual orientation being one of them. One good resource developed to model LGB-affirmative practice is the Department of Health's document 'Reducing health inequalities for Lesbian, Gay, Bisexual and Transgendered people' (Department of Health, 2007). Another positive way to promote an accepting and validating service for LBG clients would be for services to start using or use more same-sex imagery in their publicity and advertising campaigns. Indirect ways in which services can help LGB clients is by improving the visibility of LGB staff groups, being represented at LGB events (such as Gay Pride), and publicly marking or commemorating certain dates (by flying the rainbow flag, permitting staff to march under the Trust's banner for Pride, etc.) such as International Day Against Homophobia and Transphobia (IDAHO; May 17th).

We would like to end this chapter by providing a first-person account of dealing with sexuality and mental health issues, and accessing services. When we informed Lucy that we were writing this piece, she was keen to lend her voice to the chapter and offered to send us a written text of her story, suggesting we use what we thought was needed. This is her story.

Lucy's Story

A bit about me, so you have some context. This is but a fragment of the story, but is a reflection on the issues you are examining.

I am now 31 years old. I got married earlier this year to my long-term partner, Amy, and we are currently planning a family. I am writing this from a place of being completely settled about my identity, but it has taken a long while to get here and could have been a much smoother path. I always knew that I wasn't straight, but didn't really understand my sexuality, or the fact that I was gay until I allowed myself to when I was much older. Instead, already struggling with an abusive past, I was confused about my sexuality. Because of earlier abusive experiences at the hands of men, I became even more perplexed as to whether I was straight or gay; I didn't want either to be because I had been abused.

I developed a strong internal dialogue about being perfect in the world. On the outside I was fine. I appeared a happy and confident teenager – a high achiever with lots of friends, but inside I was developing increasing problems. I felt ashamed about who I was in every way, and my sexuality was an extra burden that I couldn't escape. I remember when I was about 12 years old, telling someone that I thought I was gay. I was bullied by my peers as consequence and I decided thereafter, from the very clear message that I was given at that age, that it was/I was unacceptable.

I come from a rural area, with a family who at times could be quite prejudiced. I was terrified that I would be rejected and so I closed down all aspects of myself that I thought other people wouldn't tolerate: my emotions, my sexuality. I became what I thought other people wanted, and became increasingly distressed by internal conflict. I threw myself into relationships with men from an early age, and almost made a very conscious decision that this was the only path I could choose. I tried to convince myself and the world around me that I could be 'ok' with that lifestyle. I wasn't.

I started to self harm at 10, but through my teens, with increasing pressure upon me in every way this escalated, and at 13 I was diagnosed with anorexia and experiencing what I now know to be flashbacks. I was diagnosed with severe PTSD in adult years. I drank to escape my distress. I began taking drugs. I cut myself. I had made my first suicide attempt at 14, and there were many, many more. Still, I maintained the charade with myself and the world, and I went from one long term relationship with a man, to another. I clung to these relationships like glue to avoid being found out and I married at 21, still convinced that this was the life that I had chosen for myself and therefore I would persist and make it work.

I became increasingly unwell and in my early twenties dropped out of work, and society, and relationships. I self harmed every day. I was suicidal and seriously underweight. I came into contact with statutory services, was offered therapy, and was experienced as a girl in crisis. No one saw the professional high achiever, or the sociable friend that had existed before. I became a number in a system, a self harmer, a drain on resources.

My marriage was in tatters, and my husband knew this. We both knew this. From the moment we married, I slept on the sofa. We were friends, living together. I started to face this. He admitted that he had always known I wasn't straight, but he thought too, that we could overcome this.

I started to move forwards tentatively with the help of therapy, and a few close friends, and part of that movement forwards was to admit to myself and others that I shouldn't be in the marriage that I was in. I was confused. I felt terrible and ashamed at the recognition that I was never going to be myself, or happy masquerading in a heterosexual relationship. Nor would I ever be happy living a lie. I was the one that had fabricated this elaborate pretence, and there I was having to face it, and start to destruct it again. Internally this was a huge struggle.

I also had to face up to the fact that I would never be able to know whether my sexuality had in any way been influenced by my abusive experiences, as the two are inextricably entwined. Rather, I had to start to prioritise my own needs, in the here and now, and accept my feelings and identity.

As a woman in the mental health system, known to have experienced trauma and violence, and who self harmed, I was already struggling to experience warmth from services. My constant crises caused fear and distress in services who kept saving my life, and it became even harder now I was leaving a marriage. I was met with rejection, and often invalidation by some staff members with whom I had contact with. From one team I was actually given the instruction that services did not and would not speak to me about my marriage, sexuality or abuse; that they were there to support me with my current mental state. But how could any of that be isolated from another? These issues for me are all a part of me, and my identity, and why I was unwell, and now . . . a part of my journey. I could not examine, or improve my mental ill health without addressing these struggles and conflict.

Professionals seemed to struggle why, when I was so vulnerable, I would be choosing to leave my marriage with a man that was so supportive. They had little ability to relate to the fact that I was gay. I surrendered to the system, and spoke only to those who would speak about it to me. The shame about who I was was further reinforced by this reaction. I had lived a straight life, as a straight woman. I had no gay friends. I didn't understand myself, or what it was to be gay. I received no support for the social isolation that this left me feeling. I was utterly certain that in my decision to leave my marriage, that I would be destined to a life alone, and without hope of ever finding friends of companionship that would understand or accept my sexuality.

Nowadays it is different. I am a professional, working in the world of mental health. Yet the pervasive ignorance about sexuality exists everywhere. I am shocked when I see the obvious discomfort amongst some peers at the conversation of sex with their clients. Yet sex, sexuality and relationships are a normal part of all of our lives. How can we adequately help and support our clients with their difficulties if we are unable to engage with the whole of them or their lives, and what does that say about us? What is the fear?

A friend said to me, in a discussion over lunch one day, that she didn't see why people who were gay always felt that they had to talk about their sexuality, or anticipated so much rejection. I was appalled. I tried to explain, that unless you had faced such pervasive ostracisation by society, you shouldn't be in a position of judging what that was like. Even my civil partnership is not the same legally as a marriage. Society tells me, that even now, I am not quite entitled to the same equality or standard of relationship as other couples. The subtleties of inequality are there in our legal system. The cutting edge of homophobia is clearer and these pervasively embed themselves within services and systems because they exist within people.

Every day I live with assumptions made about me and choices repeatedly over whether to come out over and over again. These assumptions are made carelessly, or ignorantly, or out of downright prejudice in both personal and professional arenas, and all of the time. People make assumptions that my partner is a him, and I get torn between 'outing' myself, or just allowing the comments to pass. Sometimes when people learn that I am in a same-sex relationship, I have received comments like: you surprise me; I would never have thought; you don't look like a lesbian!

As a woman with profound mental health difficulties, and absolutely no self esteem to mention, the double stigma of being gay and having a mental health problem was too much to bear. I had to be in a state of better health before I started to even consider publicly sharing any aspects of my sexual identity, or sharing my new relationship as it developed. Apart from two professionals who were amazing, I can't think of any other positive contact or experience that I had about this issue. It was overlooked at best.

I am often struck by how much thought goes into being gay. The constant concern that a new relationship, professional or personal, may be invaded by prejudice should that person find out that I am gay. I almost feel compelled to tell people so that we both know, but I don't. I do not require other people to tell me their sexuality in order for me to understand them, or know them, or work with them, so why should I have to do this simply because I am gay?

I also witness staff members struggling over how to respond to sexuality as an issue for their clients. Yet it is essential that staff appreciate and understand the different worlds that a gay individual may face. It seems to be a perception that a person's sexuality is not the place of a mental health worker to attend to, or that if a client has LGB issues or needs that they be placed with a staff member who is also LGB. This isn't a sensitive or helpful response to a client with LGB needs. It sends the clear message that you should stay amongst your own. Of course, at times people may request a staff member from a particular demographic and this can be appropriate but this should not be an automated, ignorance-led practice. We need to establish with each of our clients, regardless of their gender, age, sexuality or race, what their individual needs and preferences are. We should not assume these, nor pigeonhole people because of stigma.

Guidelines for Good Practice

- Be curious and ask about your client's experiences of mental health services and their expectations of your service in relation to acceptance of non-heterosexual lives.
- Be prepared to be an ally for non-heterosexual people. This may involve challenging colleagues or advocating for changes in the place you work. Such work would include conducting an anonymous audit of the views of non-heterosexual service-users who access your service. Taking such a stance may result in others questioning your own sexuality, notice how this feels and what you learn from this.
- It is important to keep the numerous contexts that influence a person's life in perspective when considering protective and destructive influences on their mental health. These include sexuality, age, race, gender, and so on.

- Consider how you might raise the issue of sex and sexuality with your clients. If you find this challenging take this to supervision.
- Share gay-affirmative literature/reports with your managers and staff team. Discuss how well the service is doing at implementing the recommendations and what could be done to improve your service.
- Clients may appreciate being linked up with supportive community-based networks, such as gay-friendly 'mad pride' events or social groups. Information about such groups can be found via local LGB helplines. It is good practice for your service to be aware of these supportive networks and make this information accessible to all clients.

References

Agara, A.J., Makanjuola, A.B. & Morakinyo, O. (2008). Management of perceived mental health problems by spiritual healers: A Nigerian study. *African Journal of Psychiatry, 11*, 113–118.

Amadio, D.M. & Chung, Y. (2004). Internalized homophobia and substance use among lesbian, gay, and bisexual persons. *Journal of Gay & Lesbian Social Services, 17*(1), 83–101. doi:10.1300/J041v17n01_06.

American Psychiatric Association (2000). *Diagnostic and Statistical Manual of Mental Health Disorders IV (Text Revision)*. Washington DC: APA.

Bartlett, A., Smith, G. & King, M. (2009). The response of mental health professionals to clients seeking help to change or redirect same-sex sexual orientation. *BMC Psychiatry. 9*(11). Retrieved 18 October 2010 from http://www.ncbi.nlm.nih.gov/pmc/articles/PMC2667504/.

Butler, C., O'Donovan, A. & Shaw, E. (2010). *Sex, sexuality and therapeutic practice: A manual for therapists and trainers*. East Sussex: Routledge.

Card, N.A. & Hodges, E.V.E. (2008). Peer victimization among schoolchildren: Correlations, causes, consequences, and considerations in assessment and intervention. *School Psychology Quarterly, 23*, 451–461.

Chan, C. (1987). Asian lesbians: Psychological issues in the "coming out" process. *Asian American Psychological Association Journal, 12*, 16–18.

Cohen, S. & Wills, T. (1985). Stress, social support, and the buffering hypothesis. *Psychological Bulletin, 98*(2), 310–357.

Cook-Daniels, L. (2007). *Transforming mental health services for older people: Lesbian, gay, bisexual and transgender (LGBT) challenges and opportunities*. A paper prepared for the AARP Diversity and Aging in the 21st Century Conference, June 21, 2007 Los Angeles, California. Retrieved 30 May 2011 from www.forge-forward.org/handouts/AARP_tranformingMH.pdf.

das Nair, R. (2006). *Metaminorities and mental health: Pathways of vulnerability for Black and Minority Ethnic queer folk*. Retrieved 12 December 2010 from http://www.inter-disciplinary.net/ci/sexuality/s2/nair%20paper.pdf.

Department of Health (2007). *Reducing health inequalities for lesbian, gay, bisexual and trans people.* London: Department of Health.

Di Giulio, G. & Reissing, E.D. (2005). *Sexual problems in clinical practice: A survey of psychologists' training, experience, and treatment techniques.* Poster presented at the Canadian Psychological Association 66th Annual Convention (June). Montréal, Canada.

Douglas-Scott, S., Pringle, A. & Lumsdaine, C. (2004). S*exual exclusion – Homophobia and health inequalities: A review of health inequalities and social exclusion experienced by lesbian, gay and bisexual people.* UK Gay Men's Health Network. Retrieved 30 May 2011 from www.spectrum-lgbt.org/downloads/health/gmhn_report.pdf.

Foucault, M. (1978). *The history of sexuality. 1: An introduction* (Trans. R. Hurley). New York, NY: Pantheon Books.

Golding, J. (1997). *Without prejudice: The MIND lesbian, gay and bisexual health awareness research.* London: MIND.

Grossman, A.H. & Kerner, M.S. (1998). Self-esteem and supportiveness as predictors of emotional distress in gay male and lesbian youth. *Journal of Homosexuality, 35*(2), 25–39.

Haboubi, N.H.J. & Lincoln, N. (2003). Views of health professionals on discussing sexual issues with patients. *Disability and Rehabilitation, 25*(6), 291–296.

Hatzenbuehler, M.L., McLaughlin, K.A., Keyes, K.M. & Hasin, D.S. (2010). The impact of institutional discrimination on psychiatric disorder in lesbian, gay, and bisexual populations: A prospective study. *American Journal of Public Health, 100,* 452–459.

Heaphy, B., Yip, A. & Thompson, D. (2003). *Lesbian and gay lives over 50.* Nottingham: York House Publications.

Herek, G.M. & Glunt, E.K. (1995). Identity and community among gay and bisexual men in the AIDS era: Preliminary findings from the Sacramento Men's Health Study. In G.M. Herek & B. Greene (eds), *AIDS, identity, and community: The HIV epidemic and lesbians and gay men.* Thousand Oaks, CA: Sage Publications.

Herek, G.M., Cogan, J.C., Gillis, J.R. & Glunt, E.K. (1998). Correlates of internalized homophobia in a community sample of lesbians and gay men. *Journal of the Gay and Lesbian Medical Association, 2,* 17–25.

Higgins, A., Barker, P. & Begley, C. (2006). Sexual health education for people with mental health problems: What can we learn from the literature. *Journal of Psychiatric and Mental Health Nursing, 13,* 687–697.

Kautz, D.D., Dickey, C.A. & Stevens, M.N. (1990). Using research to identify why nurses do not meet established sexuality nursing care standards. *Journal of Nursing Quality Assurance, 4*(3), 69–73.

King, M., McKeown, E., Warner, J., Ramsay, A., Johnson, K., Cort, C., Wright, L., Blizard, R. & Davidson, O. (2003). Mental health and quality of life of gay men and lesbians in England and Wales: Controlled, cross-sectional study. *The British Journal of Psychiatry, 183,* 552–558.

King, M., Semlyen, J., Tai, S., Killaspy, H., Osborn, D., Popelyuk, D. & Nazareth, I. (2008). A systematic review of mental disorder, suicide, and deliberate self-harm in lesbian, gay and bisexual people. *BMJ Psychiatry, 8*(70). Retrieved 18 October 2010 from http://www.ncbi.nlm.nih.gov/pmc/articles/PMC2533652/.

Kitzinger, C. & Perkins, R. (1993). *Changing our minds: Lesbian feminism and psychology.* New York, NY: New York University Press.

Lindquist, N. & Hirabayashi, G. (1979). Coping with marginal status: Case of gay males. *Canadian Journal of Sociology, 4,* 87–104.

Lister, L. (Ed). (1986). *Human sexuality, ethnoculture, and social work.* Binghampton, NY: The Haworth Press.

McCann, E. (2003). Exploring sexual and relationship possibilities for people with psychosis: A review of the literature. *Journal of Psychiatric and Mental Health Nursing, 10,* 640–649.

McCann, E. (2010a). Investigating mental health service user views regarding sexual and relationship issues. *Journal of Psychiatric and Mental Health Nursing, 17,* 251–259.

McCann, E. (2010b). The sexual and relationship needs of people who experience psychosis: quantitative findings of a UK study. *Journal of Psychiatric and Mental Health Nursing, 17,* 295–303.

Meyer, I. (2003). Prejudice, social stress, and mental health in lesbian, gay, and bisexual populations: Conceptual issues and research evidence. *Psychological Bulletin, 129,* 674–697.

Newcomb, M.E. & Mustanski, B. (2010). Internalized homophobia and internalizing mental health problems: A meta-analytic review. *Clinical Psychology Review, 30*(8), 1019–1029. DOI: 10.1016/j.cpr.2010.07.003.

Noret, N., Rivers, I. & Richards, A. (2006). *Out but not left out: Mental health service provision for LGBs living in Leeds: An assessment of service needs and mapping of service provision in the city.* A report for the Leeds LGB Mental Health Partnership. York: York St John University.

Office of the Deputy Prime Minister (2004). *Mental health and social exclusion.* Social Exclusion Unit Report. London: ODPM.

Prince, M., Patel, V., Saxena, S., Maj, M., Maselko, J., Phillips, M. & Rahman, A. (2007). No health without mental health. *The Lancet, 370*(9590), 859–877.

Quinn, C. & Browne, G. (2009). Sexuality of people living with a mental illness: a collaborative challenge for mental health nurses. *International Journal of Mental Health Nursing, 18,* 195–203.

Repper, J. (2000). Social inclusion. In T. Thompson & P. Matthias (Eds.), *Lyttles' mental health and disorder (3rd Edn).* London: Baillere Tindall.

Repper, J. & Perkins, R. (2003). Social inclusion and recovery: A model for mental health practice. London: Baillere Tindall.

Richards, A. (2010). *Closing the gap – Service needs and prohibitions to access: The LGB community, self-harm, suicidal ideation and suicide.* Retrieved 25 November 2010 from http://www.volition.org.uk/documents/Closingthe GapLGBreportFeb10.pdf.

Rivers, I. (1995). The victimization of gay teenagers in schools: Homophobia in education. *Pastoral Care, 13*(1), 35–41.

Ross, L., Dobinson, C. & Eady, A. (2010). Perceived determinants of mental health for bisexual people: A qualitative examination. *American Journal of Public Health, 100*(3), 496–502.

Ryan, C., Huebner, D., Diaz, R. & Sanchez, J. (2009). Family rejection as a predictor of negative health outcomes in White and Latino lesbian, gay, and bisexual young adults. *Pediatrics, 123*(1), 346–352.

Shaw, L. Butler, C. & Marriot, C. (2008). Sex and sexuality teaching in Clinical Psychology courses. *Clinical Psychology Forum, 187*, 7–11.

Stokes J.P. & Peterson, J.L. (1998). Homophobia, self-esteem, and risk for HIV among African American men who have sex with men. *AIDS Education and Prevention 10*(3), 278–292.

Stonewall (2007). *The school report.* Retrieved 12 December 2010 from www .stonewall.org.uk/educationforall.

Stonewall (2009). *The teachers' report.* Retrieved 12 December 2010 from http:// www.liverpool.gov.uk/Images/tcm21-166559.pdf.

Szymanski, D.M. & Kashubeck-West, S. (2008). Mediators of the relationship between internalized oppressions and lesbian and bisexual women's psychological distress. *The Counseling Psychologist, 36*, 575–594.

Taylor, I. & Robertson, A. (1994). The health needs of gay men: A discussion of the literature and implications for nursing. *Journal of Advanced Nursing, 20*(3), 560–566.

Taylor, K. (2004). *The mental health support needs of lesbian, gay & bisexual people: A Sheffield based research project.* Sheffield: Sheffield Care Trust.

Uribe, V. & Harbeck, K.M. (1992). Addressing the needs of lesbian, gay, and bisexual youth: The origins of PROJECT 10 and school-based interventions. In K.M. Harbeck (ed.) *Coming out of the classroom closet: Gay and lesbian students, teachers, and curricula.* Binghampton, NY: The Haworth Press.

Vanden Berghe, W., Dewaele, A., Cox, N. & Vinckle, J. (2010). Minority-specific determinants of mental well-being among lesbian, gay, and bisexual youth. *Journal of Applied Social Psychology, 40*(1), 153–166.

Volman, L. & Landeen, J. (2007). Uncovering the sexual self in people with schizophrenia. *Journal of Psychiatric and Mental Health Nursing, 14*(4), 411–417.

Warner, J., McKeown, E., Griffin, M., Johnson, K., Ramsay, A., Cort, C. & King, M. (2004). Rates and predictors of mental illness in gay men, lesbians and bisexual men and women: Results from a survey based in England and Wales. *The British Journal of Psychiatry, 185*, 479–485.

Weber, G. (2008). Using to numb the pain: Substance use and abuse among lesbian, gay, and bisexual individuals. *Journal of Mental Health Counseling, 30*(1), 31–48.

Weeks, J., Heaphy, B. & Donovan, C. (2001). *Same sex intimacies: Families of choice and other life experiments.* London, UK and New York, NY: Routledge.

Williamson, I. (2000). Internalized homophobia and health issues affecting lesbians and gay men. *Health Education Research 15*(1), 97–107.

Williamson, I. & Hartley, P. (1998). British research into the increased vulnerability of young gay men to eating disturbance and body dissatisfaction. *European Eating Disorders Review, 6*, 60–70.

Wintrip, S. (2009). *Not safe for us yet: The experiences and views of older lesbian, gay men and bisexuals using mental health services in London (A scoping study).* London: Polari Housing Association.

World Health Organisation (1994). *ICD-10 Classifications of mental and behavioural disorder: Clinical descriptions and diagnostic guidelines.* Geneva, Switzerland: WHO.

Yang, B. & Clum, G.A. (1994). Life stress, social support, and problem-solving skills predictive of depressive symptoms, hopelessness, and suicide ideation in an Asian student population: A test of a model. *Suicide and Life-Threatening Behavior, 24*, 127–139.

9

Disability

Catherine Butler

Research on disabled men and women seems to simply assume the irrelevance of gender, race, ethnicity, sexual orientation, or social class. Having a disability presumably eclipses these dimensions of social experience (Asch & Fine, 1988, p.3).

When areas of social difference intersect, a person faces discrimination on multiple levels. And yet, the majority of texts that write about areas of social difference take a single-issue focus, for example, disability texts frequently fail to mention race (Begum, 1992) or sexuality (Sherry, 2004). This chapter considers the interaction between disability and belonging to a sexual minority, with an acknowledgment that issues of race, class and gender are not explored in the depth they should be. The chapter starts by considering the discrimination that lesbian, gay and bisexual (LGB) disabled people face in different contexts: the dominant mainstream, LGB communities, and the disability movement. A model of identity development is then described, followed by considerations of 'coming out' versus 'passing'. The interaction between sexual identity and disability is then considered in the contexts of growing up, forming relationships and sex. Finally, to redress Thompson *et al.*'s (2001) critique that the social model of disability focuses on those with physical disabilities and excludes people with learning disabilities (pld), there is a dedicated section addressing the unique issues for sexual minority pld. A separate section follows to address issues of HIV/AIDS, which of themselves may not cause impairment, but for which stigma and prejudice result in disability and oppression. This chapter finishes with a good practice guide for clinicians and researchers working with disabled

Intersectionality, Sexuality and Psychological Therapies: Working with Lesbian, Gay and Bisexual Diversity, First Edition. Edited by Roshan das Nair and Catherine Butler.
© 2012 John Wiley & Sons, Ltd. Published 2012 by John Wiley & Sons, Ltd. and the British Psychological Society.

LGB people. In this chapter the term 'disabled people' is used: Oliver (a disability rights campaigner) believes this to be a proud and defiant label (Oliver, 1992).

Intersectionality

Society rejects me for being Deaf.
The Deaf community reject me for being a lesbian.
The Lesbian community reject me for not being able to hear them.
The Deaf-Lesbian community rejects me for being into S&M[1].
The S&M community rejects me for being Deaf (Renteria, 1993, p.38).

At any one time, an area of social difference may be more significant to an individual than at another time. For someone with a disability who is also a sexual minority, either of these could be more significant depending on that time in the person's life, contemporary significant events or the context (to be lesbian may be more important in LGB venues and to be disabled more important in a disability rights meeting). The challenge of writing and working in this area is to hold multiple identities in mind and consider their interaction:

... the new challenges that disability advocates now face is to critically recon-
ceptualise disability within a specific and interlocking context that can also
account for their experiences of oppression on the basis of race, class, caste,
gender and sexual orientation (Erevelles, 1996, p.520).

Discrimination in Dominant Society: The Heterosexual Non-Disabled Mainstream

O'Toole and Bregante (1992) draw together the common myths upheld about disabled people's sexuality (p.166):

- All sex is heterosexual;
- Only independently functioning disabled people can handle sexual re-
lations;
- Disabled people should be 'grateful' for a sexual relationship;
- Disabled people who are not married are celibate;

[1]   S&M is an abbreviation for Sadomasochism. Practitioners also refer to themselves and/or their practice as SM or S/M. This is not viewed here as a 'paraphilia'.

- Disabled people cannot be parents;
- If a parent comes disabled, the children are not getting a 'real' parent;
- If in a relationship with a nondisabled person, that person runs the relationship;
- Disabled people are too fragile for vigorous sexual activity.

In addition, Saxton (1987) notes the myths that 'disability may be contagious and that sex is somehow a rare and precious commodity that should be reserved for highly-valued people, that is, the attractive and able-bodied' (p.48).

Disabled people are mostly considered asexual, 'or at best sexually inadequate, that we cannot . . . have orgasms, erections, ejaculations or impregnate' (Morris, 1991, p.20). In addition to this and in contrast to it, pld can alternatively be viewed as 'oversexed' and out of control (Thompson *et al.*, 2001). When sexuality for disabled people is addressed it has traditionally been from a 'protective' and 'controlling' standpoint: either to prevent abuse (Burns, 1993) or provide birth control. Whitney (2006) proposes that there has been a recent shift in the recognition and assertion of the sexual rights of disabled people, however, these are still assumed to be heterosexual. For LGB disabled people, their sexual needs remain invisible unless they choose to declare them, which may be at the cost of discrimination and rejection (O'Toole & Bregante, 1992).

When disabled people do express sexual desires/needs they can be positioned as deviant or dangerous (Shapiro, 1993), particularly if these desires/needs are of the same-sex variety. A sexual minority identity can be read as resulting from disability rather than as a conscious choice (Shakespeare *et al.*, 1996); for example, a disabled lesbian interviewed by O'Toole (2000) described:

> one myth that bothers me the most is the idea that we sleep with women because we have no other choice . . . the problem with this myth is that it is just a derivation of the idea that disabled women are asexual (p.209).

If born with a disability, a person may be assumed asexual all their life. He/she may be reliant on professional support or live in supportive institutions, which might provide no sex education or encouragement, even less in relation to LGB identities and sexual practices. Hingsburger (1993) investigated care staff attitudes towards homosexual behaviour and found that it was disapproved of significantly more (70–74%) when compared to heterosexual intercourse (28–30%), heterosexual 'petting' (23–40%), masturbation (3–4%) and receiving sex education (2–5%). Similar findings were presented more recently by Clarke and Finnegan (2005) who found that 76 per cent of staff would encourage a heterosexual relationship, while only 41 per cent a same-sex one. However, these authors did not ask specifically about sexual behaviour. Hingsburger (1992) suggests that these attitudes have become more severe since the advent of HIV/AIDS as now staff are more worried about client infection and death than pregnancy. It is therefore unclear whether staff might be more tolerant of lesbian sexuality, given that there is no risk of pregnancy and low risk of HIV transmission. More encouraging, Jones (1995) (cited in Bennett & Coyle, 2001) found that 76 per cent of care staff for pld said they would value an LGB lifestyle equally to a heterosexual one; however, only one third had actually discussed LGB sexuality with clients (even when the client was thought to be lesbian or gay), compared to two thirds who had discussed 'sexuality in general'. It is also worth noting that in Jones' (1995) study a third of staff still found it difficult to talk about sexuality in general. Stevenson (2010) provides direct advice to help staff develop these skills.

This lack of support in developing and expressing an LGB identity can result in internalised homophobia, confusion, or resistance: relabelled 'challenging behaviour'. For pld, the majority report being bullied or harassed when their sexuality was known, most often by close family members, but also by staff (Abbott & Howarth, 2005). For disabled people not living in residential communities, but who have personal assistances come into their home, they still remain vulnerable to the prejudices and discrimination of their carers. These considerations add a sensitive area of discussion to interviews with potential carers, in addition to whether they will be a good carer and get on with friends and family.

Fortunately, there are pockets within mainstream society that offer welcoming and supportive spaces. An example of this is the club night 'Night of the Senses', which attracts about a thousand people at each event and sells itself on accepting everyone however 'disabled or fit, kinky or straight, nervous or courageous, lonesome or gregarious. We believe everybody should have the chance to express their sexuality and enjoy themselves to the full[2]'. Clubs such as this provide a vital space to value and honour disabled people's sexuality.

Discrimination in LGB Communities

Acceptance of disability within LGB communities is hindered by both attitudes and physical restrictions. The assumption of asexuality ironically

---

[2] From www.nightofthesenses.com.

exists, but less as a sexual identity and more in terms of physicality. One of Appleby's (1992) research participants summed up this asexual positioning as, 'to be regarded as a potential partner, it's part of it isn't it? If you are just going to be a friend, lesbian sister, it's denying sexuality' (p.26). A number of authors suggest that the LGB community has particular issues that make acceptance of disability more difficult. Another of Appleby's (1992) interviewees suggested that 'disability means weakness, and the whole focus of building a lesbian community is about women uniting in strength . . . Basically disability issues aren't about strength.' (p.23). Shakespeare (1999) also discussed that the words used in LGB liberation, 'strength' and giving 'voice', can unintentionally exclude those with disabilities.

Disabled people may break norms of what it means to be lesbian, bisexual or gay, the latter particularly emphasising a body beautiful politic. However, while gay men may be attributed to conforming to an Adonis image of body beauty, this also extends to lesbian communities: 'You only have to go to a disco to realize to what extent lesbians have bought the idea of the slim, agile, symmetrical body' (Hearn, 1991, p.50). In Shakespeare *et al.*'s (1996) research, they found that many LGB disabled people did not feel that conventional ideas of masculine and feminine, straight and gay, applied to them. This is also captured by a participant in Whitney's (2006) study:

> . . . this whole bullshit idea of normal that really doesn't apply to anybody . . . nobody really fits into that anyway and I especially don't and there is no way I'm going to even if discrimination against queer people ends (p.46).

Lack of access to a sexual minority community can exclude an individual from access to support and a sense of belonging, to protect against heterosexism. This includes a lack of role models and examples of 'successful gay/lesbian stories' that would make identifying as a sexual minority legitimate and rewarding and help the development of a positive gay identity (Bennett & Coyle, 2001). The consequences of this exclusion can be 'exhausting, isolating, and lead to internalized ableism and homophobia' (Whitney, 2006, p.40).

Problems with physical access include restrictions to and in clubs and venues that may be up stairs, with poor lighting and very loud music. Shakespeare *et al.* (1996) suggest that 'commercial imperatives make it unnecessary for promoters and owners to cater to the small (and impoverished) disabled market' (p.161). Once in a club, the attitudes of others present can be all too apparent. This includes other customers, for example, Dafydd describes (in Shakespeare *et al.*, 1996):

> ... in the process of trying to move through the club, this guy is trying to get around me, instead of waiting for me to pass, he climbs on me, literally, puts one foot on my knee, puts another foot on the handle, and climbs right over me, thinking that's nothing, I'm just a piece of furniture (p.160).

as well as employees, for example, Sara remembers (Shakespeare *et al.*, 1996): 'I was told that two people must be with me at all times ... I was a fire risk.' (p.161). Disabled people may internalise some of these messages and feel that they are not 'measuring up', which can have a negative impact on self-esteem, as without a perfect body, or financial and social leverage, disabled people are at the bottom of the 'gay pecking order' (Thompson *et al.*, 2001).

With the advent of the Disability Discrimination Act (2005) and Disability Rights Commission, disabled people could no longer be denied access to goods, facilities and services. These provisions were replaced by The Equality Act (2010), which also makes reference to 'dual discrimination', thereby further attesting to the potential discrimination that disabled LGB people face. While this is a positive, and in some respects exemplary, move made by the Government, some beliefs, attitudes, and actions, cannot be legislated against. For instance, the experiences of Dafydd and Sara may only be minimised with such legislation.

Discrimination in the Disability Movement

> Just as we lesbians and gay men have been told our sexuality is not an issue in the campaign for civil rights for disabled people, so have people from black and ethnic communities. There are (at least) two major flaws in this thinking!! Firstly, the lesbian and gay community has been engaging in civil rights struggles for twenty plus years since the historic events of the STONEWALL riots in the USA, which served as a catalyst for a powerful, unapologetic, multifaceted campaign for lesbian and gay rights. The tactics used and the lessons learned from the black civil rights struggle virtually continuous since the boycott of buses in Alabama in defiance against segregation, are the very tactics we now employ in the disability movements in Britain ... Do we really want to exclude those from whom we have so much to learn! (Gillespie-Sells, 1992, p.23).

O'Toole and Bregante (1993) describe disability rights organisations as operating on the level of 'rampant heterosexism'. Examples such as Julie's experience (Shakespeare *et al.*, 1996) illustrate this: 'On a "Rights not Charity" march a group of deaf disabled marchers refused to march alongside those of us carrying the Lesbians and Gays with Disabilities Banner. They said they didn't want to be associated with perverts' (p.166).

Fortunately, there are Disability rights groups which counter this prejudice, such as *REGARD*, which was set up to campaign and support LGB and transsexual disabled people. REGARD worked with the media to raise awareness, for example to gain wheelchair and British Sign Language access to films during the Lesbian and Gay Film Festival held annually at the National Film Theatre, London. REGARD also represented LGBT disabled people on the UK Disabled People's Council, speaking at their conferences and meetings. Other Disability rights groups have also supported LGB people, while not being exclusively for this purpose, for example *RESPOND* supports adults and children with LD who have been abused, and *The Elfrida Society* is active in supporting people with LD in gaining their sexual rights. The *Outsiders Trust* describes itself as a 'Microcosm of Acceptance' for people with physical and social disabilities and supports people in finding partners, as well as running a sex and disability helpline.

Forming an Identity

Many models of multiple identity take an 'add-on' approach, where a person may be disabled but also LGB, or vice versa, with both identities assumed to be separate and distinct (Sherry, 2004). An alternative to this view is the idea of holding multiple identities at the same time, acknowledging their interaction, the shift from foreground to background with different contexts and the complexities this brings. Sontag (1988) does this in her examination of the cultural constructs of AIDS, by exploring the combined effects of homophobia, ablism and racism. Carrol (2009) refers to this latter approach as a 'layered' rather than 'mosaic' approach.

Some aspects of identity will hold greater or lesser social value than others (Carrol, 2009), for example, heterosexuality is generally prized over sexual minority identities and able-bodiedness over impairments. Some aspects of identity are also more visible than others; a person might choose to emphasise an invisible but valued part of their identity to make it more obvious to others (e.g. a lesbian might cut her hair and wear 'coded' accessories, such as a labrys[3] necklace), or else adapt situations to make their identity less obvious (e.g. a person with dyslexia may avoid writing on a flipchart during a workshop). The significance of 'coming out' or passing (hiding) aspects of one's identity is further discussed in the next section.

A number of identity development models exist which focus on a single aspect of identity, for example, for LGB people, Cass (1979); for black people, Cross (1971); for disabled people, Shakespeare (1996) explores different models and the complexities of a disabled identity within each. However, these single-issue and stage-based models fail to incorporate 'the complex, dynamic and interwoven nature of identities' (Carrol, 2009, p.110). For example, holding multiple identities may require the person to negotiate conflicting allegiances and values of different communities at different times (Garnets, 2002). Alternative 'interactional' models exist which allow for fluidity, and incorporate biology, cognition, history and context (Cramer & Gilson, 1999), for instance, Eliason's (1996) model of lesbian identity development, Gill's (1997) model of identity formation for disabled people, and Collins' (2000) model of biracial identity development. While these models remain single-issue, they all present four components which could be combined to create an identity development model that is applicable to every aspect of identity (Figure 9.1).

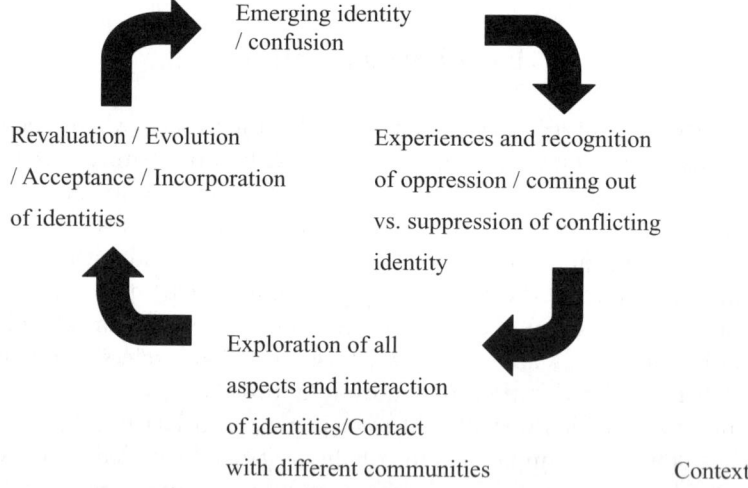

Emerging identity / confusion

Revaluation / Evolution / Acceptance / Incorporation of identities

Experiences and recognition of oppression / coming out vs. suppression of conflicting identity

Exploration of all aspects and interaction of identities/Contact with different communities

Context

Figure 9.1 **Model of multiple identity development.**

---

[3]   A labrys is symmetrical double-headed axe, which has come to be used as a lesbian symbol.

This combined model could 'start' at any point for any aspect of identity development. Jane's story provides us with a working example.

Jane's Story

Jane had polio as a child that resulted in her walking with callipers. She attended a mainstream school and had good friends. However, during her adolescence she always felt on the fringe of things and different to her friends. At first she put this down to her impairment, however, as she grew older and started to reflect on her desires and feelings, she found herself attracted to other young women. This caused her distress and confusion as she did not know who to speak to about it or how to look into it. She picked up though tentative remarks to friends and a teacher that this was not something safe to talk about. She stopped mentioning the issue but started to search the internet for information on her own. She found exciting and inspiring stories by lesbians and information about a local gay youth group. After weeks of thinking about it, she phoned the group and arranged to meet a peer supporter first before attending. At the arranged meeting she was dismayed when the peer supporter was unable to hide her surprise at seeing her callipers. The meeting was still useful and Jane arranged to attend the group, although her nervousness at the group's reaction to her impairment was very present. Jane was relieved when she was met with a mixed reaction, finding new friends and after a number of months starting a relationship. This support helped her to tell her school friends, who also reacted with surprise, but eventual acceptance. After a number of years of developing a life in the lesbian community, Jane noticed a re-emergence of a discomfort and anger at the ignorance and prejudice she encountered at various times towards her impairment. She again did some research and came across Gemma, a network of disabled lesbian and bisexual women. She felt more confident this time to introduce herself to the group, having developed a pride in her lesbian identity as well as an existing acceptance and politicisation of her disabled identity. Jane became an active member and worked on a number of awareness campaigns, alongside maintaining good connections with the different groups of friends she had made along her journey.

At any time a person may become aware of experiences of oppression and so choose to hide or emphasise one aspect of their identity over others. Later, the same individual may start to explore all aspects of their identity and seek out contact with others, and through this develop a sense of belonging and community. This leads the individual to revaluate the various aspects of their identity and integrate the different parts, leading to a more established emerging identity that may be presented to others. However, the dynamics of time and place may lead to further confusion with the newly emerged identity that could in turn lead to further oppression, as well as connection with others, etc. This model sits in a box called 'context' (see Figure 9.1) to emphasise that depending on the current context, different parts of the self will be oppressed or affirmed, brought to the fore or background, however, all parts of the self will continue to develop.

Another important identity interaction to consider is that of gender and its interaction with disability and sexual orientation. In Britain there are more disabled women than men (Martin *et al.*, 1988; Department of Work and Pensions, 2010), and these women have lower incomes, less employment and lower educational achievements (Hanna & Rogovsky, 1991). Stereotypical ideas of both women and disabled people of being 'passive' interact, so that disabled women are viewed as dependent, vulnerable and frail (Shakespeare *et al.*, 1996). Disabled men are also disadvantaged by stereotypical ideas of masculinity, these being about strength without vulnerability (Morris, 1991), and images of disabled masculinity focussing on 'perceived impotence and lack of manhood' (Shakespeare *et al.*, 1996, p.97). The privileges that patriarchy awards non-disabled men may not be awarded to those with disabilities (Shakespeare *et al.*, 1996). Gerschick and Miller (1995) summarise three ways of coping with these issues, taken from their interviews with disabled men but applicable to all genders. These are to reformulate and redefine what masculinity/femininity mean to the person, internalise traditional ideas of gender and try and live up to them, or reject outright perceived notions of gender and create alternative identities and subcultures. Interestingly, the second way of coping was met with the most problems in their study. Being a member of the disability movement could help achieve the first and third strategy, with alternative ideas of attractiveness, different values and support (Shakespeare *et al.*, 1996). However, it is contestable how different ideas of body beauty are between non-disabled culture and LGB communities, with lesbian and gay communities having embraced 'the cult of the body' (Shakespeare *et al.*, 1996, p.71) as mentioned previously.

The idea of an integrated identity being an achievable goal is currently under question. For example, Halbertal and Koren (2006) found that Orthodox Jewish gay men and lesbians were unable to integrate these two aspects of their identity, but both aspects remained valued and so participants founds ways to negotiate, rather than integrate, the two. We are at a pivotal point in postmodernism where an integrated model of identity is crying out to be developed to accommodate multiple sites of belonging, why some identities will be fore-grounded over others, and the differences between visible/invisible identities.

Coming Out Versus Passing

Majority groups may discriminate against the minority identity(ies) held by an individual, which may make the person try to hide their discouraged identity and 'pass' as either heterosexual and/or non-disabled to find social acceptance and approval (O'Toole & Bregante, 1992). Morris (1991) picks up on this desire to pass as 'normal' for disabled people and the stresses it can place on an individual, suggesting to resist this internal stigmatisation as a member of the disability rights movement is to 'challenge[s] our own prejudices about ourselves, as well as those of the non-disabled culture' (p.37). Saad (1997) goes as far as to suggest that passing is harmful to one's health. There are parallels between this and coming out as lesbian, bisexual or gay: this literature also contains writers who purport that to hide ones sexuality places the individual under psychological stress that is detrimental to overall wellbeing (e.g. McCormick, 1994). However, coming out has also been deemed a privilege of those who are a majority group member in all other parts of their identity, for instance, being white, living in the Western world, and so on. Most coming out research has been conducted with white participants, which fails to account for 'white privilege' and the cultural pressure in some communities to be heterosexual (Smith, 1997). The intersectionality of social difference must be considered when describing the complexities of coming out as lesbian, bisexual, gay and/or disabled. People may choose to be selectively out about their impairment or their sexuality depending on the context, choosing to come out at times when it has most personal and political significance (Hillyer, 1993), or only with people considered safe to disclose to.

Shakespeare *et al.* (1996) suggest that coming out as disabled is primarily a political identity as people refer to the 'disability movement' rather than the 'disability community', reflected in the fact there is not a broad based social scene as there is for sexual minorities (with the exception of the deaf community). Coming out and accepting ones impairment are not the same, people may feel they are not disabled 'enough' to take on this identity, which Shakespeare *et al.* (1996, p.53) suggest is because 'disabled people are made to feel guilty or grateful for any concessions which they enjoy, this feeling of fraudulence is common . . . and is part of the internalized oppression'. An advantage to 'coming out' and taking on a political identity is that it grants access to membership of a wider community of support and reinforcement. Shakespeare *et al.* (1996) found that for those who had come out as disabled it involved 'redefining disability as a political oppression; identifying collectively with other disabled people and with disability culture; overcoming the internalised oppression' (p.58): all of which are described as steps in forming a positive identity earlier, and which apply to multiple oppressed identities (also see Chapter 8 on *Mental Health*). However, Shakespeare (1999) reports that people find more support and primarily identify with the community they have been in for longest, whether this is LGB or disability. Other authors suggest that, like 'add-on' models of identity development, individuals 'compartmentalize themselves into multiple persons, seeking the comfort of different homes for different needs' (Boykin, 1996; p.122). Sara describes how her needs for support shifted after she became disabled (Shakespeare *et al.*, 1996, p.172):

> I did feel a need to meet other disabled people. I felt I did not belong fully to the lesbian scene any more, but neither did I fit in with disabled heterosexuals. I felt very alone and isolated for the first time in my life.

However, understanding from other LGB disabled people may not be assured, for example if people have a different impairment that resulted in disability.

Growing Up

Disabled LGB people may lack support from their family when growing up, where they may well be the only LGB and only disabled member. Forming a positive identity as either disabled or LGB may be actively discouraged (Shakespeare *et al.*, 1996). Shuttleworth (2000), in his interviews with men with cerebral palsy, found that a factor which made forming relationships in adulthood difficult was 'socio-sexual isolation during formative years' (p.265), a time when other non-disabled peers where learning how to flirt and negotiate sexual intimacy. Linked to this were parents sending negative messages about the possibility of having a fulfilling sex life. Indeed, many disabled people speak about being treated differently from non-disabled siblings; they were discouraged to be curious about sex/relationships (Shakespeare *et al.*, 1996). In addition, disabled people may lack privacy to learn about their sexuality, bodies, or to masturbate if parents and/or carers are often present, this may be particularly so if the young person is seeking out information on LGB matters.

Many disabled adults today were children at a time when segregation in education was encouraged for disabled children, boarding in 'special schools' where sex, particularly same-sex sexuality, was excluded from curriculum and informal discussions with staff. However, this did not mean that young people were not experimenting with sex and relationships, as described by Daniel (Shakespeare *et al.*, 1996, p.22):

> . . . a special school for boys where there was plenty of opportunity for sex and I had a lot of sex there with a lot of different boys. Looking back it was the best thing about boarding school. The most desirable boys were the haemophiliacs because they were closest to being non-disabled, almost god-like. The least desirable were those with muscular dystrophy, and I felt I was somewhere in the middle.

While Daniel found opportunities for positive sexual exploration in his school, sadly such institutions also create opportunities for abuse, as described so eloquently by Cross (1994, p.165):

> There are the ones who are chosen because they cannot speak of the horror. There are the ones who are chosen because they cannot run away, and there is nowhere to run. There are the ones who are chosen because their very lives depend on not fighting back. These are the ones who are chosen because there is no one for them to tell. There are the ones who are chosen because no one has even taught them the words. There are the ones who are chosen because society chooses to believe that, after all, they don't really have any sexuality, so it can't hurt them.

Relationships

The pecking order of desirability held by disabled and non-disabled people, described previously in Daniel's experience of school, continues in adult life. Non-disabled people have their choices questioned and scrutinised if they choose to date a disabled person (Bullard & Knight, 1981). Cynical reasons given to such a partnership might include 'desire to hide his/her own inadequacies in the disabled partner's obvious ones; an altruistic and saintly desire to sacrifice their lives to our care; neurosis of some sort, or plain old fashioned fortune-hunting' (Morris, 1991, p.22–23). Partners may themselves be viewed as nonsexual caregivers (O'Toole & Bregante, 1992). When non-disabled partners are involved in care and support it can place a strain on the relationship with shifting dynamics of power. This might be because of a pressure to not upset the non-disabled partner in case they withdraw their support. This might include hiding feelings of tiredness or pain and lead the disabled partner to doubt whether they are equally contributing to the relationship.

Opportunities to meet potential partners might be limited when social venues are unaccommodating. The internet, phone lines and lonely hearts columns might provide some alternative, although a person may feel the need to carefully monitor the information they reveal about themselves in the early stages of contact (Shakespeare *et al.*, 1996). When starting to date, a disabled person may struggle with deciding the best time to tell their new interest that they have a chronic illness or disability (Pakenham *et al.*, 1996). This may be particularly the case for LGB people who use internet dating/sex sites to meet potential partners. Sadly, Shakespeare *et al.* (1996) report that disabled people who could 'pass' as non-disabled were more successful at meeting partners.

If a disabled person is single it is often assumed that it is because they cannot find a partner rather than that this was their choice (Morris, 1991). Similarly, if a disabled person dates another disabled person this can also be assumed as because they cannot meet a non-disabled person who would date them (Morris, 1991). Morris (1991) suggests that 'when we choose 'our own kind' in this way the able-bodied world feels relieved, until of course we wish to have children; then we're seen as irresponsible' (p.22–23). This is particularly so for disabled LGB parents who also face the homophobia and heterosexism directed at LGB parents in general, as well as ableist discourse that disabled people cannot be good/capable parents. While Shakespeare *et al.* (1996) report that initially disabled people may avoid dating others with disability, once they 'come out' as disabled and become politically active, many disabled people meet disabled partners and find strength and support in a shared understanding of social oppression. Pansexual clubs and dating agencies exist to help disabled people meet other disabled people for sex and relationships (e.g. www.DisabilityMatch.co.uk).

Sex

Tepper (2000) argues that 'sex is portrayed as a privilege of the white, heterosexual, young, single and non-disabled' (p.285). It is used in marketing as a reward for buying the right product or wearing the right clothes: 'sexual portrayals of people who are older, who are larger, who are darker, who are gayer, who are mentally or physically disabled, or who just do not fit the targeted market profile have been conspicuously absent in mainstream media' (p.285). Tepper goes on to point out that these groups are also absent from discussions about pleasure in medical and scientific research literature. Disabled people are also deeply influenced by the high status of sex, as captured by Frances: 'It is almost as if to have sex as a disabled person is "Phew, I've made the grade and joined the club"' (Shakespeare *et al.*, 1996, p.93).

Comfort, back in 1978, highlighted that:

> ... individuals whose mobility is limited or whose deformity is evident are exposed to other forms of attack upon their sense of worth and desirability. Cultural constructs, such as a wholly unrealistic emphasis on physical beauty or strength as an index of being desirable, and the practical barriers of finding a partner, all combine to make the aim of sexual self-validation seem better given up (p.3).

These sentiments are echoed in 2000 by Shakespeare who states that sexuality 'has been an area of distress, and exclusion, and self-doubt for so long, that it was sometimes easier not to consider it' (p.160). Tepper (2000) also proposes that the combination of low self-esteem and physical limitations (such as difficulties with orgasm or arousal) 'may affirm unexpressed beliefs of asexuality, and may lead to the conclusion "why bother"' (p.288). However, it is worth noting that for some people, whether heterosexual or LGB, disabled or non-disabled, an asexual identity fits with their sense of self (Prause & Graham, 2007). The importance emphasis is whether this identity has been chosen as an affirmation of self or from an oppression of the sexual self.

For those with acquired disability, measuring oneself against what was previously possible links to cultural ideas of sex being about genitals and orgasm, perfect performance and body perfection, which combine to lower sexual self-esteem (Tepper, 2000). These are the consequences of relying on a fantasy model of sex, which disables both those with and without disability. For those who have expanded the definition of sex, rejected ableist and sexist ideals and accepted and accommodated impairments, great sex is still possible (Tepper, 2000), as described by Don Smith (in Bullard & Knight, 1981, p.16):

> I felt asexual for a long time because a man's sex was supposed to be in his penis, and I couldn't feel my penis. So that contributed to my feelings of being asexual; it didn't occur to me that it felt good to have the back of my neck licked, or that it felt good to have my arms stroked lightly. Stroking the wrists,

then to the arms, then up the arms, is a sequence that I've since learned can be very exciting.

Several interviewees of Shakespeare *et al.* (1996) took this one stage further and suggested that actually sex was better because of the interaction with disability, either in having to use one's imagination and be creative in what could be done, or needing sexual partners to talk more explicitly about what was possible. Thus perspectives on what is sex can run counter to 'traditional' ideas which stress the importance of the sexual response cycle (desire/arousal/orgasm/resolution). Such a model might position disabled people as having sexual problems, when they may not themselves consider this the case. A breaking of sexual and gendered cultural norms is a lesson non-disabled people would be wise to learn. One could argue that lesbians and gays have already broken the definition of sex = penis entering vagina, and so the variety of what is possible and what is sexy has already been opened up for exploration.

However, a celebration of sexual diversity may not be the case for every-one, as described by Beth who has a degenerative condition (Shakespeare *et al.*, 1996, p.105):

> There are now physical difficulties in having sex . . . I can never do what I want to do without help. Sometimes this is not important, at other times it makes me feel that I am a failure.

In Britain, the area of sexual facilitators (where carers are present and activity help people have sex, e.g. getting into a comfortable position) is a controversial area. Carers may offer this but it is rarely openly advertised, and may be an issue hard to raise in an interview. Most agencies that provide carers would not have a policy about this and so carers would be acting outside of their legal/contractual remit. Such services may be even more limited for same-sex sex. Other countries, such as The Netherlands, are much clearer about this as a service, as well as that of *sexual enablers*: sex workers who have been trained to work with sexual dysfunction and physical obstacles. However, the *Tender Loving Care Trust* exists to link sex workers with disabled people (www.tlc-trust.org.uk). The volunteers that run the website are keen that 'disabled people do not live their lives in frustration, and can grown and learn from sex workers in order to follow their sexual dreams'.

An aspect of sex where disabled people have been actively involved and welcomed for a long time is in the area of BDSM (Bondage/Discipline, Dominance/Submission, Sadism/Masochism). It has been suggested that this is because this community accommodates different bodies and plays with the boundaries between pleasure and pain experienced within said bodies (Reynolds, 2007). The performance artist Bob Flanagan captured this relationship in his work and challenged assumptions of disability being about weakness, dysfunction and asexuality (Reynolds, 2007). Mistress Steel (on www.steel-door.com) suggests that trust and avenues for clear communication are especially important in BDSM relationships that involve disabled participants, as there are potentially greater degrees of risk and difficulty, e.g. it may take a disabled submissive longer to heal if bruising or injuries occur. She describes how 'Tops' or 'Dominants' may bring an assistant to a 'scene' to act as their hands/eyes/ears; or if not using an assistant, a dominant may create an 'escape avenue' for the submissive, in case the dominant begins to experience difficulties in finishing a scene. An in-depth exploration of how some disabled people involve their impairments in their BDSM play is given by Robert Rubel and Angela Stassinopoulos (2007) in their book *Playing with Disabilities* (Power Exchange Books). Examples of this might include making a submissive tow a wheelchair by attaching it to their harness.

Learning Disabilities

Little has been done to operationally encourage sexual and romantic relationships for people with learning disabilities (pld) (Brown, 1994), particularly for those who seek same-sex connections, despite much work on asserting the sexual rights of pld with sex education, staff training and policy development. For example, *Valuing People* by the Department of Health (2001) made it clear there needs to be access to sex education and support to form relationships. Similarly, the NHS in Scotland has several clear policies for those working with pld to support their sexuality, including same-sex relationships and LGB identities (e.g. Highland Learning Disabilities and Relationships Group [HLDRG], 2007; Health Scotland, 2008). There are resources for pld about their sexual rights, including same-sex relationships (e.g. City of Westminster *et al.*, 2010). Numerous voluntary sector organisations also that provide social and relationship support but these are not necessarily LGB organisations.

However, in practice pld are rarely supported to live as couples, but instead as small groups of adults with careful maintenance of sexual boundaries between them (Brown, 1994). Brown (1994) suggests that living as a couple is a reward for 'independence skills and financial autonomy' (p.127). Some pld form same-sex relationships because of being segregated into same-sex living arrangements or because they were discouraged from forming heterosexual relationships (HLDRG, 2007). In addition, the sex education that is provided tends to have a heterosexual focus and is mainly about biology rather than social/emotional aspects of relationships and sex (Brown, 1994). There is therefore the assumption of 'compulsory heterosexuality' (Rich, 1980). Interestingly, Appleby (1993) has criticised this term when it is applied to women with disabilities as she maintains that these women are still considered asexual, while being at greater risk of (hetero)sexual abuse and rape. McRuer (2002) expands this idea to suggest that 'compulsory heterosexuality' is inextricably linked to 'compulsory able-bodied-ness', in that 'hegemonic heterosexuality is premised upon a lack of disability, and 'compulsory able-bodied-ness' likewise demands heterosexuality' (Sherry, 2004, p.778).

Those who experience same-sex attraction are rarely encouraged to form a positive identity and any resulting sexual behaviour is likely to be covert rather than seen as a positive choice (Brown, 1994). And yet pld have specifically asked for concrete support around meeting other LGB people and that staff see this as a legitimate part of their work (Abbott & Howarth, 2005). However, it should be remembered that not all pld may feel confident or comfortable being 'out', for example because of fear of rejection from services (Abbott & Howarth, 2005). This is particularly important given that, compared to non-disabled peers, pld are more likely to be socially isolated and have fewer close friends (Bayley, 1997), and less variety of places to meet potential partners (e.g. work, college, etc.: Shakespeare, 2000). Unfortunately, staff often report not being skilled enough or having the confidence to do this work, and those who are LGB themselves are rarely out to service-users (Abbott & Howarth, 2005).

Stauffer-Kruse (2007) captures the multiple barriers for pld in developing a positive LGB identity:

- Pld have internalised more negative attitudes towards relationships and sexuality than the general public.
- Pld may struggle to assess the attitudes of others and be able to identify a support network.
- Pld may struggle to manage relationship conflicts and complex emotions associated with relationships.
- Pld may be poorly informed or able to assert themselves to look after their sexual health and ask for what they want.
- Pld are unfortunately vulnerable to exploitation and sexual abuse, and it may be hard to distinguish between a potential sexual partner and the deceptive lure of a violent homophobe.

Moving forward from this state of affairs not only needs clear policy, staff training and support, but also work with pld themselves to break down internalised homophobia. Pld may be unaware that there are LGB communities, and only aware of the stigma associated with the identity label (Thompson *et al.*, 2001). Brown (1994) suggests to would be helpful for staff to conceptualise Weeks' (1991) idea of 'elective communities' when considering how to support LGB pld. These involve support groups around particular issues and it might be that someone is a member of multiple groups to reflect the multiple aspects of their identity. Fortunately, Abbott and Howarth (2005) found many examples of good work done by care staff in this area. This was particularly when staff felt they had their manager's support, clear policies and training and had thought through equality and diversity issues. This was reflected in the views of pld they interviewed, who reported what a difference it made to have non-judgemental, open and accepting staff who helped them feel accepted and offered practical support. Even practices such as having photographs of same-sex couples displayed in day centres or residential settings had a tremendous impact on feelings of acceptance and belonging.

Abbott and Howarth (2005) found that women who have same-sex feelings were more hidden that men. For their national survey, they found it 'relatively easy' to find men to interview, but struggled to interview women and finally only found nine who identified as lesbian or bisexual. However, for those they interviewed, it is encouraging that the majority of stories were of survival and success. Those who did best were members of learning disability advocacy organisations which emphasised the importance of social activities. Carson and Docherty (2002) suggest that such groups are better suited than residential or day centre staff at supporting services-users in friendships and relationships.

HIV/AIDS

Following the advent of AIDS in the 1980s and the associated stigma it attracted not only to those who were infected, but all 'homosexuals', it was hoped by the early 90s that AIDS would assist disabled LGB people:

> It could be said that disabled lesbians and gays have gained because of AIDS. It has forced the gay community to recognise human frailty and to start living at a rate and in a manner that will include all of us (Hearn, 1991, p.37).

Sadly this did not come to pass as the gay scene remains focussed on beauty being young, able, bodies without imperfections (Bennett & Coyle, 2001). This image holds true today for the gay scene, but Wendell (1996) highlights that the image of 'the ideal body' changes in different cultural context and through time. This pressure can be oppressive for those with and without disabilities but for those with disabilities/HIV there is also a shared experience of stigma and oppression about the disability/virus, a tension Corbett (1994) refers to as 'cultural dissonance' (p.345). For those living with the virus who are fit and well, HIV sits like a 'hidden impairment' with ethical issues about if/when to come out and disclose ones status. Fear of rejection, or of people spreading the information, make this a difficult decision. In Sweden it is a legal requirement to disclose one's HIV status if positive before having sex, whether or not a condom is used. In Britain, people have been prosecuted for infecting others with HIV through sex and not disclosing their status, yet no law exists to protect the uninfected from other transmittable diseases such a pneumonia or tuberculosis. These laws perhaps reflect a wider prejudice against those most affected by the virus: Africans, injecting drug users and gay men.

For those who are more advanced in the condition, opportunistic infections (such as cancers, pneumonia, eye conditions, etc) may result in acquired impairments, with a more marked shift to an identity as disabled as personal assistance or aids such as wheelchairs are needed. O'Brian *et al.* (2008) developed an 'episodic disability framework' to capture the experiences of disability for HIV positive people, based on the episodic nature of illness and health. This framework is made up of three components:

1. Dimension of disability: symptoms and impairments, uncertainty, difficulties with day-to-day functioning and social inclusion.
2. Contextual factors: support, stigma, strategies to cope.
3. Life events: diagnosis, starting medication, serious illness, loss of others from AIDS.

Their framework unites elements of the medical and social model of disability, and may be a useful guide to exploring the impact of HIV/AIDS on a person's life.

However, there is some resistance within the disability movement to accept those with an AIDS defining illnesses as disabled, with resentment towards its high profile and support services available (Shakespeare *et al.*, 1996). This also perhaps reflects prejudice against already stigmatised groups. People with HIV may therefore face discrimination from both those within and outside disability movements. However, some campaigning alliances have successfully been formed, such as between REGARD and the *UK Coalition of People Living with HIV and AIDS.*

Conclusion

Like Shakespeare (2000), I would also like to conclude by invoking Weeks (1998), as a kind of manifesto for change. Weeks suggests that to become sexual citizens, and here disabled sexual citizens, we need to:

1. Demand control: of our bodies, feelings and relationships.
2. Demand access: to be represented, to public spaces and to relationships.
3. Demand choice: about our identities, lifestyles and gendered experiences.

Guidelines for Good Practice

A useful position to adopt for a therapist or researcher working in this area is one of 'non-expert' (Anderson & Goolishan, 1992). This position allows the professional to bring their expertise (in the form of theory, questions, techniques) but to be openly curious about their client's ways of viewing and living in the world: leaving 'behind her own cultural biases and pre-understandings, to enter the experience of the other' (Laid, 1999, p.75). This is particularly essential if the professional has a different sexuality or disability status to the client. Such a non-expert position allows the professional to directly address issues of identity, including (Carroll, 2009, p.119-120):

- 'How to integrate the sometimes divergent aspects of identity. . .
- How to understand the impact such identities have on their relationships with others;
- How to grasp a sense of pride and privilege at being a member of a particular group;
- How to get clients to ask directly about any concerns they might feel working with therapist who are in either a minority or a majority culture.'

In addition, professionals would do well to increase the basics of their knowledge in this area by:

- Becoming familiar with support systems and organisations, while recognising that some may not be welcoming to LGB people. Professionals can use such support organisations to become more familiar with the issues clients may present with (e.g. SHADA: the Sexual Health and Disability Alliance who run conferences and a phone line, and have a resources section on their website; www.shada.org.uk).

- Invite clients to talk about sex and relationships and model that you are comfortable discussing this topic.
- Consider your privilege from whatever position you take in terms of sexuality and disability. Reflect on how this might influence therapy/ research.

In addition to the content of therapy/research itself, professionals should consider whether their work premises are physically accessible (including accessibility of information, e.g. could a wheelchair users reach the leaflet rack?), what messages are given by the images (or lack of) that are displayed on the walls and notice boards, and what policies and training is in place to ensure equality for all service-users.

References

Abbott, D. & Howarth, J. (2005). *Secret loves, hidden lives? Exploring issues for people with learning difficulties who are gay, lesbian or bisexual.* Bristol: The Policy Press.

Anderson, H. & Goolishian, H. (1992). The client is the expert: A not-knowing approach to therapy. In S. McNamee and K. Gergen (Eds.), *Social construction and the therapeutic process.* Newbury Park, CA: Sage.

Appleby, Y. (1992). Out in the margins. *Disability and Society,* 9(1), 19–32.

Appleby, Y. (1993). Disability and 'compulsory heterosexuality'. In C. Kitzinger & S. Wilkinson (Eds), *Heterosexuality.* London: Sage.

Asch, A. & Fine, F. (1988). Introduction: Beyond pedestals. In M. Fine & A. Asch (1988). *Women with disabilities: Essays in psychology, culture, and politics.* Philadelphia: Temple University Press.

Bayley, M. (1997). *What price friendship: Encouraging the relationships of people with learning difficulties.* Wootton Courtnay: Hexagon Publishing.

Begum, N. (1992). Disabled women and the feminist agenda. *Feminist Review, 40,* Spring, 70–84.

Bennett, C.J. & Coyle, A. (2001). A minority within a minority: Identity and well-being among gay men with learning disabilities. *Lesbian and Gay Psychology Review, 2,* 9–15.

Boykin, K. (1996). *One more river to cross: Black and gay in America.* New York: Bantam Doubleday Dell.

Brown, H. (1994). 'An ordinary sexual life?': A review of the normalisation principle as it applies to the sexual options of people with learning disabilities. *Disability and Society,* 9(2), 123–144.

Bullard, D.G. & Knight, S.E. (1981). *Sexuality and physical disability: Personal perspectives.* New York: Mosby.

Burns, J. (1993). Sexuality, sexual problems and people with learning disability. In J.M. Ussher & C.D. Baker (Eds), *Psychological perspectives on sexual problems: New directions in theory and practice.* London: Routledge.

Carroll, L. (2009). *Counseling sexual and gender minorities.* New Jersey: Merrill.

Carson, I. & Docherty, D. (2002). Friendships, relationships and issues in sexuality. In D. Race (Ed), *Learning disability: A social approach.* London: Routledge.

Cass, V.C. (1979). Homosexual identity formation: A theoretical model. *Journal of Homosexuality, 9,* 105–126.

City of Westminster, NHS Westminster, Image in Action and FPA (2010). *Personal and sexual relationship policy for adults with learning disabilities.* London: pwp:fs (Available on *The Outsiders* website).

Clarke, S. & Finnegan, P. (2005). *One law for all? The impact of the Human Rights Act on people with learning difficulties.* London: Values into Action.

Collins, J.F. (2000). Biracial-bisexual individuals: Identity coming of age. *International Journal of Sexuality and Gender Studies, 5*(3), 221–253.

Comfort, A. (1978). *Sexual consequences of disability.* Philadelphia: George F. Stickley Company.

Corbett, J. (1994). A Proud Label: Exploring the relationship between disability politics and gay pride. *Disability and Society, 9*(3), 343–357.

Cramer, E. & Gilson, S. (1999). Queers and crips: Parallel identity development processes for persons with non-visible disabilities and lesbian, gay and bisexual persons. *Journal of Gay, Lesbian, Bisexual Identity, 1*(1), 23–37.

Cross, M. (1994). Abuse. In L. Keith (Ed), *Mustn't grumble.* London: Women's Press.

Cross, W.E. (1971). The negro-to-black conversion experience. *Black World, 20*(9), 13–27.

Department of Health (2001). *Valuing People: A new strategy for learning disability for the 21st century.* London: Her Majesty's Stationery Office.

Department of Work and Pensions (DWP) (2010). *Family resources survey, 2008-9.* London: DWP.

Eliason, M. (1996). An inclusive model of lesbian identity assumption. *Journal of Gay, Lesbian and Bisexual Identity, 4*(1), 23–73.

Erevelles, N. (1996). Disability and the dialectics of difference. *Disability and Society, 11,* 519–537.

Garnets, L.D. (2002). Sexual orientations in perspective. *Cultural Diversity & Ethnic Minority Psychology, 8*(2), 115–129.

Gerschick, T.J. & Miller, A.S. (1995). Coming to terms. In D. Sabo and D. Gordon (Eds), *Men's health and illness.* London: Sage.

Gill, C. (1997). Four types of integration in disability identity development. *Journal of Vocational Rehabilitation, 9*(1), 39–46.

Gillespie-Sells, K. (1992). Sing if you're happy that way! *Rights Not Charity, 1,* 23–24.

Halbertal, T.H. & Koren, I. (2006). Between 'being' and 'doing': Conflict and co-herence in the identity formation of gay and lesbian orthodox Jews. In D.P. McAdams, R. Josselson & A. Lieblich (Eds), *Identity and story: Creating self in narrative.* Washington, DC: American Psychological Association.

Hanna, W. & Rogovsky, B. (1991). Women with disabilities: Two handicaps plus. *Disability, Handicap and Society, 6*(1), 49–63.

Health Scotland (2008). *Sexual health and relationships: A review of resources for people with learning disabilities.* Edinburgh/Glasgow: Health Scotland.

Hearn, K. (1991). Disabled lesbians and gay are here to stay! In T. Kaufmann and P. Lincoln (Eds), *High risk lives.* Bridport, CT: Prism Press.

Highland Learning Disabilities and Relationships Group (HLDRG) (2007). *Work-ing with people with learning disabilities about relationships and sexual-ity: Good practice guidance for staff.* Retrieved 5 September 2011 from www.highland.gov.uk.

Hingsburger, D. (1992). Human rights and HIV/AIDS: Recommendations con-cerning the rights of people with developmental disabilities. *Canadian Journal of Human Sexuality, 27*(2), 18–20.

Hingsburger, D. (1993). Staff attitudes, homosexuality and developmental disabil-ity: a minority within a minority. *The Canadian Journal of Human Sexuality, 2*(1), 19–22.

Hillyer, B. (1993). *Feminism and disability.* Norman: University of Oklahoma Press.

Jones, V. (1995). *Heterosexism and homosexual oppression in the provision of services to support the sexuality of people who have a learning difficulty.* Unpublished manuscript, Winchester: Kings Alfred's College.

Laid, J. (1999). Gender and sexuality in lesbian relationships: Feminist and con-structionist perspectives. In J. Laird (Ed), *Lesbians and lesbian families.* New York: Columbia University Press.

Martin, J., Meltzer, H. & Elliot, D. (1988). *The prevalence of disability among adults.* London: HMSO.

McCormick, N.B. (1994). *Sexual salvation: Affirming women's sexual rights and pleasures.* Westport, CT: Praeger.

McRuer, R. (2002). Compulsory able-bodiedness and queer / disabled existence. In S.L. Snyder, J. Brueggeman & R. Garland-Thomson (Eds), *Disability studies: Enabling the humanities.* New York: The Modern Language Association.

Morris, J. (1991). *Pride against prejudice.* London: Women's Press.

O'Brian, K.K., Bayoumi, A.M., Strike, C., Young, N.L. & Davis, A.M. (2008). Explor-ing disability from the perspective of adults living with HIV/AIDS: Developing a conceptual framework. *Health and Quality of Life Outcomes, 6,* 76. Retrieved 6 September 2010 from http://www.hqlo.com/content/6/1/76.

O'Toole, C.J. (2000). The view from below: Developing a knowledge base about an unknown population. *Sexuality and Disability, 18*(3), 207–224.

O'Toole, C.J. & Bregante, J.L. (1992). Lesbians with disabilities. *Sexuality and Dis-ability, 10*(3), 163–172.

O'Toole, C.J. & Bregante, J.L. (1993). Disabled lesbians: Multicultural realities. In M. Nagler (Ed), *Perspectives on disabilities* (2nd edn.). Pale Alto, CA: Health Markets Research.

Oliver, M. (1992). Changing the social relations of research production. *Disability, Handicap and Society, 7,* 157–166.

Pakenham, K.I., Dadds, M.R. & Terry, D.J. (1996). Adaptive demands along the HIV disease continuum. *Social Science and Medicine, 42*(2), 245–256.

Prause, N. & Graham, C. (2007). Asexuality: Classification and characterization. *Archives of Sexual Behaviour, 36,* 341–356.

Renteria, D. (1993). Rejection. In R. Luczak (Ed), *Eyes of desire: a deaf gay and lesbian reader.* Boston, US: Alyson Publications.

Reynolds, D. (2007). Disability and BDSM: Bob Flanagan and the case for sexual rights. *Sexuality Research and Social Policy: Journal of NSRC, 4*(1), 40–51.

Rich, A. (1980). Compulsory heterosexuality and lesbian existence. In C. Stimpson & E. Person (Eds), *Women, sex and sexuality,* Chicago, IL: University of Chicago Press.

Saad, S.C. (1997). Disability and the lesbian, gay man or bisexual individual. In M. Sipski & C. Alexander (Eds), *Sexual function in people with disability and chronic illness: A health professional's guide.* Gaithersburg, MD: Aspen Publications.

Saxton, M. (ed.) (1987). *With wings: An anthology of literature by and about women with disabilities.* New York, NY: Feminist Press at the City University of New York.

Shakespeare, T. (1996). Disability, identity and difference. In C. Barnes & G. Mercer (Eds), *Exploring the divide.* Leeds: The Disability Press.

Shakespeare, T. (1999). Coming out and coming home. *Journal of Gay, Lesbian and Bisexual Identity, 4*(1), 39–51.

Shakespeare, T. (2000). Disabled sexuality: Toward rights and recognition. *Sexuality and Disability, 18*(3), 159–166.

Shakespeare, T., Gillespie-Sells, K. & Davies, D. (1996). *The sexual politics or disability: Untold Desires.* London: Cassell.

Shapiro, J. (1993). *No pity.* New York, NY: Random House.

Sherry, M. (2004). Overlaps and contradictions between queer theory and disability studies. *Disability and Society, 19*(7), 769–783.

Shuttleworth, R.P. (2000). The search for sexual intimacy for men with Cerebral Palsy. *Sexuality and Disability, 18*(4), 263–282.

Smith, A. (1997). Cultural diversity and the coming-out process: Implications for clinical practice. In B. Green (Ed), *Ethnic and cultural diversity among lesbians and gay men.* Thousand Oaks, CA: Sage.

Sontag, S. (1988). *AIDS and its metaphors.* New York, NY: Farrar, Straus & Giroux.

Stauffer-Kruse, S. (2007). Gay men with learning disabilities: UK service provision. *Journal of Gay and Lesbian Psychotherapy, 11*(1/2), 145–152.

Stevenson, C. (2010). Talking about sex. In C. Butler, A. O'Donovan & E. Shaw (Eds.), *Sex, sexuality and therapeutic practice.* London: Routledge.

Tepper, M.S. (2000). Sexuality and disability: The missing discourse of please. *Sexuality and Disability, 18*(4), 283–290.

Thompson, S.A., Bryon, M. & de Castell, S. (2001). Prospects for identity formation for lesbian, gay, or bisexual persons with developmental disabilities. *International Journal of Disability, Development and Education, 48*(1), 53–65.

Weeks, J. (1991). Questions of Identity. In *Against nature. Essays on history, sexuality and identity*. London: Rivers Oram Press.

Weeks, J. (1998). The sexual citizen. *Theory, culture and society, 15*(3–4), 35–52.

Wendell, S. (1996). *The rejected body: Feminist philosophical reflections on disability*. New York: Routledge.

Whitney, C. (2006). Intersections in identity – Identity development among queer women with disabilities. *Sexuality and Disability, 24*(1), 39–52.

10

Age and Ageing

Stuart Gibson & Susan Hansen

Lifespan developmental psychology is based primarily on heterosexual samples. In this chapter we consider the issues faced by lesbian, gay and bisexual (LGB) people during different stages of life. We consider the role of generational effects in determining the life experiences, survival strategies and challenges faced by young, middle aged and older LGB people. Today's older LGB people grew up in a blatantly intolerant social and legislative environment. This is very different from the apparently more liberal and 'tolerant' socio-political environment in which LGB adolescents are coming to terms with their sexuality today. Indeed, the age at which young LGB people report their first same-sex experience is dropping in inverse proportion to the increase in rights, recognition and media visibility of LGB people. Although we discuss some key aspects of life experience for LGB people in youth and early adulthood, a good deal of this chapter is devoted to the experience of 'getting older'. This is because much of the literature on LGB people is 'youth oriented' and tends to neglect the experiences of older LGB people.

Young People

Adolescence is a key life stage for LGB people, as it is during this stage that sexuality becomes increasingly salient. There is considerable literature on the process of 'coming out' or the process of coming to identify as lesbian or gay (e.g. Cass, 1979; Coleman, 1982). More recently, researchers have explored models of coming out and identity development for bisexuals (e.g. Gurevich

Intersectionality, Sexuality and Psychological Therapies: Working with Lesbian, Gay and Bisexual Diversity,
First Edition. Edited by Roshan das Nair and Catherine Butler.
© 2012 John Wiley & Sons, Ltd. Published 2012 by John Wiley & Sons, Ltd. and the British Psychological Society.

et al., 2007; Weinberg *et al.*, 1994). Such stage models have been subject to considerable critique (e.g. Clarke *et al.*, 2010) as they tend to neglect socio-historical and cultural context, and to assume that developing an identity as LGB is a straightforward sequential process of 'self-discovery'. Such models also do not take into account the possibility of any fluidity in sexual identity over the lifespan. Savin-Williams (2005) notes that many young people may actively resist sexual identity 'labels' and may experience attractions to, and relationships with, people of all sexes without consequently identifying as LGB. However, there is more research on the fluidity of sexual identity in young women than in young men. Diamond (2008) studied the sexual identity development of 79 non-heterosexual young women (18–25) over a ten-year period and found considerable fluidity at the level of both identification and sexual practice. After ten years, 67 per cent had altered their sexual identity category. Sixty per cent of 'lesbian' young women reported having had sexual contact with a man during this period. Notably, 80 per cent reported adopting the labels 'bisexual' or 'unlabelled' at some point during the ten-year period of the study. This challenges the notion that bisexuality is a 'transitional' identity. As we will also see, there is some fluidity of sexual identity in older women, too.

Non-heterosexual adolescents are more likely than are heterosexual adolescents to engage in sexual activity at a younger age, including both same-sex activity and heterosexual intercourse. Young LGB people are also more likely to engage in 'risky' sexual behaviours, including unprotected heterosexual intercourse, the reasons for which are many (and covered in Chapter 6). Such behaviours are also related to problematic levels of substance use, including alcohol. Higher levels of problematic alcohol use in young LGB people are in part a product of community events based around pub, cabaret and nightclub socialising. The consumption of alcohol is often positively regarded in such community spaces and illicit drugs may also be readily available at some of these venues, whilst other more 'family oriented' venues have a firm ban on illicit substance use by their patrons, on or off site.

LGB adolescents are particularly vulnerable to mental health problems, and adverse experiences of discrimination and harassment, relative to their heterosexual peers. However, although much of the focus of the literature remains on the heightened risk of mental health, social and health problems for non-heterosexual youth, an emerging focus points to the resilience of many young LGB people in the face of such adversity (e.g. Savin-Williams, 2001). Supportive families of origin, strong interpersonal relationships, and tolerant school environments may protect many younger LGB people from experiencing the full impact of the material and psychological stress associated with coming to terms with and disclosing their sexuality. However, as discussed in Chapter 6, the extent to which young people are resilient to such stressors is dependent on the classed resources available to them in their immediate family, school and community.

Young LGB people are more likely than heterosexual youth to become homeless, due to experiencing prejudice, discrimination, intolerance, bullying and harassment from peers; to the emotional distress and social isolation produced by being rejected by family and friends; and to mental health problems associated with coming to terms with being LGB. D'Augelli (1998) asserts that many school problems of LGB pupils, including 'poor academic performance, truancy, and dropping out of school, are direct or indirect results of verbal and physical abuse perpetrated by peers or others in school' (p.200). More recently, Daley *et al.* (2008) explored the intersectionalities evident in LGB young people's experiences of bullying. They assert that 'bullying related to sexual orientation should not be assumed to be the only or primary form of violence shaping the lives of LGBT youth' (p.10). Daley *et al.* found that LGB youth who were recent immigrants were most vulnerable to bullying, and were also subject to xenophobia and racism, as well as classism and homophobia. More generally, they found that some young people were unsure as to whether their ethnicity or their sexual orientation provided the primary 'motivation' for bullying by their peers, and that their families were sometimes a further source of victimisation. Across class and ethnicity, LGB young people who presented in gender non-normative ways (particularly 'feminine' boys) were at heightened risk of victimisation and harassment at school.

Midlife Concerns

According to popular wisdom, 'middle age' begins as soon as one realises that life is 'half over' as opposed to 'half begun'. This signifying event may be prompted by an unwanted age-related physical change such as greying hair or fat accumulation around the waist. However, for many it is an age-related *social event* that triggers membership in this life-stage, for example, facing the demise of a parent, children moving out, or flipping through a gay magazine to notice that all of the pictures are of bare-chested fit younger men. This section focuses primarily on issues related to forming relationships, parenting and families. However, these are certainly not the only midlife concerns of LGB people and it might be argued that such concerns reflect those of heterosexuals. In this section we also cover issues relating to bisexuality in more depth than in other chapters in this book, although other chapters examine other midlife concerns not covered here, such as physical health (Chapter 7).

Unlike earlier generational cohorts, LGB people in the UK have been able to establish legally recognised civil partnerships since 2005. However, it is important to remember that not all LGB people wish to have and recognise such monogamous couple relationships. Some prefer non-monogamous or polyamorous relationships that are not recognised by existing legislation. However, there is a developing literature on the impact of the legal recognition of same-sex relationships (e.g. Clarke *et al.*, 2007). For example, Rothblum *et al.* (2006) found that same-sex couples who had entered into legally recognised partnerships reported stronger extended family relationships with both their families of origin and their in-laws.

By midlife, somewhere between 10–20 per cent of gay men, and about a third of lesbians are parents (Clarke *et al.*, 2010) (by later life, this figure may increase for gay men). Many older LGBs continue to nurture and benefit from connections to their families of origin, which contrasts to some common stereotypes of sexual minorities distancing and disconnecting themselves from their families of origin. However, Heaphy *et al.* (2004) report that 22 per cent of their sample of gay men and 34 per cent of lesbians were no longer in regular contact with their families of origin, on account of their sexuality. While it seems to be the case that older LGB people are indeed less likely than older heterosexuals to draw on members of their biological family as sources of social support (Cronin & King, 2010) and that some older LGBs may not be 'out' to all members of their biological family, nearly two thirds of older LGB people consider their relationship with their biological family to be 'important'. This is likely to translate to some level of social, practical and emotional support. For instance, lesbians are twice as likely as gay or bisexual men to be providing care to biological family members (Shippy, 2007) reflecting the gendered division of care that may persist in families of origin.

Heaphy *et al.* (2004) also found that the quality of LGB parent relationships with their adult children depended on a variety of factors. Some of the parents chose to 'live in the closet' for the sake of maintaining ties with their children, whereas some others had to accept the loss of close family relationships because they felt the need to be open and honest about their sexuality. However, it appeared that many of the LGB parents in this study had been able to negotiate close bonds and regular contact with their children and other immediate relatives in the midst of living openly and 'out of the closet'.

There is a large literature on LGB parenting, which was initially focused on finding 'no differences' in the development of children from same-sex versus heterosexual households. Beginning in the 1970s, this affirmative research (e.g. Golombok *et al.*, 1983) began in response to custody battles where the sexuality of LGB parents was often described as 'dangerous' to children, and as sufficient reason to deny custody. However, contemporary critics (e.g. Stacey & Biblarz, 2001) argue that such comparative research treats difference as deficiency and does not capture the ways in which LGB people may actively seek to 'do family differently'. Recent research on LGB families (e.g. Goldberg, 2007) has focussed on the lived experiences of those families, rather than pursuing a comparative research agenda.

However, even in such contemporary research, the issue of 'difference' remains clearly relevant to participants when describing their experiences as parents, and their children's experiences at school. Clarke *et al.* (2004) assert that the issue of the homophobic bullying that may or may not be experienced by children raised in same-sex households is a delicate one for LGB parents because this is a 'problem' that has long been used to undermine LGB families. For instance, it has been given weight in recent custody cases where custody was denied to the LGB parent on account of the judge's reservations about the 'stigmatisation', teasing and bullying likely to be experienced by their children at school (e.g. Falk, 1989). Many psychological studies, including an influential report by the American Psychological Association (1995), have minimised this impact of homophobic bullying on children from same-sex headed families, and Clarke *et al.* (2004) argue that lesbian and gay parents also produce 'normalising' and 'minimising' accounts of the incidence and impact of bullying when describing their children's experiences at school. They assert that this is the result of lesbian and gay parents' acute awareness of the extent to which they are held publicly morally accountable, as good or bad parents, for their children's wellbeing.

Outside of raising children, LGB people live a myriad of relationship forms and living arrangements, which reflects the importance and value of friendships, community and 'kinship' for LGB people. Heaphy *et al.* (2004) found that the vast majority of participants chose to live close to their friends and not their families of origin. Other authors have referred to such arrangements as 'families of choice' (e.g. Weston, 1991; Weeks *et al.*, 2001). Thus, LGB people in midlife have established cohesive networks of friends and lovers who provide support, care and commitment to each other in relationships that are 'fluid, flexible and adaptable' (Weeks *et al.*, 2001, p.5). This shared sense of identity and history can be a source of great strength as members grow and age together. Lesbians in particular may report that ex-partners are key members of their friendship support groups, perhaps due to the permeable boundaries many lesbians draw between relationships based on love and friendship (Kitzinger & Perkins, 1993). Many rural lesbians travel out of their geographical area to forge and maintain social networks with other lesbians and often have few familial supports, relying instead on sometimes geographically dispersed friendship networks (Comerford *et al.*, 2004). Masini and Barrett (2008) report that for older LGB people, support from close friends rather than biological family was associated with better mental health and lower rates of anxiety, depression and internalised homophobia. However, the single-generational composition of many families of choice can also result in amplified experiences of grief and loss, as was particularly the case in the 1980s when gay men were likely to have lost many friends, lovers and ex-lovers from HIV-related causes.

Bisexual Experiences

Our understanding of what it might be like for bisexual men and women to age is based on a small number of studies with a limited number of participants. For example, only 25 bisexual men and nine bisexual women responded to Grossman and D'Augelli's landmark study on ageing with sexual minorities (Grossman, 2006). As a result, the unique experiences of bisexuals are poorly understood, largely because of their invisibility within the broader communities of sexual minorities. According to Dworkin (2006) this risk of invisibility increases as bisexuals grow older because of what happens when they enter into long-term committed relationships. As they stay in these relationships bisexual men and women may begin to identify, act, and appear to others as straight, gay or lesbian, depending on the gender of their partner. As a result, their visibility as something that is readily identifiable, separate and distinct may begin to diminish.

However, not all bisexuals choose to develop (long-term) coupled relationships. The nature of loving relations for bisexuals can take a variety of shapes and forms. For example, they may choose to be in relationships with more than one person at a time (as might any other sexuality). This variety of relationship forms contrasts with early models of sexual identity development that have tended to be linear and sequential in nature with dichotomous categories of lesbian/gay or straight. The fluid and flexible nature of sexual identity has been minimised or even ignored. As a result, bisexuality has been relegated into the awkward and undesirable position of being seen as less valued, transitional in nature, or a conscious choice for some driven by fears of being identified as lesbian or gay.

Another reason for not understanding the ageing process for bisexuals is the lack of clarity and consistency in distinguishing different forms of bisexuality. It has become popular to categorise bisexuality into four different types, including transitional, historical, sequential, and concurrent (Klein, 1993). *Transitional bisexuality* refers to a temporary state which is followed by a transition to more 'stable' identification with a straight, gay or lesbian identity. *Historical bisexuality* refers the scenario described above by Dworkin (2006) when a bisexual individual enters a monogamous relationship but continues to experience sexual attraction to male and female genders. *Sequential bisexuality* refers to when individuals experience sexual attraction to male and female genders but they make a choice to have only one monogamous (sexual) relationship at a time. Their bisexuality is regarded as sequential because their next sexual relationship with another person could be of a different gender. This differs from *concurrent bisexuality* which refers to when individuals experience sexual attraction to all genders but do not restrict their sexual relations to any particular gender at the same time.

At first glance it may appear useful to create such distinctions. However, problems abound. Do sequential bisexuals become historical by default if their monogamous relationships prevail? In essence, the fluidity and flexibility inherent with bisexuality is difficult to capture with such fixed categorisations. Another potential problem with using such categories is that they can be used in value-laden and pejorative ways. There are longstanding stereotypes of bisexuals as promiscuous, unhealthy, mixed up and unable to remain in committed relationships. Typologies such as Klein's can be used to substantiate such stereotypes which do nothing to improve our understanding of the lived experiences of bisexuals.

So what do we know about the ageing experience for bisexual men and women? One longitudinal study has been following a number of bisexuals based in San Francisco since the early 1980s. At the beginning of this study, Weinberg *et al.* (1994) suggested a common developmental path for bisexuality starting with initial confusion, followed by acceptance in applying the bisexual label to the self, followed by a period of settling into the identity. The researchers initially concluded that 'continued uncertainty' prevails in midlife because of the amorphous nature of bisexuality. However, they have since amended their developmental model in more positive terms based on their continued investigation (Weinberg *et al.*, 2001). These findings contrast with that of Grossman (2006) and Grossman *et al.* (2001). Generally speaking, their small subset of bisexuals reported lower self-esteem and felt less positive feelings about their sexuality as compared to lesbians and gay men. This study also found marked gender differences. Bisexual men reported more problematic levels of alcohol use and more recent suicidal thinking than bisexual women, whereas bisexual women were more open about their sexuality and more integrated with the LGB community than were bisexual men (Grossman, 2006). That studies so far have produced contradictory results suggests that not much is known about life experiences for bisexuals and that more research is needed.

Older Adults

Many older LGB people are in long-term relationships within a well-connected network of friends and family. Depression and other signs of psychological difficulties in older LGB people are no different in size or scope from that of the general population (Dorfman *et al.*, 1995). In essence, older LGB folk are – more often than not – healthy, satisfied with life, sexually active, productive and connected to others (Grossman, 2006). If there are difficulties or vulnerabilities in growing old, then it is more likely to be influenced by factors other than sexual identity (Lee, 1990). This said, psychological research into LGB ageing is still a developing field (Gabby & Wahler, 2002; Herdt & de Vries, 2004; Kimmel *et al.*, 2006; Kimmel & Sang, 1995; and Reid, 1995). Researchers have debunked the longstanding assumption that growing up in a society that has pathologised and criminalised homosexuality must leave some kind of lasting negative impact on adjustment and life satisfaction in later life. However, it has been argued by some that there may be some protective or even enhancing elements from 'coming to terms' with one's sexual identity in early adulthood for later-life adjustment. Berger (1996), Kehoe (1989), and Kimmel (1978) have discussed how the crisis of 'coming out' could prepare one for the 'crisis' of midlife and growing old because it generates skills and competencies for facing such developmental challenges. Despite its intuitive appeal, this proposition has not been supported by research (Baron & Cramer, 2000). In fact, Lee (1987) has argued that positive adjustment to old age has more to do with more generic developmental challenges. He has argued that having sufficient financial resources, acquiring advanced education, maintaining good physical health and enjoying support from living with a partner have more impact on psychological adjustment and life satisfaction in old age than sexuality itself (Baron & Cramer, 2000). It is important to remember that most, if not all of this research has been based on white middle-class urban Canadians or Americans and that these findings might not readily translate and apply to the lived experience of older LGB people from other cultures and social classes.

One such American study became an influential authority in our understanding of ageing for sexual minorities in North America, conducted by Arnold Grossman and Anthony D'Augelli, in collaboration with other researchers (D'Augelli *et al.*, 2001; Grossman, 2006; and Grossman *et al.*, 2001). This relatively large and comprehensive self-report study collected information on physical and mental health, life satisfaction and social functioning with various self-report measures from more than 400 LGB people aged 60 to 91 years. Approximately half of the respondents (50% women and 47% men) reported being in a committed relationship with an average length of nearly 15 years. However, only 29 per cent of the respondents said they were living with their partners as the majority (63%) lived alone. The researchers did not ask for 'reasons' regarding their living arrangements but it can be assumed that some of these respondents were living apart from their partners for fears of being identified as LGB. Other potential reasons include financial incentives to living separately or being in a long-distance relationship. Nearly two thirds of the women and 41 per cent of the men reported having children, and most of them had regular contact with them. This suggests that a substantial number of older LGB are connected to family networks as parents, grandparents or even great-grandparents. This counters one of the long lasting myths of disconnection and isolation from families of origin for older LGB people.

The vast majority of older lesbian and gay respondents reported good physical health with active lifestyles, and similar to the community at large, people living with their partners reported better physical health than those living alone. Those with higher household incomes also appeared to enjoy better physical health and more active lifestyles. In terms of mental health, people generally reported feeling satisfied and happy with their lives. Statistical analyses failed to identify any differences in mental health between women and men or between gay men, lesbians and bisexuals. The only differences identified were that older people living with their partners reported better mental health than those living on their own and people with higher household incomes reported relatively higher levels of mental health. The reasons for higher levels of mental health for older people living with their partners are unclear and warrant further investigation. How does living alone put older LGB people at risk for loneliness or depression? Is it simply a matter of living with someone else on a daily basis that protects against loneliness and sadness? Or do older people living together enjoy more opportunities for social connectedness and social participation with others?

Despite the large proportion of respondents who reported satisfaction with life and good mental health, a small proportion reported serious mental health problems. For example, 4 per cent admitted having contemplated suicide over the past year. However, Grossman *et al.* (2001) were unable to identify any significant differences in suicidal thinking between those living alone and those living with partners. They also failed to find significant differences between women and men or between gay men, lesbians or bisexuals. Household income, social network size and degree of involvement with lesbian/gay community groups were not related to recent suicidal thinking. It is important to note that this rate of suicidal contemplation in older LGB people is somewhat lower than that of the general population of older people. In a review of recently published research, Yeates and Duberstein (2005) reported that 9 per cent of 156 Americans over the age of 60 reported suicidal thinking over the past year, and 7 per cent of 125 British people over the age of 80 reported the same over the past two years. However, it is difficult to know how meaningful this difference is to the general population. Studies examining suicidal ideation in older people are problematic. They can only be based on self-reports, and various studies use differing definitions and time frames. Some studies refer to specific thoughts of suicide whilst others refer to a more generalised 'thoughts of death', and the timeframes for such thoughts vary between the past week and the past two years.

As expected, some of the respondents (11%) reported a history of mental health difficulties, illness and disability (Grossman *et al.*, 2001). Those who acknowledged such difficulties also tended to report lower levels of current mental health, more lifetime suicidal ideation and more suicidal ideation associated with difficulties in accepting their sexual orientation. People who reported having a diagnosed mental disorder also reported lower levels of self-esteem, more negative views of their sexual orientation, more loneliness and more substance misuse. Nearly 70 per cent of the respondents reported drinking alcohol over the past year, although only 9 per cent of the respondents could be classified as 'problem drinkers'. Men reported significantly more problematic levels of drinking than women. This is comparable to recent findings from the US Department of Mental Health who found problematic levels of alcohol usage in 11 per cent of men and 9 per cent of women over the age of 65 (Blazer & Wu, 2009). Older LGB people are thus just as likely as anyone else to drink alcohol, sometimes to excess. However, illicit drug use appears not as common as alcohol use. More than 80 per cent of the respondents in Grossman *et al.*'s (2001) study denied any illicit drug use over the past year.

A recent study by Heaphy *et al.* (2004) took a different approach in assessing LGB ageing and later life. This British study explored how ageing is influenced by relational and social contexts. Heaphy *et al.* (2004) used both quantitative and qualitative methods to explore the living circumstances and experiences of more than 250 LGBs between the ages of 50 and 90. They found that ageing is experienced, approached and negotiated in a variety of ways by LGB people. The personal meanings of 'ageing' and 'old age' were varied because they were seen to be fluid and context driven. Some participants claimed that they were unaware and/or unaffected by the ageing process. Some did not see themselves as 'old' and did not see much impact of ageing on their day-to-day lives or connections with others. However, many more participants felt that the youth-oriented and commercialised gay scene made them acutely aware of their age to the point of feeling marginalised and excluded. As to be expected, this was the case for men more than women (Herdt & de Vries, 2004; Kimmel & Sang, 1995).

Much like the North American studies, a large number of participants in Heaphy *et al.*'s (2004) study were in 'significant' relationships (almost 60% women and 40% men), with younger participants more likely to be in relationships than older participants. However, a large proportion did not live together: nearly half of the women were living with their partners, but only 27 per cent of the men. There were a variety of reasons for couples not living together, ranging from not wanting their sexuality to be advertised, to being less inclined to live with a new partner if recently bereaved, and not feeling ready to live with a new partner.

During experiences of extreme distress, for example bereavement, many older LGB people attempt to access non-heterosexual organisations and groups for support (Heaphy *et al.*, 2004). It should be noted, however, that ageism is unfortunately sometimes encountered by older LGB people seeking help from community groups, as such groups are not always positioned to offer support for older people. Cronin and King (2010) note that not all older LGB people have access to wider LGB social networks or families of choice. Moore (2002) reports that older LGB people living in rural settings may feel particularly isolated, may feel 'invisible' to healthcare professionals, and are increasingly reliant on support with transport to maintain their social support networks as they become less mobile. Some older LGBs may be effectively excluded from such social networks due to their geographical location (Bell & Valentine, 1995), 'lifestyle choices' (Heaphy, 2007), or to factors related to their age-related identity cohort (Rosenfeld, 2009) such as differential values associated with being 'out'.

Coming out is often assumed to be an unambiguously positive experience, a prerequisite for psychological adjustment and life satisfaction. However, as Rosenfeld (2009) points out, for older generations, coming out may not necessarily be regarded as a positive and liberating act by which one's sexuality achieves a publicly recognised status. Rather, coming out may be seen as self-destructive, self-indulgent or even foolish. Older LGB people may view their sexuality as a private stigma likely to provoke negative reactions if publicly acknowledged. Thus for some older LGB people, remaining closeted may be seen as the more positive, prudent and self-protective course of action. For instance, some older lesbian women may resist associating with more 'obviously' lesbian women, fearing the 'shame' of public exposure and unwanted attention (Rosenfeld, 1999). Another older lesbian interviewed by Rosenfeld (1999) reported experiencing social rejection from other older lesbians due to her 'public visibility' as an out lesbian:

> I'm a very obvious lesbian. And I find that a lot of lesbians don't want to hang too much with obvious lesbians. They're not out out . . . I understand there are places where I just don't fit in, because of the way I am (p.132).

Older LGB people may also not desire to be included in public LGB community events, such as Pride, and may thus resist attempts at inclusion by younger members of the community.

Heaphy *et al.* (2004) found that a significant number of women and men believed that their sexuality had had an enormous impact on their lives. However, the nature of this impact varied considerably. More than 80 per cent of women and 62 per cent of men said that their lives had been enriched by their sexuality. While the majority of the participants claimed that they were pleased with how their lives had turned out, 21 per cent of women and 35 per cent of men reported feeling lonely and isolated which they attributed to their sexuality. Clearly a significant proportion of older LGB people displayed strength and self-confidence despite growing up in times when same-sex attraction and sexual relations were pathologised and criminalised. However, a sizeable minority also appeared to have been negatively affected by these historical and cultural forces. In summary, it appears that many of the older LGB who participated in this UK study are resilient, content and self-confident. However, like the American studies, the respondents may represent only a slither of the entirety of LGB communities.

Sexuality in Later Years

Senior citizens, particularly older women, are assumed to be asexual, or at least no longer actively sexual. However, as Knauer (2010) asserts, we ordinarily define LGB people as such by their sexuality. By this commonsensical logic, senior citizens cannot possibly be LGB! Conversely, when older LGB people are regarded as sexually active, they may encounter pernicious and hurtful stereotypes regarding sexual predation: these apply particularly to older gay men, but arguably this stereotype is sometimes applied to older lesbian women (see for example, Judy Dench's character in the 2007 film *Notes on a Scandal*, Dir. Richard Eyre).

Despite stereotypes to the contrary, older LGB people report that sex is a vital and defining part of their relationships (Garnets & Peplau, 2006; Pope *et al.*, 2007). As we have noted, 60 per cent of the older lesbians, and 40 per cent of older gay men in Heaphy *et al.*'s (2004) sample were in a couple relationship, though not all of these respondents were sexually active.

The 'invisibility' of sexuality in 'sweet old ladies'

One potentially distressing aspect of sexuality in later life is that getting older can make one's status as a lesbian in a relationship invisible. Traies (2009) asserts that older lesbians can effectively 'disappear': as old women tend to be oriented to as 'grandmothers', they are thus assumed to be both heterosexual in orientation and celibate in practice. Thus, even two older women living together may find themselves becoming invisible as a couple as they age, and may be referred to by others as 'flat mates' or as 'friends' living together out of financial necessity rather than partnership and love. The lack of recognition and acknowledgement of one's sexuality may be a frustrating and disheartening experience for older lesbians. Grossman (1997, p.17) quotes an older lesbian:

> ... we can walk down the street holding hands affectionately and kissing – without an eyebrow being raised because no one notices us – we have become invisible! We certainly do not regret the lack of reprisals. What is devastating is that with age we have become non-persons.

A significant number of lesbians do not act on their attraction to women until much later in life (see *Alice and Betty's story* below). Some researchers account for this phenomenon by drawing attention to the greater fluidity in women's sexuality over the lifespan whilst others argue that this is due to the pressure of heteronormative social expectations lesbians may experience during young adulthood: many older lesbians met such social expectations earlier in life by entering into heterosexual marriages and having children. Often they may have waited until their children reached adulthood before entering into a relationship with a woman (Traies, 2009). Those older lesbians that exited a heterosexual marriage whilst their children were younger are likely to have faced hostility in the family courts, and may even have lost custody of their children on account of their sexuality (Golombok *et al.*, 1983).

Contrary to widespread assumptions, nearly three quarters of women who identify as lesbian have had a sexual experience with a man (Herbert, 1996). Kehoe (1986) reports that for older lesbians who reported having had sexual experiences with both men and women, sexual relationships with women were reported to be more sexually satisfying, less sexually demanding, and more emotionally fulfilling and reciprocal than those with men. Tracey and Junginger (2007) found that, like heterosexual women, as lesbians grow older they may report a gradual decline in desire for sexual activity, more problems with lubrication during sexual activity, and decreased levels of arousal and pleasure. However, Beaber and Werner's (2009) study of the relationship between anxiety and sexual functioning in lesbians and heterosexual women shows that despite this apparent 'decline', older lesbians report higher levels of sexual functioning – level of arousal and reaching orgasm – than do heterosexual women. Furthermore, older heterosexual women were more likely than older lesbians to be *anxious* about sexual functioning, lubrication, orgasm and pain. These authors also noted that for older lesbians, deficits or 'declines' in sexual functioning were often effectively offset by relationship satisfaction. That is, the more satisfied older lesbians were with their significant relationship, the greater their reported arousal, orgasm and satisfaction, and the fewer problems they reported with lubrication and sexual functioning. Notably, this is also true of lesbians experiencing menopause. Unlike their heterosexual counterparts, menopausal lesbians do not report complaints or discomfort from their partners, and are less likely to pathologise menopause as a symptom of sexual decline and ageing. Indeed, many older lesbians regard their sex lives as at least as enjoyable, if not more so, after menopause (Garnets & Peplau, 2006).

Any existing 'age-related decline' in physiological aspects of sexual functioning may be exacerbated if a chronic illness, such as cancer, is diagnosed. Boehmer *et al.* (2009) note that one of the more distressing side effects of chronic illnesses is a decrease in sexual function. They note encouragingly that lesbians may experience fewer associated difficulties in their sexual relationships and report having more empathic, understanding and supportive partners than heterosexual women. However, they note that lesbians may have more difficulties than heterosexual women in accessing support and information regarding challenges with sexual functioning from medical professionals.

Of course, not all older lesbians are in a 'significant' relationship. However, single older lesbians may actually have more chances of finding a new romantic or sexual partner than older heterosexual women (Garnets & Peplau, 2006). This is for several reasons. Firstly, women have greater longevity than men, which means that after middle age there may simply be a larger pool of potential female partners than male partners. Secondly, lesbians tend not to be as youth-oriented in their selection of partners as do either heterosexual or gay men. However, some older single lesbians may find it difficult to meet prospective partners due to geographical and social isolation and care-giving responsibilities.

Sexuality and older bisexual women and men

There is far less research on sexuality in older bisexual women and men. According to the longitudinal research of Weinberg *et al.* (2001), for many bisexual men and women, sexual activity decreases in midlife because of less interest in sex, diminished energy and increased childrearing and work responsibilities. By midlife nearly half of their bisexual participants were in monogamous relationships. Nearly one third were having sexual relations with only members of the 'opposite sex' and 'moving towards monogamy' whereas about 20 per cent were now exclusively in same-sex relationships. It appears that many of the bisexual women were giving up on finding men who were interested or capable in accepting their bisexuality whereas the bisexual men were just finding it 'easier' to have sex with men. Despite these apparent changes in sexual partners and relationship forms in midlife for bisexuals, the researchers discovered that bisexual feelings and attractions had not gone away. Interest in sex may play a less important role in their lives but attraction to both genders prevails.

Sexuality and older gay men

Many gay men in their 50s and 60s report higher levels of sexual activity than earlier in life. This may be in part due to the 'rewards' of growing older: higher levels of self-acceptance, increased free time, and lower levels of stress. Despite reporting higher levels of sexual activity in later life, older gay men experience similar physiological changes in sexual functioning as do older heterosexual men (Kimmel & Sang, 1995). Erectile dysfunctions and ejaculation problems may ensue. However, some older gay and bisexual men may use erectile enhancing medication (EEM) to augment their sexual experience. As is the case with younger gay men's use of EEM, when used recreationally, this may be correlated with a range of health risk behaviours, such as unprotected sex. Pope *et al.* (2007), however, report that many older gay men focus on the development of sexual and emotional intimacy rather than sexual performance alone.

Elford *et al.* (2008) note that older gay men living with HIV are just as likely to report high risk sexual behaviour as are younger gay men, and that a third of HIV positive gay men over the age of 50 years were diagnosed in their 50s or 60s: thus this is not an ageing cohort of men who became positive when they were younger. Schmid *et al.* (2009) assert further that older men may be disadvantaged within the medical system as HIV may not always initially be considered as a likely cause of illness for seniors (who may be assumed to be heterosexual and/or celibate). This means that there is often a much shorter time from diagnosis to onset of AIDS for older men.

Although some degree of ageism may be feared or encountered when older single gay men seek new sexual partners, Pope *et al.* (2007) found that older gay men are usually ultimately successful when actively searching for new partners. However, Fox (2007) reports that some older gay men may feel inhibited when attending community social events and particularly when interacting with younger gay men, as they are aware of the stereotypical perception of the older gay male as a 'sexual predator' and may be wary of being subject to such judgements. The phenomenon of 'accelerated ageing' may also play a role. Accelerated ageing refers to the finding that the feeling of being noticeably 'old' occurs at a much younger age for gay men than for heterosexual men (Bennett & Thompson, 1991). Gay men may report feeling 'old' and thus vulnerable to negative and exclusionary stereotypes after the age of just 35! This is arguably in large part a consequence of a youth-oriented gay culture.

Caveats

Without a doubt the studies presented in this chapter provide a detailed picture of what life is like for LGB people in contemporary society. However, our appreciation of their experience from this type of research is limited for a variety of reasons. The mixture of self-report inventories, focus groups and semi-structured interviews provides multiple means of gathering information. However, the recruitment methods suffer from the same limitations as most research in this field. Recruiting participants by advertising in gay media, approaching community groups and using personal connections is not only effective but expedient. However, it limits our ability to generalise the results to the broader community of sexual minorities. Therefore most research has tended to recruit educated and financially secure white gay men who live in urban settings; for example, only 8 per cent of the participants in the study by Grossman *et al.* (2001) identified themselves as bisexual, and more than 97 per cent of the participants in the Heaphy *et al.* (2004) study reported 'White British' ethnicity. These researchers also struggled to get women over the age of 60 to respond to their surveys. In the end, some may argue that these proportions may be a relatively accurate reflection of the number of self-identified bisexuals in North America or the number of sexual minorities in the UK who are non-white. But this is difficult to prove as many people who might be considered part of this community continue to remain 'invisible' and elusive to reach for researchers. In the end, researchers have to rely on accessing sexual minorities who are interested and motivated to participate in such research. Unfortunately this will not generate findings that can reflect the reality for everyone in these communities. A further important point is that generational cohort effects permeate this field. Ageing is embedded in a social and historical context. It is essential to consider this when using research to draft policy, develop service programmes and improve therapeutic interventions. As stated by Kimmel *et al.* (2006), 'the intersection of social change and historical cohort is profound' (p.6) in that the experience of ageing today is inevitably going to be different from ageing tomorrow.

Diversity in Practice

Acknowledging and appreciating diversity is essential if health and social care professionals want to respond effectively to LGB people (Pugh, 2005). LGB people's experiences over the lifespan are historically, socially and culturally particular. Health and social care professionals need to identify, appreciate, respect and respond to these differences if they want to provide appropriate care and support. Thus, providing psychological support to a 72–year-old gay man who is mourning the sudden loss of his lifetime partner will depend on knowing something about his personal circumstances and 'gay' life history. Where did he grow up and what was it like to be 'gay' when he first started to explore his own sexual identity? Did he come out? When did he come out to himself and others? Did he ever come out to his family? If not, what did they know about this relationship? What support has he had from family and friends over the years, especially when he was having difficulties with his partner? How connected was his partner to his own family of origin? Did they ever forgive him for failing to follow through with his arranged marriage to a young woman from his homeland? How many friends have they lost over the years to HIV? Why did they never live together? How financially secure will he be without his partner's financial support? Why did his partner not nominate him as the beneficiary for his estate? How involved is his partner's family in looking after him? The questions, and the answers, are potentially endless.

Alice and Betty's Story

Alice is 62 years of age and Betty is 44. They have been in a relationship for ten years and lived together for seven. Two years before they met, Alice divorced her husband after 15 years of marriage. Alice had been aware of her attraction to women since her early 30s when her daughter was young. After the divorce and when her daughter left home, Alice began to explore her sexual attraction to women. Betty was the first woman to move in with Alice.

Alice and Betty are very happy together but they struggle on occasions, especially in terms of Alice's relationship with her daughter and extended family. Alice's adult daughter is recently divorced, and she and her child may have to move in with Alice for a while. Alice would also like to have this opportunity to be around her grandson as being a grandparent is something that Alice has always cherished and looked forward to. Betty would like to support Alice in her decision to offer her daughter the chance to move in. However, this situation has stirred up some apprehension and resentment for Betty as Alice is not 'out' to her child, while Betty has always been open with her family and friends about her sexual identity. Since Alice doesn't see her family very often, they have managed to avoid this situation with little conflict. However, this situation with Alice's daughter has brought this problem to the fore.

Betty and Alice have begun to argue about this situation without much resolution. Alice would like Betty to move into one of the spare bedrooms in preparation for her daughter's arrival next month. Betty is refusing so they are at an impasse. They decide to go for some couple counselling so they can discuss how to resolve their difficulties.

This story presents a variety of issues for consideration. The most obvious issue is the apparent discord between Betty and Alice in their openness about their sexual identities. While this may not be a source of tension on a daily basis, it appears to surface when Alice interacts with her family. Perhaps this couple has been able to create some harmony for themselves while avoiding this inevitable conflict until now. This is something that many sexual minority couples have to face at some point regardless of age. Open communication with a willingness to accept a partner's different approach to family relations is required. To help with this, Betty could be reminded of the challenges Alice must have faced many years ago when she became aware of her sexual attraction to women at a time when homosexuality was still a crime and considered a psychiatric disorder. Because of her lack of personal experience with this, Betty may have some difficulties in appreciating the lasting legacy of such circumstances on self-acceptance and openness. However, Alice needs to appreciate Betty's personal experience in coming to terms with her sexual identity during more accepting and permissive circumstances. Betty's family and friendship networks appear to have been accepting and comfortable with her sexual identity from the very beginning in late adolescence. Alice may need to be reminded that Betty does not share the same desires and interests in being a grandparent or other aspects of the 'traditional' family life cycle. Hopefully Betty and Alice will be able to use counselling for discussing their feelings and thoughts about these differences so they can develop a shared understanding and acceptance of them. How they decide to manage these differences will depend on how they can learn more about each other and themselves.

Guidelines for Good Practice

Good clinical practice in working with LGB clients requires some degree of familiarity with developmental lifespan issues. These guidelines are important to consider:

- It is paramount to identify and recognise the influence of historical (generational) cohort effects on development. The experience of coming to terms with one's sexual identity in contemporary society is very different from someone who grew up in the 1950s when homosexuality was still considered a mental illness and was criminalised.
- Do not assume that the developmental experiences of a bisexual male or female will resemble that of a gay male or lesbian, respectively. The lived experience of a bisexual is unique and distinct from that of other sexual minorities.
- Do not assume that older LGB people have stopped having sex. Older LGB people may manage some of the physiological changes associated with ageing and sexuality more positively than their heterosexual counterparts, but they may also find it harder to obtain support and information regarding challenges with sexual functioning from professionals.

- It is essential to familiarise yourself with published research on lifespan developmental issues for LGB people. However good clinical practice also requires you to identify and appreciate each individual client's unique circumstances that pertain to their problems and difficulties. Acknowledging and appreciating diversity is essential for effective clinical practice.

References

American Psychological Association (1995). *Lesbian and gay parenting: A resource for psychologists.* Washington DC: American Psychological Association.

Baron, A. & Cramer, D.W. (2000). Potential counselling concerns of aging lesbian, gay, and bisexual clients. In R.M. Perez, K.A. DeBord & K.J. Bieschke (Eds.), *Handbook of counseling and psychotherapy with lesbian, gay, and bisexual clients.* Washington, D.C.: American Psychological Association.

Beaber, T. & Werner, P. (2009). The relationship between anxiety and sexual functioning in lesbians and heterosexual women. *Journal of Homosexuality, 56*(5), 639–654.

Bell, D. & Valentine, G. (1995). *Mapping desire: Geographies of sexualities.* London: Routledge.

Bennett, K. & Thompson, N. (1991). Accelerated aging and male homosexuality: Australian evidence in a continuing debate. *Journal of Homosexuality, 20*(3/4), 65–75.

Berger, R.M. (1996). *Gay and gray: The older homosexual man* (2nd edn.). New York, NY: Harrington Park Press.

Blazer, D.G. & Wu, L.-T. (2009). The epidemiology of at-risk and binge drinking among middle-aged and elderly community adults: National survey on drug use and health. *American Journal of Psychiatry, 166*, 1162–1169.

Boehmer, U., Potter, J. & Bowen, D. (2009). Sexual functioning after cancer in sexual minority women. *Cancer Journal, 15*(1), 65–69.

Cass, V. (1979). Homosexual identity formation: A theoretical model. *Journal of Homosexuality, 4*(3), 219–235.

Clarke, V., Burgoyne, C. & Burns, M. (2007). Romance, rights, recognition, responsibilities and radicalism: Same-sex couples views on civil partnerships and marriage. In V. Clarke & E. Peel (Eds.), *Out in psychology: Lesbian, gay, bisexual, trans and queer perspectives.* Chichester: John Wiley & Sons, Ltd.

Clarke, V., Ellis, S., Peel., E. & Riggs, D. (2010). *Lesbian, gay, bisexual, trans and queer psychology: An introduction.* Cambridge: Cambridge University Press.

Clarke, V., Kitzinger, C. & Potter, J. (2004). Kids are just cruel anyway: Lesbian and gay parents talk about homophobic bullying. *British Journal of Social Psychology, 43*(4), 531–550.

Coleman, E. (1982). Developmental stages of the coming out process. *Journal of Homosexuality, 7*(2/3), 31–43.

Comerford, S. Henson-Stroud, M., Sionainn, C. & Wheeler, E. (2004). Crone songs: Voices of lesbian elders on aging in a rural environment. *AFFILIA 19*, 418–36.

Cronin, A. & King, A. (2010). Power, inequality and identification: Exploring diversity and intersectionality amongst older LGB adults. *Sociology, 44*(5), 876–892.

D'Augelli, A.R. (1998). Developmental implications of victimization of lesbian, gay, and bisexual youths. In G.M. Herek (Ed.), *Stigma and sexual orientation: Understanding prejudice against lesbians, gay men, and bisexuals.* Thousand Oaks, CA: Sage.

D'Augelli, A.R., Grossman, A.H., Hershberger, S.L. & O'Connell, T.S. (2001). Aspects of mental health among older lesbian, gay, and bisexual adults. *Aging & Mental Health, 5*(2), 149–158.

Daley, A., Solomon, S., Newman, P. & Mishna, F. (2008). Traversing the margins: Intersectionalities in the bullying of lesbian, gay, bisexual and transgender youth, *Journal of Gay & Lesbian Social Services, 19*(3), 9–29.

Diamond, L. (2008). Female bisexuality from adolescence to adulthood: Results from a 10 year longitudinal study. *Developmental Psychology, 44*(1), 5–14.

Dorfman, R., Walters, K., Burke, P., Hardin, L., Karnik, T., Raphael, J. & Silverstein, E. (1995). Support in the aging process for gays and lesbians. *Journal of Gerontological Social Work, 24*(1/2), 29–44.

Dworkin, S.H. (2006). The aging bisexual: The invisible of the invisible minority. In D. Kimmel, T. Rose & S. David (Eds.) *Lesbian, gay, bisexual and transgender aging: Research and clinical perspectives.* New York, NY: Columbia University Press.

Elford, J., Ibrahim, F., Bukutu, C. & Anderson, J. (2008). Over fifty and living with HIV in London. *Sexually Transmitted Infection, 84*, 468–472.

Falk, P.J. (1989). Lesbian mothers: Psychosocial assumptions in family law. *American Psychologist, 44*, 941–947.

Fox, R.C. (2007). Gay grows up: An interpretive study on aging metaphors and queer identity. *Journal of Homosexuality, 52*, 33–61.

Gabby, S.G. & Wahler, J.J. (2002). Lesbian aging: Review of growing literature. *Journal of Gay and Lesbian Social Services, 14*(3), 1–21.

Garnets, L. & Peplau, L. (2006). Sexuality in the lives of aging lesbian and bisexual women. In D. Kimmel, T. Rose & S. David (Eds.), *Lesbian, gay, bisexual, and transgender aging: Research and clinical perspectives.* New York, NY: Columbia University Press.

Goldberg, A. (2007). Talking about family: Disclosure practices of adults raised by lesbian, gay and bisexual parents. *Journal of Family Issues, 28*(1), 100–131.

Golombok, S., Spencer, A. & Rutter, M. (1983). Children in lesbian and single parent households: Psychosexual and psychiatric appraisal. *Child Psychology and Psychiatry, 24*, 551–572.

Grossman, A.H. (2006). Physical and mental health of older lesbian, gay, and bisexual adults. In D. Kimmel, T. Rose & S. David (Eds.), *Lesbian, gay, bisexual and transgender aging: Research and clinical perspectives.* New York, NY: Columbia University Press.

Grossman, A.H. (1997). The virtual and actual identities of older lesbians and gay men. In M.B. Duberman (Ed.), *A queer world: The center for lesbian and gay studies reader.* New York, NY: New York University Press.

Grossman, A.H., D'Augelli, A.R. & O'Connell, T.S. (2001). Being lesbian, gay, bisexual and 60 or older in North America. *Journal of Gay and Lesbian Social Services, 13*(4), 23–40.

Gurevich, M., Bower, J., Mathieson, C. & Dhayanandhan, B. (2007). What do they look like and are they among us?: Bisexuality, (dis)closure and (un)viability. In V. Clarke and E. Peel (Eds.), *Out in psychology: Lesbian, gay, bisexual and trans perspectives.* Chichester: John Wiley & Sons, Ltd.

Heaphy, B. (2007). Sexualities, gender and ageing: Resources and social change. *Current Sociology, 55*(2), 193–210.

Heaphy, B., Yip, A.K.T. & Thompson, D. (2004). Ageing in a non-heterosexual context. *Ageing & Society, 24,* 881–902.

Herbert, S. (1996). Lesbian sexuality. In R.P. Cabaj & T.S. Stein (Eds.), *Textbook of homosexuality and mental health.* Washington, DC: American Psychiatric Press.

Herdt, G. & de Vries, B. (Eds.) (2004). *Gay and lesbian aging: Research and future directions.* New York, NY: Springer Publishing Company.

Kehoe, M. (1986). Lesbians over 65: A triply invisible minority. *Journal of Homosexuality, 12*(3–4), 139–152.

Kehoe, M. (1989). *Lesbians over sixty speak for themselves.* New York, NY: Haworth.

Kimmel, D.C. (1978). Adult development and aging: A gay perspective. *Journal of Social Issues, 43,* 113–120.

Kimmel, D., Rose, T., Orel, N. & Green, B. (2006). Historical context for research on lesbian, gay, bisexual, and transgender aging. In D. Kimmel, T. Rose & S. David (Eds.), *Lesbian, gay, bisexual and transgender aging: Research and clinical perspectives.* New York, NY: Columbia University Press.

Kimmel, D.C. & Sang, B.E. (1995). Lesbians and gay men in midlife. In A.R. D'Augelli & C.J. Patterson (Eds.), *Lesbian, gay and bisexual identities over the lifespan.* Oxford: Oxford University Press.

Kitzinger, C. & Perkins, R. (1993). *Changing our minds: Lesbian feminism and psychology.* London: Onlywomen Press.

Klein, F. (1993). *The bisexual option* (2nd edn.). New York, NY: Harrington Park Press.

Knauer, N. (2010). *Gay and lesbian elders: History, law, and identity politics in the United States.* London: Ashgate.

Lee, J.A. (1990). Aging. In W.R. Dynes (Ed.), *Encyclopedia of homosexuality.* London: St James Press.

Lee, J.A. (1987). What can homosexual aging studies contribute to theories of aging? *Journal of Homosexuality, 13*(4), 43–71.

Masini, B. & Barrett, H. (2008). Social support as a predictor of psychological and physical well-being and lifestyle in lesbian, gay and bisexual adults aged 50 and over. *Journal of Gay and Lesbian Social Services, 20*(1/2), 91–110.

Moore, W. (2002). Connecting care providers through a telephone support group. *Journal of Gay and Lesbian Social Services, 14*(3), 23–41.

Pope, M., Wierzalis, E., Barret, B. & Rankins, M. (2007). Sexual and intimacy issues for aging gay men. *Adultspan, 6*(2), 68–82.

Pugh, S. (2005). Assessing the cultural needs of older lesbians and gay men: Implications for practice. *Practice, 17*(3), 207–218.

Reid, J.D. (1995). Development in late life: Older lesbian and gay lives. In A.R. D'Augelli & C.J. Patterson (Eds.), *Lesbian, gay and bisexual identities over the lifespan.* Oxford: Oxford University Press.

Rosenfeld, D. (2009). Heteronormativity and homonormativity as practical and moral resources: The case of lesbian and gay elders. *Gender & Society, 23,* 617–638.

Rosenfeld, D. (1999). Identity work among lesbian and gay elderly. *Journal of Aging Studies, 13*(2), 121–144.

Rothblum, E., Balsam, K., Todosijevic, J. & Solomon, J. (2006). Same-sex couples in civil unions compared with same-sex couples not in civil unions and heterosexual siblings: An overview. *Lesbian and Gay Psychology Review, 7*(2), 180–188.

Savin-Williams, R. (2005) . *The new gay teenager.* Cambridge, MA: Harvard University Press.

Savin-Williams, R. (2001). A critique of research on sexual minority youths. *Journal of Adolescence, 24*(1), 5–13.

Schmid, G.P., Williams, B., Garcia-Calleja, J., Miller, C., Segar, E., Southworth, M., Tonyan, D., Wacloff, J. & Scott, J. (2009). The unexplored story of HIV and ageing. *Bulletin of the World Health Organisation, 87*(3), 162–162A.

Shippy, R. (2007). We cannot go it alone: The impact of informal support and stressors in older gay, lesbian and bisexual caregivers. *Journal of Gay and Lesbian Social Services, 18*(3/4), 39–51.

Stacey, J. & Biblarz, T. (2001). (How) does the sexual orientation of parents matter? *American Sociological Review, 66,* 159–183.

Tracey, J.K. & Junginger, J. (2007). Correlates of lesbian sexual functioning. *Journal of Women's Health, 16,* 499–509.

Traies, J. (2009). *"Now you see me": The invisibility of older lesbians.* Unpublished MPhil Thesis. Birmingham: Birmingham University.

Weeks, J., Heaphy, B. & Donovan, C. (2001). *Same sex intimacies: Families of choice and other life experiments.* London: Routledge.

Weinberg, M.S., Williams, C.J. & Pryor, D.W. (1994). *Dual attraction: Understanding bisexuality.* Oxford: Oxford University Press.

Weinberg, M.S., Williams, C.J. & Pryor, D.W. (2001). Bisexuals at midlife: Commitment, salience and identity. *Journal of Contemporary Ethnography, 30*(2), 180–208.

Weston, K. (1991). *Families we choose: Lesbians, gays, kinship.* New York, NY: Columbia University Press.

Yeates, C. & Duberstein, P. (2005). Suicide in older adults: Determinants of risk and opportunities for prevention. In K. Hawton (Ed.), *Prevention and treatment of suicidal behaviour: From science to practice.* Oxford: Oxford University Press.

11

From Invert to Intersectionality: Understanding the Past and Future of Sexuality

Esther D. Rothblum

I cannot tell you what a source of both inspiration and pleasure The Ladder contained for me within its pages. I, as an invert, can only know of what momentous importance such a movement as yours can mean, for the ultimate good of all of us.

Like so many others . . . I am living a completely repressed existence, sublimating my nature, whenever possible, in my profession.

One of the insertions in The Ladder caught my attention and I could not help but muse over it with some irony. The part about "Come out of hiding." What a delicious invitation, but oh, so impractical. I should lose my job, a marvelous heterosexual roommate, and all chances of finding work . . . I would be blackballed all over the city.

I am interested-very much interested in becoming a member of the Daughters of Bilitis. Although at present discretion prevents me from making any moves to help the cause . . . there is one very effective weapon we, who must fight from a hiding place, still have – the fountain pen and the typewriter (J.M. Cleveland, Ohio The Ladder, October 1956, p.14.).

Progress

As non-heterosexual activists, we tend to focus on oppression, on remaining sources of internalised heterosexism, and on the limitations of clinical practice. Yet we also need to celebrate how far we have come, as the quote above illustrates. Non-heterosexual issues and communities are portrayed in the news and popular media, and increasing numbers of people know someone who is non-heterosexual. Gay Pride parades in many countries

Intersectionality, Sexuality and Psychological Therapies: Working with Lesbian, Gay and Bisexual Diversity,
First Edition. Edited by Roshan das Nair and Catherine Butler.

reflect the increasing gender, ethnic, religious, ability/disability, cultural, and age diversity of our communities. The United Nations has promoted LGBTI (lesbian, gay, bisexual, transgender and intersex) rights as human rights, and we read about non-heterosexual milestones in politics, the law, education, health, mental health, popular culture, athletics, and the arts, among others. Nevertheless, limitations of early research and writing meant that we knew the most about non-heterosexuals who were white, middle class, able-bodied, highly educated, and willing to be out.

It is important to identity risk factors of being non-heterosexual in a heterosexist society, as reviewed in this volume by Jowett and Peel about physical health (Chapter 7) and by das Nair and Fairbank about mental health (Chapter 8). However, it is also important to focus on the benefits. For example, women who exclusively have sex with women do not need to practice birth control, and thus don't have to consider the risks of the various contraceptive methods. Women who have sex with women are also at lower risk for HIV than are women or men who have sex with men. Because men still earn significantly higher incomes, in general, than do women, two men in a couple will have more economic resources. My research has found that non-heterosexual women report finding more support from their communities during times of stress or hardship than do heterosexual sisters (Rothblum, 2008; 2010); also non-heterosexual men and women are more highly educated than their same-gender siblings (Rothblum & Factor, 2001). As Gibson and Hansen state in this volume (Chapter 10), '. . . the crisis of "coming out" could prepare one for the crisis of midlife and growing old because it somehow generates skills, competencies or mastery for facing such developmental challenges'.

Conversely, it is important that non-heterosexuals not be unduly influenced by what 'mainstream' society considers beneficial. Not everyone necessarily wants to join the military, get legally married, rear children, or join the middle class, to name just a few examples. Reducing heterosexism should not mean assimilating to the point of diluting our vibrant and diverse non-heterosexual rituals and communities.

Intersectionality as a Continuum

Psychological research, grounded in a positivist methodology, likes to form categories. A great deal of research compares a treatment to a placebo, people who are high or low on measures of mental health, or women to men. Just as we regard age as falling on a continuum (39 is not that different from 40, even though they represent different decades), so it is important to view all dimensions of intersectionality as continuums. Sexuality itself is complex and multi-dimensional, including sexual identity, sexual fantasies, sexual attraction, sexual relationships, degree of outness to others, and participation in political and social activities, among others. A man who identifies as gay may be currently in a sexual relationship with a woman. The research of Lisa Diamond (2008) with a cohort of young women found that love and desire are more fluid than constant, so that the woman whose sexual identity remains lesbian, or heterosexual, over time are the exception rather than the norm. Butler (this volume) states that, due to internalised oppression, some people may not feel disabled 'enough'. Our research found over 30 terms used by individuals who do not identify fully with the concept of binary gender (Factor & Rothblum, 2008). As Riggs and das Nair state (Chapter 1), 'Chicana lesbian might be an identity in itself...' rather than a combination of 'Chicana' and 'lesbian'.

Riggs and das Nair state in Chapter 1 to this anthology that there has been an assumption that 'cultural categories' remain stable over time. Yet we need to understand that all dimensions are flexible. A Native American woman visiting South Africa may be startled to be identified as white. There are many degrees of mobility, or vision, or hearing. In Robinson's (2010) recent book *Disintegration*, he describes how the concept of 'the Black community' in the US has evolved into disparate communities, such as immigrants from Africa, biracial and multiracial families, and African Americans from wealthy, middle class and poor backgrounds, so that being black in the US is increasingly less cohesive.

Gibson and Hansen emphasise in this volume that we must be aware of the 'generational cohort' of non-heterosexual people, given that older people grew up in a more heterosexist society than those who are younger. Both Diamond (2005) and Savin-Williams (2005) have conducted longitudinal research with non-heterosexual youth, and found that sexual identity is more fluid and flexible, more resistant to easy categorisation, and can be independent of sexual behaviour. As members of this age cohort enter adulthood, they may appear markedly different from older generations. Much of the research conducted on non-heterosexuals, including the life experience of therapists, may be inapplicable to this younger generation.

Locating Ourselves and Our Intersecting Identities

Psychology as a discipline has been influenced by feminist, disability and critical race theorists. In the early part of the last century, academic articles about psychological research did not regularly mention the gender or race of 'subjects' (presumed to be white and male unless stated otherwise). Now psychology journals typically require that research articles describe the demographics of participants, including gender and race/ethnicity. Grant applications such as those of the US National Institutes of Health include a section on 'inclusion of women and minorities' where research applicants must explain how they will ensure that women and people of colour will be included in the study (though there is no requirement to explain how researchers will ensure diversity of sexuality, social class, or ability/disability, for example).

Whereas in the past psychology journals used the passive voice ('it was found', 'it is believed') and discouraged use of the first person or in fact any identifying information about authors, this has changed thanks to feminist methodologies (e.g. Hesse-Biber & Yaiser, 2004). Understanding that 'the personal is political', it is more common (though certainly not yet the norm) for authors to locate themselves in their research.

When the academic journal *Feminism & Psychology* published a call for papers for a thematic issue on 'representing the other', they received 150 inquires and 80 submissions (Wilkinson, 1996). Authors described dilemmas such as teaching disability studies as an able-bodied woman, studying incest in South Africa as a white woman, women rearing sons, and women conducting research on male murderers, among many others.

If we view intersectionality as multiple, continuous dimensions, then this blurs the boundaries of self and other. If I interview non-heterosexual women about what the 'women's community' means to them, then there will be a plethora of ways that respondents define 'woman', 'non-heterosexual', and 'community'. Furthermore, they may see me as same or other, not necessarily due to demographic information, but because of politics, attitudes, interests, and so on.

Traditionally, therapists were trained to self-disclose as little as possible (although certain information, such as their gender expression, race, age cohort, and accent may have been easy to discern). As Riggs and das Nair state in Chapter 1, therapists too should assess their own social location. Whether to share this with clients is a decision that must be taken in full consideration of the impact upon the client and any potential for misunderstanding the motivation for disclosure.

Because the discipline of psychology is primarily focused on the individual, and therapy on empowering the individual, this is problematic from a feminist and activist perspective. In their book *Changing Our Minds: Lesbian Feminism and Psychology,* Kitzinger and Perkins (1993) argue that this de-politicised approach to women's concerns has moved the focus from our societies and communities to the individual 'client'. Furthermore, they describe how psychology has appropriated feminist concerns such as violence against women, but reversed them, so the discourse has changed from 'what are the causes of violence against women?' (e.g. patriarchy, unemployment) to 'what are the consequences of violence against women?' (e.g. post-traumatic stress disorder, depression, anxiety). In fact, the Code of Ethics of the (former) Feminist Therapy Institute (1995, p.40) focused on 'cultural diversities and oppression', power differentials, and social change.

Furthermore, therapists from all social class backgrounds are trained in knowledge arising from middle class values, and therapy is accessible more to economically advantaged individuals (see das Nair & Hansen, this volume). Alternatives to therapy, such as family of origin and religious organisations (see das Nair and Thomas, this volume, Chapter 6) may not be accepting of people who are not heterosexual. Consequently, non-heterosexuals may want to create alternatives to therapy that take advantage of the social networks in diverse non-heterosexual communities, including the formation of religious or spiritual resources as well as resources for what das Nair and Thomas term 'non-believers'.

It is not just psychology, but western societies in general, that individualise problems and solutions. For example, the concept of 'falling in love' and choosing one's spouse or partner for romantic or sexual reasons are not only historically recent phenomena, but are not the case in non-western societies that are more communal and collectivistic, such as China, Pakistan, or Japan (c.f. Dion & Dion, 1993). As Higgins and Butler argue in this volume, non-heterosexuals who seek asylum in the UK need to prove their 'gay identity' which is complicated when they come from countries without language or belief in individual sexual identities. Consequently, therapists and researchers should use as an example das Nair's model for 'Metaminorities and mental health' (in das Nair & Fairbank, this volume, Chapter 8) that focuses on external and social contributors to mental health in addition to internal and psychological factors.

Looking to the Future

> I know it's going to be a long, hard pull before
> we are accepted as we really are. You and I,
> and our contemporaries, will probably never
> see the free world we are seeking. There
> have been pioneers in all causes and I
> sincerely hope that you, who are pioneering
> in this particular cause, will eventually win so
> that those who come after us will have a
> happier world to live in.
>
> (The Ladder, February 1960, p.23).

Riggs and das Nair emphasise that the goal of intersectionality is to *add* to complexity. The goal of intersectionality is not to create a new grid say, of five genders × eight social classes × ten religions × 18 ethnic groups × 12 categories of disabilities, to use an exaggerated example. Instead, we must view our clients, research participants, friends, neighbours, co-workers – as well as ourselves – as forming multiple, interlocking dimensions, each one adding colours, shades and hues to a rainbow tapestry.

References

Diamond, L.M. (2005). A new view of lesbian subtypes: Stable versus fluid identity trajectories over an 8-year period. *Psychology of Women Quarterly, 29*, 119–128.

Diamond, L. (2008). *Sexual fluidity: Understanding women's love and desire.* Cambridge, MA: Harvard University Press.

Dion, K.K., & Dion, K.L. (1993). Individualistic and collective perspectives on gender and the cultural context of love and intimacy. *Journal of Social Issues, 49*(3), 53–69.

Factor, R.J., & Rothblum, E.D. (2008). A study of transgender adults and their non-transgender siblings on demographic characteristics, social support, and experiences of violence. *Journal of LGBT Health Research, 3*(3), 11–30.

Feminist Therapy Institute (1995). Feminist therapy code of ethics. In E.J. Rave and C.C. Larsen (Eds.)*Ethical decision making in therapy: Feminist perspectives* (pp. 38–41). NY: Guilford Press.

Hesse-Biber, S.N. & Yaiser, M.L. (2004). *Feminist perspectives on social research.* New York, NY: Oxford University Press.

Kitzinger, C. & Perkins, R. (1993). *Changing our minds: Lesbian feminism and psychology.* New York, NY: New York University Press.

Robinson, E. (2010). *Disintegration: The splintering of Black America.* New York, NY: Doubleday.

Rothblum, E.D. (2008). Finding a large and thriving lesbian and bisexual community: The costs and benefits of caring. *Gay and Lesbian Issues and Psychology Review, 4*, 69–79.

Rothblum, E.D. (2010). Where is the "women's community"? Voices of lesbian, bisexual, and queer women and their heterosexual sisters. *Feminism & Psychology, 20*(4), 454–472.

Rothblum, E.D. & Factor, R. (2001). Lesbians and their sisters as a control group: Demographic and mental health factors. *Psychological Science, 12*, 63–69.

Savin-Williams, R.C. (2005). *The new gay teenager.* Boston, MA: Harvard University Press.

Wilkinson, S. (1996). Representing the other—Part I. *Feminism & Psychology, 6*(1), 43–44.

Index

Intersectionality, Sexuality and Psychological Therapies: Working with Lesbian, Gay and Bisexual Diversity,
First Edition. Edited by Roshan das Nair and Catherine Butler.
© 2012 John Wiley & Sons, Ltd. Published 2012 by John Wiley & Sons, Ltd. and the British Psychological Society.